Globalization, Communication and the Workplace

D1449360

Related titles available from Continuum:

English for Occupational Purposes
Dan Kim

Workplace Discourse
Almut Koester

Globalization, Communication and the Workplace

Talking Across the World

Edited by
Gail Forey and Jane Lockwood

continuum

Continuum International Publishing Group

The Tower Building	80 Maiden Lane
11 York Road	Suite 704, New York
London SE1 7NX	NY 10038

www.continuumbooks.com

© Gail Forey, Jane Lockwood and contributors 2010

All rights reserved. No part of this publication may be reproduced or transmitted in any form or by any means, electronic or mechanical, including photocopying, recording, or any information storage or retrieval system, without prior permission in writing from the publishers.

British Library Cataloguing-in-Publication Data
A catalogue record for this book is available from the British Library.

ISBN: 978-0-8264-4607-7 (hardcover)

Library of Congress Cataloging-in-Publication Data
Globalization, communication and the workplace: talking across the world / edited by Gail Forey and Jane Lockwood.
    p. cm.
Includes bibliographical references and index.
ISBN: 978-0-8264-4607-7
1. Interpersonal communication. 2. Intercultural communication.
3. Discourse analysis. 4. Communication in organizations. I. Forey, Gail, 1961–
II. Lockwood-Lee, Jane.

P94.6.G59 2010
302.3–dc22   2009048035

Typeset by Newgen Imaging Systems Pvt Ltd, Chennai, India
Printed and bound in Great Britain by the MPG Books Group

Contents

Notes on Contributors

Deborah Cameron is the Rupert Murdoch Professor of Language and Communication at Oxford University. Her research areas and publications cover a wide range of areas including sociolinguistics, language and gender, language attitudes and ideologies, language and media. She is author of a number of books one of which is "Good to Talk?" (Sage 2000), which is one of the first books to discuss call centres from a sociolinguistic perspective.

Claire Cowie is a Lecturer in Linguistics and English Language at the University of Edinburgh, where she teaches and researches on English as a Global Language. She is interested in accent norms and accent training in call centres in India, as well as the sociolinguistics of English in India more broadly.

Alan Davies is Emeritus Professor of Applied Linguistics at the University of Edinburgh. He has taught and researched English and Applied Linguistics in Kenya, Nepal, Australia and Hong Kong. His recent publications include *An Introduction to Applied Linguistics* (2007 2nd ed. Edinburgh University Press) and *Assessing Academic English* (2008, Cambridge University Press).

Neil Elias set up, and is Country head of, Logica Philippines, an offshore service provider for the Logica group in Europe. Prior to this, he was founding president of the first offshore BPO and call centre operation for the AIG financial group, based in Manila, and has worked in Europe, Australia and North America. Neil has presented at international conferences on the intercultural issues in training for the workplace and has recently co-authored a journal article on BPO quality assurance communications assessment.

Gail Forey is an Associate Professor and Associate Director for The Research Centre for Professional Communication at the Hong Kong Polytechnic University (PolyU). She has carried out research and published in the areas of written and spoken workplace discourse, SFL discourse analysis, language education and teaching development.

Eric Friginal is an Assistant Professor at the Department of Applied Linguistics and English as a Second Language at Georgia State University, Atlanta, GA, USA. He specializes in (applied) corpus linguistics, sociolinguistics, analysis of spoken discourse, technology in the classroom, English for specific purposes, cross-cultural communication and technical and professional writing.

Jane Hayman is an intercultural trainer at the International Consultants Centre, Melbourne. Jane has over twenty years' experience as a TESOL teacher, teacher trainer, manager and materials writer and is a national panellist for English language centre accreditation. Jane's research interests include comparing different approaches to culture and language awareness in corporate and educational contexts.

Susan Hood is a Senior Lecturer in Applied Linguistics and TESOL at the University of Technology, Sydney. Her research interests are in interpersonal meaning and the ways such meanings are enacted in different contexts from written academic encounters to spoken call centre interactions, and in the modalities of language, gesture and image.

Jon S. Y. Hui teaches and coordinates Discipline Specific English courses in the Department of English at City University of Hong Kong. Prior to his current profession, Jon worked in the radio and datacommunication sector over 20 years and held positions ranging from research and development engineer to regional manager. His current research interests include professional and interpersonal communication.

Anna Kristina Hultgren is a postdoctoral research fellow at the University of Copenhagen. Her recently completed doctoral thesis (Oxford) looks into communication training practices in the globalized call centre industry and the extent to which this is or can be followed in practice. Her research interests include language and gender and language and globalization.

Li Lan is an Assistant Professor in the Department of English, Hong Kong Polytechnic University, and a Fellow of Chartered Institute of Linguist, UK. With MPhil and PhD degrees in Applied Linguistics from Exeter University, her research interests and publications cover lexicology, lexicography, professional communication, corpus linguistics and sociolinguistics.

Jane Lockwood is currently Head of the Centre for Language in Education at the Hong Kong Institute of Education. Before that she founded FuturePerfect Business English Specialists (Manila). From 1995–2003 she headed up the Centre for Professional and Business English at the Hong Kong Polytechnic University and completed her PhD at Hong Kong University entitled Language Training Design and Evaluation Processes in Hong Kong Workplaces in 2002. She has published widely in the area of workplace curriculum and assessment development specific to the business processing outsourcing area.

Lucy MacGregor has a PhD in psycholinguistics from the University of Edinburgh. As a Research Associate in the English Department at the Hong Kong Polytechnic University she worked on various projects relating to the use of English by non-native speakers. She is currently a Research Fellow at the University of Leeds.

Lalita Murty is a lecturer in linguistics in the Norwegian Study Centre at the University of York, UK. Her research interests are mainly in the area of intelligibility of native varieties of English in the context of BPOs and call centres in India.

Catherine Nickerson is an Associate Professor in the College of Business Sciences at Zayed University in the United Arab Emirates. She has lived in India, the United States, the Netherlands and the United Kingdom. She has been teaching and researching the use of English as an international business language for the past fifteen years.

Barry Tomalin is Director of Cultural Training at International House, London and Visiting Lecturer in Intercultural Communication at the University of Westminster. Among his publications are 'The World's Business Cultures and How to Unlock Them' (Thorogood 2007), 'Cultural Awareness' (OUP 1995) and 'International English for Call Centres', (Macmillan India 2009), as well as monographs on France, Germany and Italy. His research interests include the theory and methodology of teaching cross-cultural skills and empathy, a study which has informed his work on language, culture and empathy in the BPO industry.

Jenny Yau Ni Wan is a full-time PhD candidate in the Department of English at the Hong Kong Polytechnic University. The topic of her thesis is 'Call Centre Communication: An Analysis of Interpersonal Meaning'. Her research interests include language of the workplace, systemic functional linguistics and discourse analysis.

Part I

Current Issues in English Communication in the Globalized Workplace

Chapter 1

Introduction

Jane Lockwood
The Hong Kong Institute of Education, Hong Kong

Gail Forey
The Hong Kong Polytechnic University, Hong Kong

The offshore and outsourcing (O&O) of various work has globally developed at a very rapid pace, especially in Asia. Parts of the O&O industry include Business Processing Outsourcing (BPO); this is where a business that was once located in the country of origin has been outsourced to an overseas destination. The key O&O destinations in this decade are India, China, the Philippines and other parts of Asia, South America and Eastern Europe (Cu 2006; NASSCOM 2009). The work in these O&O destinations typically comprise a range of back office functions including call centres, animation, legal advising, medical transcriptions, etc. Today the level of skills O&O have exceeded simply 'back office support', to the extent that the BPO industry is now transforming itself into what is termed in the industry Knowledge Processing Outsourcing (KPO). In KPOs the service offered is more professional and requires greater professional qualifications and skills than simple back office, administrative duties. Both the BPO and KPO services are housed within the Information Technology Enabled Services (ITES). ITES is a general term to refer to work that is supported through the use of technology, primarily telecommunications and internet transmission. Many of these terms O&O, BPO, KPO and ITES will be referred to throughout the book. In recent years, the outsourced work to developing countries has become more complex and professionally challenging, putting even great pressure on the workforce to communicate effectively in English. One young Indian IT support engineer reported recently that he feels huge responsibility to his USA and European- based IT clients and colleagues who look to him for a range of complex IT solutions that keeps USA and Europe functioning. When we were visiting him and gathering data in one of the BPO sites, he was solving a major refrigeration problem that was causing ice cream across America to melt.

The benefit and the rise of ITES can be attributed to economic gains, where an organization reduces overheads by O&O work. Many within the industry also argue that O&O often leads to improved quality levels due to a well-qualified and willing graduate workforce wanting to work. This is truly a globalized workplace stage where English language communication skills are being performed and tested. Until recently however, little international research was being carried out in this area, particularly in the area of English language communication. Given that many of these outsourced destinations are ex-colonies of the UK and USA and have a legacy of speaking English, one critical question that the book poses is whether these levels of English language communication are yielding the kind of quality the multinationals are expecting. What exactly are the communication problems, and how does this industry contribute to our understanding of World Englishes in an international business context? What can we learn from this multicultural discourse? What is the impact on language in the home and the world outside work in these destination?

Some of these questions are addressed in this volume although the research into this field has only just begun. This edited volume brings together an exciting agenda of recent research on this new globalized emerging discourse, focusing on issues where English language plays a key role in the discourse and beyond in the social context of customer service and implications for the offshore destination. The following broad themes, issues and questions are addressed in this volume.

In the first section, the book outlines some of the current issues in English communication in the globalized workplace. Li and MacGregor present the outcomes of a case study in email communication across 20 Hong Kong-based companies that deal with international clients. The authors of these business emails are L2 speakers of English and in their texts the findings reveal that these L2 writers over compensate in their use of politeness markers, which affects the main point of the communicative function of the business email. Nickerson also focuses on the nature and level of English communication currently being used in international business settings. She specifically discusses the context of the ITES industry world wide. She argues for the 'commodification' of English as a 'flattener' in the emerging economies that form part of the ITES industry and challenges the 'native speaker' model as the one to strive for in this increasingly multinational and globalized context. Finally in this section, Hultgren and Cameron provide a useful insight in to the communication problems found in an L1 context. This focus on concerns related to communication between the customer and Customer Service Representative (CSR) who are both first language (L1) English speakers, provides us with a clear understanding of the business and structural issues that may negatively impact communication above and beyond the ability to speak very good English. As a backdrop to the other articles in this volume, Hultgren and Cameron provide some important contextual issues for us to consider as smooth communication in the ITES industry cannot solely be related to English proficiency.

The second section of the volume goes straight into the heart of the interpersonal complexity of the language used in the call centre industry. This research is exciting because analysis of the actual authentic interaction on the phones has rarely been seen within the field of applied linguistics. This is pioneering work. A group of systemic functional linguists have focused on different aspects of the discourse to deconstruct the interpersonal nature of the discourse. Hui applies Appraisal theory (Martin and White 2005) to both a written and spoken text, where the field of the texts is similar, in that they are both complaints. Hui highlights some interesting characteristics related to making a complaint whether spoken or written. Hood also uses Appraisal theory and explores the issue of naming and negotiating relationships in the call centre interaction. She suggests that there is a repertoire of ways to build and repair relationships in the interaction and these are done strategically by both the agent and the customer. This repertoire of resources includes something as unexpected as 'shifts in the register', i.e. how in some customer service interactions may appear to be closer to a friendly 'chat' than a service call. Hood systematically demonstrates the register shifts found in the data with revealing examples and a rigorous analysis. Wan, again following Appraisal theory, analyses how interpersonal meaning is construed in the call centre interaction through voice quality. This article has far-reaching implications for training in the BPO industry where 'accent neutralization' training is widespread, and she argues such training misses how important the prosodic features are in the interaction for making meaning. Cowie and Murty also explore the issue of pronunciation, phonological or accent choices of Indian call centres agents when interacting with American English speakers. Their data is based on simulations between a CSR and a North American English speaker, and they analyse features typical of North American English speakers which are found in the Indian CSR's discourse. They found that some of the Indian CSR's are able and prepared to accommodate a North American accent while others consciously choose to retain their Indian identity when speaking English.

The third section explores some of the practicalities in providing communications training. These chapters focus on a variety of intercultural training issues, as well as language curriculum development issues for pre-hire training in the call centres. Hayman explores the interface between language and intercultural training in international business settings and provides suggestions for methodological approaches which facilitate intercultural training in the workplace. Elias focuses specifically on current approaches to intercultural training in the Indian and Filipino call centres and provides authentic examples of current intercultural training programmes. He argues that current practice lacks a principled frameworks for practice and suggests we need better definitions of culture that cross into the boundaries of linguistics, education and psychology. Tomalin provides an engaging description of some of the very serious issues that confront intercultural trainers in India. He highlights a number of linguistic resources which cause difficulties for the customer, such as word stress and rhythm, specific sounds and issues of accent. He compares some of the differences between L1 British English CSRs and Indian, L2 English-speaking CSRs and highlights relevant points about the length of the utterance and the accent. Friginal, reporting on data collected in the Philippines, outlines the key benefits for the country and those working in the call centres. He then moves on to discuss the need for cross-cultural competences and the importance of cross-cultural training. Lockwood provides insight into the planning principles and processes of communications training in the call centres and argues that call centre trainers are being asked to construct programmes with little or no background in curriculum design and materials development, often with disastrous results.

The fourth section is concerned with the issue of communication assessment. Communication assessment is a crucial issue for the BPO industry where millions of dollars are spent by companies trying to source good communicators for their call centres, and an equal amount of money is spent on quality assurance assessment once the CSR is recruited. Lockwood argues that much of this money is wasted on invalid and unreliable ways of assessing and further suggests that the commercial solutions in the market place are inappropriate for this industry. Davies describes how crucial skills such as clarity, intelligibility and rapport can be assessed and the need for such assessment in this new globalized workplace. Davies raises a number of difficulties which arise when speaking about assessment of informal spoken discourse, and he provides practical suggestions which could be adopted for assessment development.

The final section, provided by Forey draws together many points raised earlier and looks beyond the industry to the social implications of call centres. Based on interview data with CSRs from India and the Philippines she raises interesting questions about the impact on family life, education and health for a generation of ITES employees who generally start work at 9pm and finish at 6 am in the morning at least 5 nights a week.

Those involved in submitting chapters for this volume discuss a new emerging discourse which is rarely considered within applied linguistics. It is easy for a customer to forget who is on the other end of the phone when they are calling and involved in a frustrating and protracted customer service interaction. It should also be noted that although in the present volume many of the chapters discuss the 'problems' or 'communication breakdown' found in call centre communication, that frequently calls are completed, the customer is happy, the company maintains a positive customer profile and generally everything goes to plan. When visiting call centres in the Philippines and India, it is clear to see that at least 90% of all calls we viewed were successful. A tantalizing and yet under-researched area related to the quality of the calls, relates to the contradictory information provided to the call centres by customer surveys and quality assurance departments. Often account managers bemoan that the high-quality scores yielded from local QA processes are not matched by the customer satisfaction surveys. This has led to the spotlight being on these second language speakers of English at work. Much has yet to be done to investigate how business practices are impacting good communication in the call centres. The size of what we, as researchers and communication consultants into the BPO industry, have seen as successful customer service encounters seems to be overshadowed by what the business has evaluated as unsuccessful calls.

It is only when academics or those within applied linguistics invest time in to exploring this fascinating site of language and communication that the true picture of the ITES industry will be known. Far greater time needs to be spent in understanding:

- the interpersonal meanings that unfold and influence customer service encounters
- the range and variation of the linguistic demands across industries and across registers
- how business practices and requirements may be mitigating good communication on the phones
- the implications of this industry on those working and living in these O&O destinations

For applied linguists, it is often reported that access to authentic data in the workplace is difficult and studies tend to focus around sites which are more 'research friendly'. However, as demonstrated in this volume, the ITES industry is an intriguing environment where language, culture, globalization and the workplace converge; where issues of assessment, social engineering, text analysis, multimodal analysis, accent, training, curriculum and many other areas relevant for applied linguists can be explored. The present volumes proceeds to provide an initial picture of some of the issues related to the BPO, but many areas remain in need of research.

References

Cu, E. L. (2006), *Philippine BPO Industry: 2005 Scorecard*. Retrieved 27 February 2006 from http://www.bpap.org/bpap/bpapresearch.asp

Martin, J. R. and White, P. (2005), *Language of Evaluation*. London: Continuum.

NASSCOM (2009), Perspective 2020: *Transform Business Transform India*. (Executive Summary) http://www.nasscom.in retrieved 27 May 2009.

Chapter 2

English in Tiers in the Workplace: A Case Study of Email Usage

Li Lan
The Hong Kong Polytechnic University, Hong Kong

Lucy MacGregor
University of Leeds, UK

This chapter is a case study of the English usage in a Small and Medium Enterprise (SME) company in Hong Kong, where English is the lingua franca for business transactions with about 20 companies worldwide. Self-report questionnaire data revealed email to be the most frequently used medium for external communication, and is the focus of the present discussion. We performed a textual analysis of 111 authentic workplace emails between the company employees and international customers. We focused on two factors that should influence the language: first that the users were non-native (L2) speakers of English, and secondly that email was the medium of communication. Although all messages were successful in terms of basic information exchange there was a wide range in the proficiency of writing and at the lowest end of the spectrum samples were littered with lexical, grammatical and stylistic errors. It is difficult to disentangle the influence of the writer's language proficiency and the effect of the email medium, but we found the emails to be characterized by a number of linguistic features – abbreviations, contractions and ellipsis – reflecting an emphasis of the communication medium on speed and efficiency. These features are similar to those observed previously in business faxes and contributed towards an informal style. Some formality was maintained by the inclusion of salutations and closings, mirroring standard business letter format. Furthermore, although most emails were 'to the point' they included many politeness markers and structures which are unnecessary for the main communicative purpose, but function instead for the benefit of the interpersonal relationship.

Introduction

The social structure, values and culture of an organization are portrayed through language in the workplace, and therefore appropriate language use is central to any successful business (Gunnarsson 2004:36). English has become the language of international business communication (Crystal 1997; Kameda 1996) which may present a challenge for employees' communicating in their non-native language.

The present study is an investigation into the actual English usage by employees in a Small and Medium Enterprise (SME) company in Hong Kong, where English is the lingua franca for business transactions which take place with about 20 companies worldwide. The study was borne out of a request by Company A for help with improving the English skills of its employees. Although the primary purpose was to identify areas of weakness and suggest a language enhancement strategy, the company agreed that the data could also be used for research purposes. Email is used frequently by the company, in line with the general trend in business communication, and is the focus of the present chapter. We report findings from a linguistic analysis of email exchanges between company employees and other non-native speakers external to the company. We consider the influence of two factors on the language output: first that the language users are non-native (L2) English speakers and second that the communication medium is email.

Background

English as a Lingua Franca of Business Communication

As much of business now operates in a global market, many business communications take place in neither party's first language and English is often the language of choice. Moreover, non-native English-speaking professionals now greatly outnumber native speakers (Crystal 2003). For international companies, the language competency of their non-native-speaking employees is of considerable importance to ensure successful communication with their business partners.

Business communication between non-native speakers of English is relevant to applied linguists interested in how language works in real-world contexts, rather than in the classroom. The issue of confidentiality makes it difficult to source authentic business communication texts (Bolt and Bolton 1996; Flowerdew and Wan 2006; Hewings 1999; Li and Bilbow 2001). This reason, explains in part the predominant focus of business writing research on writing produced specifically for public purposes, for example CEOs' letters (Bowman 1984; Hyland 1998), financial reports (Coutis 1986), promotional materials (Cheung 2006; Connor and Gladkov 2004; Pilegaard 1997; Zhu 1997). However, such publically available texts are normally substantially edited and can be regarded as standard English. Another common source of business discourse research comes from simulated business writings produced in educational settings (Cheng and Mok 2006; Louhiala-Salminen 1996). Ten years ago

Akar and Louhiala-Salminen observed that, 'research into business communication in general, and especially English business communication from the L2 user's point of view, remains a sparsely populated area'(Akar and Louhiala-Salminen 1999:135). There is now increasing recognition of the need to locate business communication research 'within the context of the social and organizational settings in which it is produced and received (Davies et al., 1999:293)'. The research reported here contributes to the burgeoning area into workplace-situated language-use.

A few studies on workplace writing have attempted to investigate authentic records of business communication (Flowerdew and Wan 2006; Kirkpatrick 1991; Kong 1998, 2006). Kong (2006) analysed 250 internal directive emails according to their semantic accounts: reason, condition, purpose, result, attribution, concession and manner, and illustrated indirectness in business interactions. In three types of relationship – peer to peer, subordinate to superior and superior to subordinate – the politeness behaviours were found to be related to the Chinese ideology of hierarchy, which stipulates absolute respect for power and authority. Kong noted that differences among the groups are attributable to politeness and mitigation of potential face-threat. His findings also highlight 'the equal concern of the Chinese employees for hierarchy and harmony in the workplace' (Kong 2006:98).

Email in the Workplace

Computer mediated-communication (CMC) is essential to modern-day business. As a major channel, email enables information to be exchanged rapidly between multiple parties in distant locations and different time zones. As a written medium, it enables a potentially permanent record of the information to be maintained. This can minimize the risk of any misunderstandings between parties, making it often preferable to telephone communication.

Email is still a relatively new communication medium and therefore the rules governing its structure and etiquette are still developing. Several studies have commented on the emergence of email language which can be characterized by abbreviations, a lack of adherence to traditional grammatical rules and an informal, colloquial, personal and friendly style (Gimenez 2000; Li 2000). However, such descriptions are probably over-generalized. Emails are multi-functional and therefore their language should differ according to the particular purpose for which they are written and the relationship between sender and receiver. It is likely that in a business context the features cited above, which contribute to an informal style, could be considered inappropriate.

Gains conducted a textual analysis of business emails sent between offices within a UK company, and showed that the majority of texts adopted a semi-formal tone and the style adhered to standard conventions in written English. For example, sentences were fully formed and grammatical and did not contain any examples of linguistic features which are commonly found in conversational discourse (Gains 1999).

Mulholland (1999) reports the results of an investigation into the language of emails which were exchanged between secretarial and administrative staff at an Australian University for the purpose of arranging meetings. Emails included frequent use of politeness markers, despite the otherwise brevity. Interestingly, politeness was typically found at the end of the text rather than throughout. The authors suggest such a placement of politeness at the end lessens its apparent importance for the writer. The choices and etiquette influencing the use of politeness are still very much developing, and education and language training developing such communication is still and does not have strict set of generic conventions. The use of 'email English' has come to the attention of many linguists, yet there is only a very limited literature on its stylistic and linguistic features. In her book entitled *Wired Style: Principles of English Usage in the Digital Age*, Hale states that 'when we turned to traditional style manuals for answers, we found them inadequate': there was nothing for what she calls 'the style maven of the post-print era'. For Hale the striking feature of email is what she calls 'screw the rules . . . Welcome inconsistency, especially in the interest of voice and cadence . . . Play with grammar and syntax. Appreciate unruliness' (Hale 1996:96). Research also found that emails between companies, or between a company and a customer show some degree of informality, and are less formal than business letters (Gimenez 2000).

Most previous studies on email have focused on internal emails (Kong 2006; Li 2000; Nickerson 1999), and often those between people with different statuses within a hierarchy. Those that have looked at information exchange between two people of similar status have focused on friends. In our email samples the two parties were of equal status, negotiating for business transaction. The relationship works to the benefit of both parties.

Given that language is a necessary element of company strategic planning for any business involved in international transactions, and 'English language expertise is a personal attribute which facilitates performance' (Wright and Wright 1994:3), our discussion focuses on: (1) the communicative functions of the emails for direct business transaction, (2) the range of language proficiencies displayed, (3) the text features which characterize the emails and (4) the overall style of the emails.

The Case Study

Background Information about the Company

Company A (not its real name), which provided the data for the present study, is a vendor in fashion-related products and supplies garments for well-known global brands, which sell mainly in the EU market. The company, which was established nearly 30 years ago and has offices in Hong Kong and in mainland China, employs over 150 professional merchandizers who are responsible for business transactions with customers in about 20 countries. The company authority is very aware of the importance of English within its business and wishes to improve linguistic skills of its employees. It approached the first author for a language assessment and staff training with the agreement that the information could also be used for research purposes.

Staff Profile

To obtain the demographics of Company A employees, a questionnaire designed by Evans and Green (2003) was completed by 38 staff members in the Shenzhen office of the company. Results show that the company has a young team both in terms of age and experience: the vast majority (82%) are under the age of 30 years and around half (53%) have been working for less than 5 years. Most of the employees (82%) have either a Higher Diploma certificate or a BA degree. It is also noted that the majority of the employees (82%) are women.

Communication in the Workplace

The official working languages of the company are English, Cantonese and Putonghua, although English is the major language used when communicating with other companies. Questionnaire data showed that almost all employees (78%) reported written English to be 'extremely important' to their current job (the highest rating on a 6 point scale). English is particularly important for email communication. The majority of employees 'often' or 'always' write (66%) and read (75%) external emails in English. These figures demonstrate the importance of English as a business lingua franca to Company A.

The Data

The data consist of 111 authentic workplace emails (10,364 words) sent to or from Company A over a period of 2 months in 2008. The data were passed to the author with subject headers removed, all proper names replaced with pseudonyms and sensitive business information, such as contact person, address, price etc., replaced with cross signs. The company released the information for the purpose of staff training and it was their decision what to provide. The data were randomly selected, reflecting a number of business transactions during the period.

English in Tiers in the Workplace

The emails were classified in three tiers according to the English proficiency: near native, fluent and flawed. Judgments were made by the authors, a non-native speaker with a background in linguistics and a native English speaker. Examples from each of the three tiers are shown in Figures 1, 2 and 3 below (errors and/or typos highlighted in italics).

HI KEN,

I RECEIVED THE FABRIC SWATCHES YOU SENT ME A FEW DAYS AGO AND WE ARE DOING SOME SIMILAR TYPES OF POLY/WOOL PLAIDS BUT THEY ARE A LITTLE DIFFERENT. I SEE THAT YOU ALSO SENT ME *SOOM* WOOL/RAYON FABRICS AND THESE ARE TOO EXPENSIVE FOR OUR LINES SO I THINK THE BETTER IDEA WOULD BE FOR ME TO SEND YOU A PACKAGE OF SOME OF THE FABRICS WE DO HERE AND THEN YOU CAN SEND ME BACK YOUR COUNTER SWATCHES. I CAN ALSO SEND YOU SOME TECH PACKS ALONG FOR PRICING JUST TO SEE IF YOUR PRICES ARE *WORKABEL* FOR US. LET ME KNOW IF YOU THINK THIS IS A GOOD IDEA AND THEN I WILL SEND OUT THE PACKAGE RIGHT AWAY. THANKS.

HAVE A GREAT WEEKEND.

B/REGARDS

John

FIGURE 1 Example of email classified as near-native

Dear John,

Thanks for *your* detailed information of your company.

Well noted that you just do the tops with no bottoms and your *minimum quantity, working procedures*. Here we would like to send you some pictures of jackets we are making for your reference.

Also we sent you some of our fabric swatches of Fall/ Winter for your reference by DHL under AWB # 195 1689 806 today. Please confirm *receipt* & comments by return.

Nice to know that you will visit China, please inform us once you fix your schedule to China. Thank you!

Best regards

Ken

FIGURE 2 Example of an email classified as fluent

```
Dear                                                    Peter,

I  don't  know  if  my  first  mail  arrived  at  your  server  about  20
minutes    ago    but    after    my    check    I    don't    think    so.

Once    more,    you    can    keep    the    goods    in    China.
On the other side you can send it to Company A and they reject it,
or  you  can  charge  Company  A,  anyway  all  points  are  not  for  a
solution    we    are    working    at    the    moment    for.

Also pls. note that they don't thread us with any penaltys at this
moment, if this will happen with a store group or mail order company
or a discounter, what do you think what they will charge us + they
don't          pay          us          the          goods          .

The onlyest thing they want is that we send them their orders after
their requests and they don't have to do rejections, therefore they
gave us the chance to re-send goods after their requests latest june
15th.          in          their          warehouse          .

Also tomorrow you will get some more explanations from Dolly reg.
the          front          length          we          are          discussing.
This was also not so easy because those creative people are normally
not    willed    so    much    to    be    involved    into    claims.
She    made    this    because    I    know    she    a    very long    time.

brgds
Joe
```

FIGURE 3   Example of an email classified as flawed

Emails were considered to be near native when they contained only typographical errors or a small number of grammatical mistakes.

Fluent emails typically contained some structurally awkward sentences.

Flawed emails were littered with grammatical mistakes, for example, subject-verb agreement and tense errors, lack of articles, pronoun misuse, awkwardly constructed sentences. They also contained some lexical mistakes and displayed an inappropriate style. Of all email samples, only 20% can be regarded as error free. This is particularly interesting given the high status of the company within its field in the global market. Importantly, we found no evidence in the emails of any miscommunication between parties, and therefore the emails were successful in terms of basic information exchange.

Structural Analysis

Business communication is a purposeful social activity which serves to manifest a goal or intent through words. We performed a rhetorical move analysis (Bhatia 1993; Swales 1990) to identify the functions of the email and the discourse structure. Since most workplace emails are short in nature, the discussion is limited to the overall functions identified and the opening and closing moves.

Functions of Email

We categorized the email exchanges according to their communicative function. In some cases the emails performed more than one function but in most cases one main function could be clearly identified. As expected all emails concerned details about the company, samples and payment. The results are shown in Table 1 below.

Openings and Closings

An analysis of inter-office emails within a company showed that the majority did not include any greeting (Gains 1999), supporting previous claims made in the literature that salutations are optional in emails (Hatch 1992). However, data in the present study are from exchanges made between members of different companies and it was expected that style might confirm more closely to formal business letters. This turned out to be true. As can be seen in Table 2, the large majority of the emails (79%) started with **'Dear'** which was typically followed by

Table 1 Functions of the emails

Communicative function	Frequency (%) of emails
Requesting information and action (samples, payment)	42.6
Providing information (samples)	41.9
Confirming receipt of information and action taken	7.8
Clearing responsibility	6.2
Promoting company	1.6

Table 2 The style of openings used in the emails

Opening	Frequency (%)
No opening	16 (14)*
Dear	88 (79)
Hi	7 (6)

* In these 16 emails it was unclear whether the opening had been removed by the company prior to sending to the author for analysis.

Table 3   The style of closings used in the emails

Closing	Frequency (%)
No closing	19 (17)*
Best regards (or contracted form)	84 (76)
Regards (or contracted form)	4 (4)
Best wishes	2 (2)
Thanks	2 (2)

* In 16 of these 19 emails it was unclear whether the closing had
   been removed by the company prior to sending to the author
   for analysis.

the recipient's first name. Occasionally (6% of the time), the more informal **'Hi'** initiated the email.

Almost all of the emails (83%) included a closing, which was typically **'Best regards'** or a contracted form of this variant (Table 3). Most email accounts have the option to automatically generate a closing and signature when the email is sent. It was not possible to tell whether the closings here were generated in this way and therefore perhaps reflect company policies rather than the preferences of the individual user. However, it is clear that a closing is a characteristic feature of these emails. The findings contrast somewhat to Gain's (1999) study of intra-company emails which showed that a large percentage (42%) concluded with the sender's name only or an informal **'thanks'** (**'thank you'**, **'many thanks'** etc.). In the present study, the closings were similar to those which would be observed in more traditional business letters although interestingly, contracted forms were considered acceptable (Table 3).

Text Features

We performed a textual analysis to identify linguistic features of the emails. We found the emails to be characterized by a number of features. Quantitative data about the emails was obtained using WordSmith Tools 5.0 (Scott 2008). The emails were short and contained many examples of abbreviations and ellipsis. These features reflect the emphasis placed on the rapid exchange of information. Interestingly, only a few examples of contractions were observed. These are discussed below.

Short Sentences

The emails were typically short, both in terms of word length and overall message length. The mean word length is only 4 letters and the mean length of the 111 emails is 84 words. The mean sentence length was 11.8. Figure 4 depicts the number of emails of different lengths and shows that almost a fifth of the emails (21) had 20 words or fewer and over 40% (46) had 40 words or fewer.

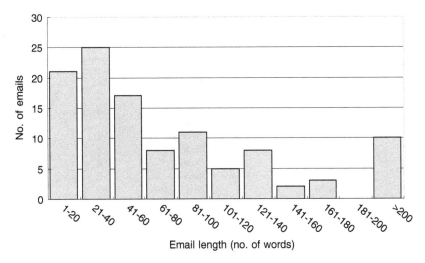

FIGURE 4 The number of the emails of different lengths (in words)

Table 4 Frequency of contractions observed in the data (111 emails, 10,364 words)

Contraction	Frequency	Full form	Frequency
Don't	14	*Do not*	16
It's	14	*It is*	14
Can't	3	*Can not/cannot*	8
Haven't	2	*Have not*	2
There're	2	*There are*	1
There's	1	*There is*	6
Isn't	1	*Is not*	7
Couldn't	1	*Could not*	0
We'd	1	*We had*	1
We've	1	*We have*	23
We're	1	*We are*	28
Let's	1	*Let us*	2
TOTAL	**42**		**108**

Contractions

Spoken language and informal written language is littered with contracted forms including negations with **'not'** and an apostrophe, for example **'don't'** (do not). Table 4 shows examples of contractions observed in the current data. Although the overall number of contractions was small, several contracted forms (e.g. **'don't', 'it's'**) occurred as often as their full equivalents, and across emails of all three proficiency levels. These findings are interesting given that contractions are inappropriate in formal writing (Bilbow 2002:36).

Table 5 Frequency of abbreviations observed in the data (111 emails, 10,364 words)

Abbreviations	Frequency	Full form	Frequency
Pls	60	Please	78
No.	13	Number	7
Asap	2	As soon as possible	0
Pc(s)	9	Piece(s)	1
Fty	5	Factory	9
Qty	3	Quantity	8
Rgds	1	Regards	3
B.rgds, brgds, b/regards, br	15	Best regards	69
Yr	4	Your	103
U	6	You	234
TOTAL	**173**		**512**

Abbreviations

The emails included many examples of abbreviations, both standard (e.g. **'no.'** = number, **'ASAP'** = as soon as possible) and domain specific (e.g. **'fty'** = factory, **'qty'** = quantity). Table 5 shows the frequency of occurrence of the abbreviations in the text.

Use of Punctuation

Compared to formal standard writing, the punctuation in many of the emails was inappropriate. For example, there were many cases where commas were used rather than periods (examples 1 and 2 below) or no punctuation was used at all (example 3). This can account for the long mean sentence length (18 words).

1. And re neckdrop C.F. for 018/027, we are afraid your measured the distance between back/front neckline, whiles from your measurement standard, it should be measured from horizon straight line, please kindly see attachment and clarify below:
2. i think for lining in 190T will be too light pls change to 210T polyester kindly advise your comments

Sentence initial words were often not capitalised (example 3)

3. me too, nice to meet u hope we can have long term business together. awaiting your prices. as per our discussion all fur trim in ur original samples are real one not fake pls reconfirm

Previous research has shown that business writing makes greater use of requests than of questions. Also, exclamation marks are rarely used, with the exception of sales letters where they function to draw the reader's attention (Bilbow 2002:56). In contrast to these findings, the workplace emails here included several examples of question marks and exclamation marks, which were overused to convey emotion. These features also contribute to an informal style, much like speech.

4. Even the mistake is not from our side, then who will pay for this???
5. . . . and both you and I will loose the job if we do business in this way!!!
6. Then where can we stand???
7. Don't you think they just think everything from their side to protect themself, always thinking without the benefit of our company???
8. I never got this, we discussed and left worksheets last novemebr??? Do you remember. . .:o))

Elliptical Forms

Another striking feature of the emails is the frequent use of ellipsis, which makes the syntax straightforward. Examples of some ellipsis from the data are given below (full forms given in parentheses).

9. Please advise the size. (Please let us know which size you require.)
10. Well received the order. (We have received the order.)
11. Pls confirm upon receipt. (Please confirm that you have received this email.)
12. New draft. (I have attached a new draft to this email.)

Colloquial Expressions

In contrast to the business emails analysed by Gains (1999), the present emails display examples of colloquial language common to speech, but which would be considered inappropriate in formal business letters (inappropriate language is underlined).

13. Yes, we are <u>doing basically</u> the same types of jackets
14. <u>To be honest</u>, we do not understand
15. We all have holiday on May 1st, <u>right??</u>
16. Could you please check again <u>on your side?</u>

Timeliness

The emails included many examples of language use which emphasize the importance placed on a fast response (indicated by underlining).

17. Looking forward to your <u>reply today</u>.
18. pls <u>send us today</u>, thank you.
19. I don't know if my first mail arrived at your server about <u>20 minutes ago</u>
20. pls advise if you can arrange the deposit <u>by tomorrow ?</u>
21. I will email you again the remade one hopefully <u>by tomorrow</u>. Regarding fabrics emailed yesterday, please let me know if you find them interested.

Politeness Strategies

The linguistic features identified above result in the email style being 'to the point'. It might therefore be expected that there would be few examples of language that does not directly contribute to achieving the main function of the message. However, the current data included many politeness markers and structures, replicating the findings of Mulholland (1999). For example, the word list generation (using Wordsmith Tools) showed that **'please'** (or its contracted form, **'pls'**) was the eighth most frequent word across all texts, occurring 138 times or on average more than once per email. Requests for action or which direct the attention of readers typically included please or made using modal verbs rather than imperatives, for example (polite language underlined):

22. <u>Thanks</u> for your reply
23. <u>Please</u> advise. . . .
24. I <u>would like</u> *to* know
25. <u>Could</u> you <u>kindly . . . .</u>
26. <u>Please kindly</u> note. . . .

The apparent emphasis on politeness can be accounted for by considering the relationship between the sender and receiver. A successful business relationship requires that the two parties establish and develop a good rapport. In the absence of cues available during face-to-face interactions (e.g., voice and gesture), the influence of the actual language on the interpersonal relationship becomes even more important.

Requests for action are frequently phrased indirectly (example 27). This is inline with Kirkpatrick's observation that 'Asian cultures are marked by circularity, implicitness and digressiveness; whereas Western cultures are characterized by linearity and explicitness' (Kirkpatrick 1991:202).

27. Looking forward to hearing from you soon.

Furthermore, some sentences which function as small talk are included (examples 28 and 29) to develop and maintain friendly business relationship.

28. Have a great weekend.
29. Hope you come back DK and have a good rest . . .

Sometimes the language functions solely for the benefit of the interpersonal relationship as in the use of appropriate opening and closings. Typically the language functions mainly to inform the other party of something, but is written in a way which also benefits the relationship. For example, acknowledging receipt of an email (example 30).

30. Thank you for your email.

An interesting use of polite language can be seen in (example 31). By asking the other party to check, and by phrasing this as a question, the user is assigning responsibility to the other side in a very polite way.

31. Can you check again on your side and clarify?

It is interesting to consider to what extent politeness strategies are used explicitly for the benefit of the relationship. If the phrases are too formulaic they may have little positive effect on the relationship between sender and receiver.

Conclusions and Implications

The challenge for email users is meeting the demand and expectation for haste while ensuring appropriate use of language. Many company employees communicating with business partners around the world face the combined challenge of using their non-native language to express information, ideas and emotions in a manner appropriate to the email medium. The emails analysed in the current study displayed a range of English proficiency, but all were successful in terms of basic information exchange and we did not observe any examples of miscommunication. As long as the function of the email is clear and the relevant information is present and accurate, then grammatical and lexical inaccuracies are less important. Perhaps more crucial is the overall style of the text. Although contractions, abbreviations and ellipsis contribute to an informal style, the presence of politeness markers and grammatical constructions meant that a degree of formality more similar to traditional business letters was maintained.

Email enables information to be exchanged quickly between multiple people simultaneously, and speed is often expected. Partly as a result of this, emails are often not subject to the same rigorous checking procedures as formal letters. Furthermore, email style is typically less formal than written letters. Although a degree of informality may be acceptable in business exchanges once a relationship has been established, language users must be aware of the appropriate standards for the mode of communication.

Business writing is social activity that creates and maintains organizations (Bargiela Chiappini and Nickerson 1999:4). Given the importance of email as a communication medium and of English as a business lingua franca, there is a clear need for teaching and learning resources suitable for non-native users of English (Gains 1999; Gains 1999; Gimenez 2000; Louhiala-Salminen 1997); familiarity with email is not enough. Users need to be aware of the norms and rules which govern the appropriate use of English in the specific context. In 1999, Gains claimed that there is 'no clear answer to the question of whether a stylistic protocol exists for the writing of email messages' (Gains 1999:82). The present research contributes to our understanding of how email language really is in the workplace more than 10 years after Gains' assertion, but future work is needed to firmly establish what is appropriate. We argue that this should be determined by members of the business community. Interesting future work could perhaps compare the perception of native and non-native users. How do those in business feel about receiving an error-ridden email? Which linguistic features are perceived to be obligatory, optional or inappropriate? To what extent does the email style influence future business transactions?

It is difficult to disentangle the effects of email being the communication medium and the user's language proficiency on the writing output. In email 'conversation', as Hale (1996:3) puts it, a line needs to be drawn between native speakers 'screwing the rules', and L2 users 'breaking the rules' or 'not knowing the rules' – although such a line might well be fuzzy at times. The workplace examples presented here display features of informality observed previously in emails by native users, but there is still much to do to improve English proficiency.

References

Akar and Louhiala-Salminen, L. (1999), Towards a new genre: A comparative study of business faxes. In Bargiela-Chiappini, F. and Nickerson, C. (eds.) *Writing Business: Genres, Media and Language.* London: Longman.

Bargiela-Chiappini, F. and Nickerson, C. (1999), Business writing as social action. In Bargiela-Chiappini, F. and Nickerson, C. (eds.) *Writing Business: Genres, Media and Language.* London: Longman, 1–32.

Bargiela-Chiappini, F., Nickerson, C. and Planken, B. (eds.) (2007), *Business Discourse.* Basingstoke, UK: Palgrave Macmillan.

Bhatia, V. K. (1993), *Analysing Genre: Language Use in Professional Settings.* London: Longman.

Bilbow, Graham, T. (2002), *Business Writing for Hong Kong,* 2nd edn. Hong Kong: Longman.

Bolt, P. and Bolton, K. (1996), The International Corpus of English in Hong Kong. In Greenbaum, S. (ed.) *Comparing English Worldwide.* Oxford: Clavendon, 197–214.

Bowman, E. H. (1984), Contents analysis of annual reports for cooperate strategy and risk. *Interfaces* 14, 61–71.

Cheng, W. and Mok, E. (2006), Cultural preference for rhetorical patterns in business writing. *Hong Kong Linguist* 26, 69–80.

Cheung, M. (2006), A discourse analysis of Chinese and English sales letters in Hong Kong. *The Proceedings of the 5th International Conference of the European Association of Languages for Specific Purposes*, Zaragoza,142–150.

Connor, U. and Gladkov, K. (2004), Rhetorical appeals in fundraising direct mail letters. In Connor, U. and Upton, Thomas A. (eds.) *Applied Corpus Linguistics: A Multidimensional Perspective*. Amsterdam; New York: Rodopi, 258–286.

Coutis, J. K. (1986), An investigation into annual report readability and corporate risk-return relationships. *Accounting and Business Research* 16, 285–294.

Crystal, D. (2003), *English as a Global Language*, 2nd edn. Cambridge, UK: Cambridge University Press.

Davies, F., Forey, G. and Hyatt, D. (1999), Exploring aspects of context: Selected findings from the Effective Writing for Management Project. In Bargiela-Chiappini, F. and Nickerson, C. (eds.) *Writing Business: Genres, Media and Language*. London: Longman, 293–312.

Evans, S. and Chris, G. (2003), The use of English by Chinese professionals in post-1997 Hong Kong. *Journal of Multilingual and Multicultural Development* 24(5), 386–412.

Flowerdew, J. and Wan, A. (2006), Genre analysis of tax computation letters: How and why tax accountants write the way they do. *English for Specific Purposes* 25 (2), 133–153.

Gains, J. (1999), Electronic mail – A new style of communication or just a new medium: An investigation into the text features of email. *English for Specific Purposes* 18(1), 81–101.

Gimenez, J. C. (2000), Business email communication: Some emerging tendencies in register. *English for Specific Purposes* 19(3), 237–251.

Gimenez, J. C. (2006), Embedded business emails: Meeting new demands in international business communication. *English for Specific Purposes* 25, 154–172.

Gunnarsson, B. L. (2004), Orders and disorders of enterprise discourse. In Gouveia, Carlos A. M., Silvestre, Carminda and Azuaga, Luisa (eds.) *Discourse, Communication and the Enterprise: Linguistic Perspectives*. Lisbon: University of Lisbon Centre for English Studies, 17–39.

Hale, C. (ed.) (1996), *Wired Style: Principles of English Usage in the Digital Age*. San Francisco, CA: Hardwired.

Hewings, M. and Nickerson, C. (1999), *Business English: Research into Practice*. Harlow, England: Longman.

Kameda, N. (1996), *Business English toward Transnationalism: The Significance of Cross-cultural Business English and its Role*. Tokyo: Bungei Shunjush.

Kirkpatrick, A. (1991), Information sequencing in Mandarin in letters of request. *Anthropological Linguistics* 33(2), 183–203.

Kong, K. C. C. (1998), Are simple business request letters really simple? A comparison of Chinese and English business request letters *Text* 18(1), 103–141.

Kong, K. C. C. (2006), Accounts as a politeness strategy in the internal directive documents of a business firm in Hong Kong. *Journal of Asian Pacific Communication* 16(1), 77–101.

Li, L. (2000), Email: A challenge to standard English? *English Today* 16(4), 23–29.

Li, L. and Bilbow, G. T. (2001), From a business corpus to a business lexicon. *Lexikos* 11, 209–221.

Louhiala-Salminen, L. (1996), The business communication classroom vs reality: What should we teach today? *English for Specific Purposes* 15(1), 316–333.

Louhiala-Salminen, L. (1997), Investigating the genre of a business fax: A Finnish case study. *The Journal of Business Communication* 34(3), 316–333.

Mulholland, J. (1999), Email: Uses, issues and problems in an institutional setting. In Bargiela-Chiappini, Francesca and Nickerson, Catherine (eds.) *Writing Business. Genres, Media and Discourses.* Harlow, UK: Longman, 57–84.

Nickerson, C. (1999), The use of English in electronic mail in a multinational corporation. In Bargiela-Chiappini, Francesca and Nickerson, Catherine (eds.) *Writing Business. Genres, Media and Discourses.* Harlow, UK: Longman, 35–56 .

Pilegaard, M. (1997), Politeness in written business discourse: A textlinguistic perspective on requests. *Journal of Pragmatics* 28(2), 223–244.

Scott, M. (2008), WordSmith Tools Version 5. Liverpool: Lexical Analysis Software.

Swales, J. (1990), *Genre Analysis: English in Academic and Research Settings.* Cambridge, UK: Cambridge University Press.

Wright, C. and Wright, S. (1994), Do languages really matter? The relationship between international business success and a commitment to foreign language use. *Journal of Industrial Affairs* 3(1), 3–14.

Zhu, Y. (1997), A rhetorical analysis of Chinese sales letters. *Text* 17(4), 543–566.

Chapter 3

English as a Key Resource to Business and Development

Catherine Nickerson
Zayed University, United Arab Emirates

In this chapter I will discuss the various ways in which English has contributed as a key resource to business and development. In doing so, I will be looking at the levels of English language proficiency available to business and industry around the globe, and the relationship that exists between high levels of English language skills on the one hand, and the emergence and development of industries such as the ITES industry on the other. I will discuss other factors that may play a role in addition to the presence of English, and I will also selectively review the most recent literature on the use of English as an international business language or business lingua franca and discuss the ITES industry as an example of the globalization not only of business, but also of communication.

Introduction: The World is Flat and English Speaking

The hugely influential 2005 publication, *The World is Flat* by Thomas L. Friedman, describes a world in which global business transcends the traditional boundaries imposed by geographical or cultural borders (Friedman 2005). The volume begins in Bangalore, India – the centre of the Indian IT sector – and discusses the impact of technological advances such as fibre optic micro cable and work flow software, which, Friedman believes, have contributed to a flattening of the playing field between the developed world and emerging economies. Such technological advances have allowed countries such as India and China to contribute to the global supply chain to an ever increasing extent and as a result to become more and more competitive with the existing industrialized nations. Friedman identifies 10 factors, or 'flatteners' which have facilitated this change in the world's economic scenario, including the development of Netscape and the development of work flow software. The fifth of these factors is 'outsourcing', i.e. the process by which corporations can divide and then subcontract their activities, e.g. service versus manufacturing, such that these activities are then completed in the most economical way. This is, of course, at the heart of the success of the ITES industry in emerging economies such as India, China and the Philippines, and in this chapter, I will be arguing that a major part of the flattening of the world has in fact taken place because of the increasing dominance – and acceptance – of English as the language of both global business and technology. In addition I will argue that without that dominance, much of what Friedman describes would have taken place at a much slower rate, or perhaps not taken place at all. In the remainder of this chapter, I will discuss outsourcing in each of the three areas of the world in which research in Business or Professional English has generally been divided; those countries in which English is used as a first language, those in which it is used as a second language and those in which it is used as a foreign language (see for example, Kachru's seminal work on World Englishes across the globe, Kachru et al. 2006). I will consider situations in which English is used as an international business language, i.e. situations that involve any speakers of English who come from two or more different nations, and situations in which it is used as a business lingua franca, i.e. situations in which none of the speakers involved speaks English as a first language (Nickerson 2010/forthcoming). In each case I will attempt to provide different examples of relevance to the ITES sector, and I will explore how the use of English underpins each one. I will start with English as a Second Language, since these are the countries in the world where the ITES industry is perhaps at its most familiar, move on to contexts in which English is used as a first language, and conclude with a discussion of the emergence of the ITES industry in countries where English is used as a foreign language.

The dominance of English as the language of global business and technology is an established fact (see Nickerson 2009 for further discussion). The teaching of English worldwide is a multi-million dollar industry, as reflected in at least two of the examples I will discuss below, and a knowledge of English is widely seen as a ticket to economic success across the globe regardless of the official language policies that may be pursued at the same time by governments or multinational corporations (MNCs). Countless books, scholarly articles, edited collections and textbooks have been published in the past two decades with a focus on areas such as English for Academic Purposes, English for Business Purposes, Business English, Business Discourse (primarily English) etc. etc. And in the last 5 years in particular, there has been a proliferation of empirical accounts of the nature and use of English in workplace contexts, including most recently within the ITES industry (e.g. Charles and Kankaanranta 2005 on meetings and email; Clark, Rogers, Murfett and Ang 2008 on call centre discourse in Singapore; Planken 2005 on negotiations; Poncini 2004 on meetings etc.). As a result of these studies, we now know quite a bit about how English is used around the globe in workplace settings, and the challenges that are faced and then met on a daily basis by those who use it. In the sections that follow I will conclude each section with a brief discussion of the relevance of existing

studies in workplace language and discourse for the ITES industry, and speculate on where such research might go in the future (see also Davies, this volume
for a discussion on the myth of the native speaker of English).

English as a Second Language

Outsourcing and English as a Second Language

Perhaps the best known examples of emerging economies in which the ITES
industry has had a major impact on the economy, are the Philippines and India
(Cowie 2007; Forey and Lockwood 2007; Pal and Buzzanell 2008; Upadhya and
Vasavi 2009). In both cases in these countries, English is spoken by a large number of people, as either a first or an additional language. In India, for instance,
90 million people claim that they speak English as a first, second or third language, and in the Philippines, around 42 and a half million speak it as a first or
additional language (Wikipedia 2009). This translates to around 10% of the
total population for India, and around 47% for the Philippines. In the
Philippines, English is one of two official languages, and in India, in addition to
the fact that English is still the official language of major institutions such as the
Parliament and the Supreme Court, it also retains a privileged unofficial status
as the language of education, technology, law and business (Gargesh 2006).
In the Indian context in particular, the dominance of English in the legal sector
has led to the recent emergence of a thriving KPO industry centred on providing legal support to the USA. This is because the recent introduction of the
e-discovery law in the US, which requires a complete document review of
electronic sources, coupled with the economic meltdown at the end of 2008
and the corresponding need to deal with the legal consequences of redundan-
cies and bankruptcies, have created the need for cost-effective LPO services,
e.g. a senior associate in USA is paid $200–300 per hour for document review
while an LPO based in India charges no more than $25–30 per hour for the
same work (*Economic Times* 2008). The emergence of the KPO-LPO industry in
India is an excellent example of the way in which an ESL background may
underpin the ITES industry, in that not only do Indian lawyers complete all of
their education in English, the Indian legal system post-Independence incorpo-
rates elements of both US and UK Law, hence providing a certain amount of
domain-based familiarity for the lawyers involved.

In both India and the Philippines, there are clearly strong historical links
with other parts of the world in which English has a large number of first language speakers, i.e. the USA (for the Philippines) and the UK (for India), and
it may also be the case that there is at least some cultural familiarity between the
USA and the Philippines and between the UK and India because of their shared
history, which allows ITES employees to attune themselves relatively easily to
the American and British customers that they interact with. It is also most

certainly the case in both contexts that levels of education are high, that English medium education is widespread, and that there is a large pool of appropriately qualified people who provide the ITES industry with a useful set of potential employees. Forey (2008) has commented for instance, that the ITES industry has provided relatively well-paid employment for large numbers of graduates in the Philippines, who would otherwise have opted for domestic work in wealthier nations such as Hong Kong or Singapore. In other words, the emergence of the ITES industry has therefore improved both the economic prospects and societal status for numerous people, and likewise, in Friedman's terms, it is clearly the case that outsourcing certain activities to either India or the Philippines is a cost-effective option for many major corporations. So is it possible to establish a link between the presence of English as Second Language spoken by large numbers of people and the emergence of the ITES industry, as long as the economic conditions are favourable, or are other factors also at play? And is one ESL context more likely to support a successful ITES industry than another?

Nigeria is listed in third place in the List of Countries by English Speaking Population (Wikipedia 2009) immediately after the USA, which has around 251 million speakers of English, and India, with 90 million. There are 79 million people in Nigeria who speak English as either a first or additional language, which is around 53% of the entire population, and English is also the official language. In addition, literacy rates are 69% – higher than in many states in India – and Nigeria also provides English medium education up to tertiary level, in a similar way to India and the Philippines. And yet, to date, Nigeria has been unable to match the success of the industry in India or the Philippines; in 2006, for instance, Ofour Direct operating in Lagos claimed to be the first commercial call centre partner in Nigeria (Ofour 2006) and a subsequent internet search failed to identify much ITES activity in Nigeria, nor did it reveal what had happened to Ofour in the intervening 2 years. There may perhaps be three reasons as to why the ITES industry would be successful in some ESL environments, but not in others. First, in the case of Nigeria, political and economic instability may have played a role in the industry's reluctance to invest. Secondly, although English medium education is available, it may not produce the same numbers of highly qualified graduates as elsewhere, e.g. in 1990, although as many as 200,000 students were enrolled at Nigerian universities or colleges at tertiary level, this represented less than 1% of the twenty-one to twenty-nine-year-old age group, the primary age group for intake into the ITES industry (Library of Congress, 1992; in July 2008, the most recent Library of Congress report on Nigeria does not provide any additional figures for tertiary education, but it does report that in 2005 only 23% of girls and 28% of boys were in secondary education suggesting that the pool of potential employees would be relatively small). Thirdly, the English that is spoken as a lingua franca in Nigeria is Nigerian Pidgin rather than a more standard Nigerian variety of English, and this may create further obstacles in developing a successful ITES industry, since the mainstay of ITES communication is the mutual intelligibility between different varieties of English, e.g. Indian English with British English. The situation may also be similar in other parts of (ESL-speaking) Africa, e.g. in Uganda, English is one of two official languages and is spoken by two and a half million speakers as an additional language (Crystal 2005), and yet the BPO industry numbers less than 1,500 and the country has only very recently recognized the potential that the industry could have (Computer World Nigeria 2008).

One other country serves to illustrate the complex nature of the relationship between English as a Second Language, a favourable, i.e. cost effective, economic climate and the emergence of the ITES industry; Singapore. A Singaporean census carried out in 2000, reports that there are just under one million eight hundred thousand speakers of English in Singapore, around 39% of the population, of which around six hundred thousand speak English as a first language and a little over one million one hundred thousand as an additional language (Wikipedia 2009). As Clark et al. report (Clark et al. this volume), Singapore has very high levels of education and technology, e.g. an internet down-time target of only 10 minutes every 10 years, but correspondingly high levels of labour costs – exceptionally high in fact compared to India and the Philippines. In other words, Singapore has identified and developed a niche in the ITES market, that being to represent the luxury end of the market for those customers who are willing to pay the price for absolute reliability. In the Singaporean case, the combination of reliability and English language skills have compensated for any obvious economic disadvantages.

Research in ESL Workplace Contexts

A number of recent studies have looked at the discourse of ITES interactions in ESL contexts like India (Cowie 2007) Singapore (Clark et al. 2008) and the Philippines (Forey and Lockwood 2007). Studies such as these provide a fruitful line of enquiry which could be expanded to other contexts to improve our understanding of the discourse features which customer service representatives (CSRs) need to master in order to get their work done successfully. This in turn has obvious implications both for training and assessment (see also Lockwood this volume on assessment). Clark et al.'s work (2008) has also shown that CSRs working in the ITES industry in Singapore need to be able to code-switch between Singaporean English and a more standard variety of English on a moment to moment basis in order to complete their work tasks. This is an interesting aspect of call centre discourse that could also characterize the work of other ESL speakers working in other parts of the world who are operating on their own domestic market, e.g. a CSR based in Bangalore working for the domestic branch of a bank would need to be able to code-switch not only across different varieties of English to meet the needs of their expatriate customers as well as their Indian customers who prefer to speak English, but also quite plausibly to switch from English to Hindi, or equally from English to one of the other languages spoken in the South of India. A study of such code-switching could make a useful contribution to the development of training materials for call centre discourse.

In other research related to ESL workplace contexts outside of the ITES industry, the focus has been on needs analysis, e.g. the Teaching English to meet the needs of business education in Hong Kong project described by Jackson (2005), on the interaction between English and other local languages, e.g. Nair-Venugopal's study of language choice and communication in Malaysian business (Nair-Venugopal 2001) and her later discussion of what actually constitutes Malaysian Business English (Nair-Venugopal 2006), and on the sociolinguistic consequences of opting or not opting for English as an official language, e.g. Gargesh's discussion of English in India in business and technology (Gargesh 2006). In addition, work by researchers such as Rogerson-Revell and Bilbow in the Hong Kong context, has revealed those discourse strategies that ESL speakers find problematic (in meeting situations) both in the production and interpretation of English (Bilbow 2002; Rogerson-Revell 1999). Rogerson-Revell's later work also provides some excellent insights into the problems faced by speakers of languages other than English, both ESL and EFL speakers, in interactions with first language English speakers (Rogerson-Revell 2007, 2008). Finally, the studies by Yeung (e.g. Yeung 2003, 2004) which contrast the discourse strategies used by Hong Kong Chinese speakers and those used by Australian speakers, and the numerous studies of the discourse strategies used by first and second language speakers of English in New Zealand that fall within the Language in the Workplace Project (e.g. Holmes 2000; Stubbe and Brown 2002), identify a number of crucial differences between the speakers of different varieties of English that could help in the design of training and assessment materials. In sum, all these studies provide approaches and/or methodologies that could be of use in understanding the interactions that take place within the ITES industry. For example, needs analysis surveys combined with the study of code-switching between English and other languages would be useful in the development of appropriate training materials, as would further work not only on the language and discourse strategies that are effective in successfully completing a transaction, but also on the discourse strategies used by first language English speakers that ESL speakers are likely to find problematic.

In this section I have looked at the relationship between English as a Second Language and its relationship with business and development. I have identified a number of factors that may combine with an ESL environment to create the conditions for the development of a successful ITES industry and I have speculated on what the existing research on ESL Workplace discourse could contribute to our understanding of the communication that takes place within the ITES context. In the next section I will look at outsourcing and English as a first language.

English as a First Language

Outsourcing and English as a First Language

The town of Ten Sleep in Wyoming in the USA has a population of around 350. It also has a fibre optic cable and is home to a thriving ITES industry that employs 300 teachers of English across Northern Wyoming, providing English language training via Skype to 15,000 students in Korea. As the CEO of Eleutian Technology, Kent Holiday, commented in December 2008, 'It's a $100 billion dollar market just between Korea, Japan and China, and so we wanted to be the leader and wanted to have millions of users' (Globe and Mail 2008). Eleutian Technology provides an excellent example of where a native variety of English, i.e. in this case American English, is being used as a resource in combination with the technology available. In the Wyoming case, at least two other factors have also contributed to the success of the Eleutian Technology venture. First, the teaching expertise is available and under-used in much the same way as the pool of highly educated ESL speakers in India and the Philippines, and secondly, there is an extensive and relatively new market for the services available as a result of the fact that English is rapidly becoming the language of Asian business. In a similar way to the recent emergence of the KPO industry in India with a particular focus on legal services, Eleutian Technology is an example of a thriving ITES KPO industry which has found a niche in the market as a result of external developments on the other side of the globe.

In other recent developments in the ITES industry, native speakers of English elsewhere in the world have also emerged – or perhaps re-emerged – onto the global ITES stage. In December 2008, for instance, much was made in the business media of the decision taken by the major Indian BPO corporations to set up offices in Belfast and Londonderry in Northern Ireland. By the end of 2008, Indian companies such as HCL Technology, Polaris, Tech Mahindra and Firstsource had already invested $300 million and created around 3,500 jobs in Northern Ireland, making India second only to the USA in terms of IT investment in the region (DNAIndia 2008). As in the case of the emergence of the ITES industry in ESL contexts like India and the Philippines, the government in Northern Ireland had made it economically attractive for overseas investors, e.g. by giving support for the costs of initial set-up, such as recruitment and training costs, and in addition, Northern Ireland also has a large pool of technical talent that provides a suitable workforce. Finally, the decision to invest in Northern Ireland can perhaps also have been made in part because of the fact that English is spoken as a first language (by all but the very smallest minority of Irish Gaelic speakers) in Northern Ireland. Firstsource, for instance, now has 36 call centres worldwide and employs more than 18,500 people across four continents, i.e. in India, the UK, the USA, Argentina and the Philippines. With the exception of Argentina, all the call centres are therefore located in regions of the world where English is spoken as either a first language or second language. Given a set of favourable economic conditions, coupled with the availability of a suitable workforce, it seems plausible that corporations would then also consider availability of English as a determining factor, since this would facilitate communication within the corporation and between the call centre agents and their corporate clients. Interestingly, Firstsource in Argentina asks for applicants that are bilingual in Spanish and English, presumably reflecting a need to interface with a set of Spanish-speaking customers, as well as with other Firstsource employees located in different parts of the world, with whom they are more likely to share English as a common language (Firstsource 2009). For the other regions of the world in which Firstsource is operating, it is only in the information for Indian applicants that English is specifically mentioned, e.g. Proficiency in written and verbal communication in English; in contrast, the Philippines asks for 'good communication skills' rather than making any specific reference to English, perhaps because English is spoken by a larger percentage of the population than it is in India (see discussion on the ESL context above).

The examples that I have given here illustrate two ways in which English may be considered as key resource to business and development. In the Firstsource example, the presence of English can be viewed as an additional resource which may be of influence in determining whether or not a corporation will invest in a particular region, if all other things are equal. And in the Eleutian Technology example, native speaker English is not only a key resource, it is also the product that drives the entire business – made feasible as a business idea by other factors relating to the increasing use of English as the global language of business and technology.

Research in First Language Research Contexts

The 2000 study by Deborah Cameron is a landmark study in the investigation of language and discourse in the ITES industry (Cameron 2000). In the study, Cameron uses a combination of observation, interviews and written materials such as employees' manuals, training packs and relevant memos, to investigate the speech styles that were prescribed to telephone call centre operators at seven centres in the UK. Cameron's work shows that the speech styles recommended for use at the call centres involved strategies such as showing rapport, asking questions, being expressive and being sincere. In other words, they were the types of strategies that are often described as 'women's language'. Bolton (2008) has discussed the transvestite community that works in call centres in the Philippines, and has suggested that they may be particularly effective as CSRs because of their expert use of such 'feminine' strategies, which are particularly appropriate in empathizing with the customer in call centre work. Cameron points out that the type of regulation that she observed in the call centres she studied – which is a common occurrence in the training given for call centre employees (Hultgren and Cameron – this volume; Friginal 2007) – is a reflection both of increasing globalization and of an awareness of the role that language can play 'as a valuable commodity, potentially a source of "competitive advantage", which needs to be "managed" rather than simply left to take care of itself', i.e. an awareness of the value that can be associated with the commodification of language (Cameron 2000:324).

Other work that has focused on the strategies used by first language speakers of English includes Yamada's work on US business meetings (compared to Japanese business meetings), Yeung's work on Australian management discourse, the work of Holmes and her colleagues within the Language in the Workplace Project, as I have discussed above, Nelson's study of UK and US Business English, which includes business meetings and negotiations, and Lampi's work on business negotiations in the UK (Holmes 2005; Holmes and Marra 2004; Holmes and Stubbe 2003; Lampi 1986; Nelson 2000, 2006; Yamada 1992; Yeung 2000, 2003). Although these studies look at genres that are clearly not completely the same as the type of interactions that take place within the ITES industry, they do however identify large numbers of the strategies that speakers use in various situations of relevance to the ITES industry, e.g. making requests, dealing with conflict, apologizing etc. Likewise, the studies by Rogerson-Revell on meeting discourse (2007, 2008), particularly her discussion on the difficulties experienced by speakers of other languages in interactions with first language speakers of English, and the strategies they use to combat these, could be of interest in training CSRs from ESL or EFL contexts (see also Charles and Marschan-Piekkari 2002 for a similar study within an MNC).

In this section I have looked at outsourcing and English as a first language, and the ways in which it has influenced the emergence and relocation of the ITES industry. I have also identified a number of studies that could be of interest in designing appropriate materials to train CSRs particularly if they need to interact with first language speakers of English. In the next section I will go on to look at outsourcing and English as a foreign language, and discuss how English has played a role in the ITES industry as exemplified by the emerging economies of China and Russia.

English as a Foreign Language

Outsourcing and English as a Foreign Language

In (Mainland) China, English is clearly not spoken as a second language and the historical ties with English-speaking countries that characterize many of the other countries in the developing world are not in evidence, apart from the special case of Hong Kong. At present there are around ten million speakers of

English as an additional language in Mainland China, and current estimates suggest that there are 300 million people currently learning the language, with English now mandatory in schools and colleges (Wikipedia 2009). Within a very short time, many of these students will complete their education, and by that time many of them will have sufficient skills in English to enter the ITES industry. As has been well-documented elsewhere, China now poses a major threat to India's dominant position within the ITES industry (see for example, Rediff 2007), not only because cities such as Dalian City in Liaoning Province have been purposefully developed as IT centres – and BPO hubs – in a similar way to Bangalore in India, but also because the Chinese industry has clearly identified a potential threat to their ability to compete with other more established (and largely ESL) locations, and they have therefore implemented compulsory English language study throughout their system in order to counter this. And at the time of writing, the Chinese government had approved Business English for the first time as an official course of study at tertiary level (personal communication, Zuocheng Zang, Professor at the University of International Business and Economy, Beijing). In other words, the economic conditions are favourable to compete on the global market, the technical skills are available and the linguistic needs to support the industry have been assessed and are currently being addressed. At the same time, English has also rapidly been gaining ground as the language of business in the Asia Pacific region in general, and this has also created the need for Mainland China to improve its English language skills and assign the necessary resources to do so, with a corresponding effect on the ITES industry.

Elsewhere in world, Russia also provides an interesting example of the role played by English in the ITES industry, albeit a fledgling industry that is unlikely to challenge the position held by India and the Philippines for some time to come. On the face of it, Russia doesn't look like a promising destination for the ITES industry, since as long ago as 2003, Hayes and MacSweeney commented in InformationWeek,

> Russia has a long way to go before it rivals India, the darling-du-jour of offshore outsourcing. Immature business and project-management skills, not enough promotion of English-language skills, and a telecommunications infrastructure in disrepair are among the challenges that have kept Russia from matching the astounding success of India, which exported nearly $10 billion in software and services last year. (InformationWeek 2003)

However, a closer look at the ITES industry in Russia, reveals that there is a small niche in the market in that the Russians may be able to fill perhaps better than their Indian counterparts, and that the reasons for this are related to language, location and culture. By September 2008, Russia was being described by an Indian BPO industry watchdog, as 'emerging as a skilled back office administration to the world's leading corporations' (BPOWatchIndia 2008).

The reasons given for the Russian success in creating a market dealing with difficult software problems in particular, are first to do with the Russian tendency towards pessimism, which some customers apparently prefer if they are dealing with a difficult problem, e.g. 'Indians always report the best possible scenario and the Russian firms always the worst possible scenario', secondly, the location of Russia in relation to many of their clients, e.g. 'Moscow and St Petersburg are a three-hour flight from Frankfurt and only two-hour time difference from Western Europe', and finally the fact that they may speak other languages in addition to English, e.g. 'Several of the firms have German and Finnish language skills, in addition to English' (Russoft 2003). In the Russian scenario then, English is viewed as necessary but not sufficient; as a linguistic resource yes, but not one that excludes other languages. This is a similar situation perhaps to the Argentinean Firstsource example that I have cited above, where English and Spanish are required to successfully enter the industry, rather than the English only requirement that has been dominant in India and the Philippines. As the market continues to develop, it will be interesting to see if more opportunities are identified that are at least partly created by the existence of a multilingual workforce.

The Chinese and Russian examples show that the historical presence of English as either a second or first language may not always be a determining factor in the success or failure of the ITES industry. In China, the efforts made to improve the English language skills across society will impact the industry as more people with better language proficiency enter the workforce, and in Russia the industry will continue to develop if the Russians can capitalize on their cultural and linguistic advantages, alongside the implementation of improvements in the infrastructure necessary to adequately support an ITES environment.

Research in Foreign Language Research Contexts

Many of the studies I have discussed above are also relevant for the ITES industry located in areas of the world where English is a foreign language, e.g. Rogerson-Revell's work on multicultural meetings and Clark et al's work on the strategies that are effective in call centre communication in Singapore. Other work specifically related to English as a foreign language may also be of relevance, including Louhiala-Salminen, Charles and Kankaanranta's 2005 study of the use of English as a Business Lingua Franca between Finnish employees and Swedish employees at two major joint ventures in Scandinavia, and the 2002 study by Gimenez of the difficulties faced by the employees of an Argentinean subsidiary in communication in English with their European Head Office. Louhiala-Salminen et al. (2005), for instance, identify considerable differences in the discourse strategies used by the Swedes and the Finns, which led to misperceptions on both sides, e.g. the Swedes were perceived by the Finns as too 'discussive' and 'wordy', whereas the Finns were perceived by the Swedes as

too 'direct' and 'economical with words' (2005:408). The study is of interest to
the ITES industry because it illustrates the way in which a speaker's national
culture may impact their discourse realizations, and that these in turn may
influence the way in which they are perceived. In the 2002 study by Gimenez,
an analysis of the fax and email communication between an Argentinean subsidiary and its European Head Office reveals that communication conflicts
occur as a result of a clash between the globally adopted conventions required
by Head Office and the locally constructed identities operating within the
subsidiary. Informal networks – or shadow structures running parallel to
the official organizational structures – had evolved within the subsidiary so that
the senior managers with lesser skills in English could cope only by relying
on their more junior colleagues who generally had better English. As the
ITES industry continues to expand across continents, as in the case of the
Indian BPOs such as Firstsource that I have discussed above, it will be interesting to see how much English language proficiency determines an employee's
success as a CSR, team leader or manager, and whether there is evidence of
disempowerment as a result of lack of language proficiency in that way that
Gimenez describes (see also Marschan-Piekkari, et al.1999, for further discussion on the evolution of shadow structures in MNCs related to language
proficiency).

To conclude this section I will discuss an on-going study of the perception of
English as a foreign language, i.e. the English produced by Dutch speakers of
English, that has clear implications for the ITES industry (Gerritsen et al.
2008). In this study, native speakers of British English were asked to listen to
three simulations of a telephone sales pitch, one involving an RP (British)
accent, one with a slight Dutch accent in English and one with a moderate
Dutch accent. The study showed that the more pronounced the accent, the
more negative the native speaker perceptions were, despite the fact that all
three speakers were rated as equally comprehensible. A great deal of time and
money is spent on accent training within the ITES industry, and, perhaps
controversially, the ability to produce an RP accent is frequently used as
a determining factor in whether or not some-one is offered a job (see also
Cowie 2007). Studies similar to that by Gerritsen and her colleagues, focusing
specifically on the ITES sector, would be very useful in establishing just what
role accent really does play in customers' attitudes to and perceptions of the
non-native English-speaking CSR.

Conclusion

In this chapter I have discussed the role that English has played in various
parts of the world as a key resource to the development of an ITES industry.
As the dominant language of global business and technology, the use of English
as a lingua franca in its broadest sense (i.e. including native speakers of

English) has both facilitated and contributed to the process of globalization that is at the heart of both the emergence and economic success of the industry. I have suggested that at the very least the presence of English can be considered as an eleventh 'flattener' or facilitator in addition to Friedman's existing list, and I would go on to say that the levelling of the playing field between the developed world and the emerging economies that are part of the ITES sector, is hard to imagine at all without the commodification of English.

In the second part of my discussion on outsourcing for each of the three ways in which English is used around the globe, I have identified research on call centre discourse along with other studies of workplace communication that offer useful insights into the interactions that take place between CSRs and their customers, and between the employees working for the large BPO corporations as those corporations become increasingly multinational. The chapters in the present volume in particular represent the cutting edge of research into the communication that takes place within the ITES industry around the globe. As such they will make an invaluable contribution to our understanding of Business English and its continuing role in the process of globalization.

References

Bilbow, G. (2002), Commissive speech act use in intercultural business meetings. *International Review of Applied Linguistics in Language Teaching* 40(4), 287–303.

Bolton, K. (2008), Asian Englishes, call centre communication and the issue of proficiency. Paper presented at the 3rd International Conference Talking Across the World, GEAR School Bangalore, 25–26 April.

BPOWatchIndia. (2008), http://www.bpowatchindia.com/bpo_industry_report/bpo_future/september-17-2008/bpo_future_global.html (accessed 25 January 2009).

Cameron, D. (2000), Styling the worker: Gender and the commodification of language in the globalized service economy. Journal of Sociolinguistics 4(3), 323– 347.

Charles, M. and Marschan-Piekkari, R. (2002), Language training for enhanced horizontal communication: A challenge for MNCs. *Business Communication Quarterly* 65(2), 9–29.

Clark, C., Rogers, P., Murfett, U. and Ang, S. (2008), Is Courtesy Enough? 'Solidarity' in Call Center Interactions. *Ross School of Business Paper No. 1103.* http://ssrn.com/abstract=1128246 (accessed 11 November 2008).

Computer World Nigeria. (2008), http://www.computerworldnigeria.com/articles/2008/10/20/uganda-develops-bpo-strategy (accessed 20 January 2009).

Cowie, C. (2007), The accents of outsourcing: the meanings of 'neutral' in the Indian call centre industry. *World Englishes* 26(3), 316–330.

Crystal, D. (2005) (1995), The Cambridge Encyclopedia of the English Language, 2nd edn. Cambridge: Cambridge University Press.

DNA India. (2008), http://www.dnaindia.com/report.asp?newsid=1208100 (accessed 10 December 2008).

Economic Times. (2008), http://economictimes.indiatimes.com/Infotech/LPOs_thrive_as_BPOs_languish_d uring_slump/articleshow/3751429.cms (accessed 24 November 2008).

Firstcource. (2009), http://www.firstsource.com/careers (accessed 24 January 2009).

Forey, G. (2008), Call centre communication research: Investigating emotional labour and emotional language. Paper presented at the 3rd International Conference Talking Across the World, GEAR School Bangalore, 25–26 April.

Forey, G. and Lockwood, J. (2007), 'I'd love to put someone in jail for this': An Initial investigation of English in the business processing outsourcing (BPO) industry. English for Specific Purposes 26(3), 308–326.

Friedman, T. L. (2005), *The World is Flat.* New York: Farrar Straus and Giroux.

Friginal, E. (2007), Outsourced call centers in English in the Philippines. *World Englishes* 26(3), 331–345.

Gargesh, R. (2006), Language issues in the context of Higher Education in India. Paper presented at the Language issues in English Medium Universities Across Asia Symposium, University of Hong Kong, Hong Kong, 8–9 June.

http://www.hku.hk/clear/doc/DAY%201/Ravinder%20Gargesh.PPT (accessed 11 November 2008).

Gerritsen, M., Nejjari, W., Van der Haagen, M. and Korzilius, H. (2008), The effect of Dutch-accented English on British RP-speakers in the onset of a telephone sales talk. Paper presented at the APacLSP Conference, Partnerships in Action: Research, Practice and Training, City University Hong Kong, 8–10 December.

Gimenez, J. (2002), New media and conflicting realities in multinational corporate communication: A case study. *International Review of Applied Linguistics in Language Teaching* 40, 323–344.

Globe and Mail. (2008), http://www.theglobeandmail.com/servlet/story/RTGAM. 20081121.wgtteach1121/ BNStory/Technology/home (accessed 22 December 2008).

Holmes, J. (2000), Doing collegiality and keeping control at work: Small talk in government departments. In Coupland, Justine (ed.) *Small Talk*, 32–61. London: Longman.

Holmes, J. (2005), Leadership talk: How do leaders 'do mentoring', and is gender relevant? *Journal of Pragmatics* 37, 1779–1800.

Holmes, J. and Marra, M. (2004), Relational practice in the workplace: Women's talk or gendered discourse? *Language in Society* 33, 377–398.

Holmes, J. and Stubbe, M. (2003), *Power and Politeness in the Workplace.* Upper Saddle River, NJ: Pearson Education.

Hultgren, A. K. and Cameron, D. (this volume).

InformationWeek. (2003), http://www.informationweek.com/news/services/show-Article.jhtml?articleID=12 802965 (accessed 20 December 2008).

Jackson, J. (2005), An inter-university, cross-disciplinary analysis of business education: Perceptions of business faculty in Hong Kong. *English for Specific Purposes* 24, 293–306.

Kachru, Braj B., Kachru, Y. and Nelson, C. (2006), *The Handbook of World Englishes.* Hoboken, New Jersey: John Wiley and Sons Inc.

Lampi, M. (1986), Linguistic *Components of Strategy in Business Negotiations.* Helsinki School of Economics, Studies B-85, Helsinki: Helsinki School of Economics.

Library of Congress. (1992) (2008), A country study: Nigeria. http://lcweb2.loc. gov/frd/cs/ngtoc.html (accessed 23 January 2009).

Louhiala-Salminen, L., Charles, M. and Kankaanranta, A. (2005), English as a lingua franca in Nordic corporate mergers: Two case companies. *English for Specific Purposes* 24, 401–421.

Marschan, R., Welch, D. and Welch, L. (1999), In the shadow: The impact of language on structure, power and communication in the multinational. *International Business Review* 8, 421–440.

Nair-Venugopal, S. (2001), The sociolinguistics of choice in Malaysian business settings. *International Journal of the Sociology of Language* 152, 21–52.

Nair-Venugopal, S. (2006), An interactional model of English in Malaysia: A contextualised response to commodification. In Bargiela-Chiappini, Francesca (ed.) *Asian Business Discourse(s) Part II.* Amsterdam: John Benjamins, 51–75.

Nelson, M. (2000), The business English lexis site. http://users.utu.fi/micnel/ business_english_lexis_site.htm (accessed 8 April 2006).

Nelson, M. (2006), Semantic associations in business English: A corpus-based analysis. *English for Specific Purposes Journal* 25, 217–234.

Nickerson, C. (2010/forthcoming), The Englishes of business. In Kirkpatrick, Thomas Andrew (ed.) *The Handbook of World Englishes.* London and New York: Routledge.

Ofour. (2006), http://www.ofour.org (downloaded 20 January 2009).

Pal, M. and Buzzanell, P. (2008), The Indian call center experience: A case study in changing discourses of identity, identification, and career in a global context. *Journal of Business Communication* 45, 31–60.

Planken, B. (2005), Managing rapport in lingua franca sales negotiations: A comparison of professional and aspiring negotiators. *English for Specific Purposes* 24, 381–400.

Poncini, G. (2004), *Discursive Strategies in Multicultural Business Meetings.* Bern: Peter Lang.

Rediff. (2007), http://www.rediff.com/money/2007/feb/09bpo1.htm (accessed 22 January 2009).

Rogerson-Revell, P. (1999), Meeting Talk: A stylistic approach to teaching meeting skills. In Hewings, Martin and Nickerson, Catherine (eds.) Business English: Research into Practice. London: Longman, 55–71.

Rogerson-Revell, P. (2007), Using English for international business: A European case study. *English for Specific Purposes* 26, 103–120.

Rogerson-Revell, P. (2008), Participation and performance in international business meetings. *English for Specific Purposes* 27, 338–360.

Russoft. (2003) (http://www.russoft.org/docs/?doc=951 (accessed 18 December 2008).

Stubbe, M. and Brown, P. (2002), *Talk that Works: Communication in Successful Factory Teams: A Training Resource Kit.* Wellington: School of Linguistics and Applied Language Studies, Victoria University of Wellington.

Upadhya, C. and Vasavi, A. R. (2009), *In an Outpost of the Global Economy: Work and Workers in India's Information Technology Industry.* Delhi: Routledge India.

Wikipedia. (2009), http://en.wikipedia.org/wiki/List_of_countries_by_English-speaking_population (accessed 30 January 2009).

Yamada, H. (1992), *American and Japanese Business Discourse: A Comparison of Interactional Styles.* Norwood, NJ: Ablex.

Yeung, L. (2000), The question of Chinese indirectness: A comparison of Chinese and English participative decision-making discourse. *Multilingua* 19, 221–264.

Yeung, L. (2003), Management discourse in Australian banking contexts: In search of an Australian model of participation as compared with that of Hong Kong Chinese. *Journal of Intercultural Studies* 24, 47–63.

Yeung, L. (2004), The paradox of control in participative decision-making: Facilitative discourse in banks. *TEXT* 24, 113–146.

Chapter 4

Communication Skills in Contemporary Service Workplaces: Some Problems

Anna Kristina Hultgren
University of Copenhagen, Denmark

Deborah Cameron
University of Oxford, UK

It is widely agreed that in the globalized service economy considerable emphasis is placed on workers' communication skills. In this chapter, we scrutinize the notion of communication skills as it is understood in call centres and point to some of its problems and limitations. Drawing on authentic audio-recorded customer service transactions collected from an onshore call centre in Scotland, we show that predetermining the spoken interaction of call centre workers is only partially possible and even potentially counterproductive.

Introduction

There is hardly any doubt that in the globalized service economy considerable emphasis is placed on workers' **communication skills** (Cameron 2000; Fairclough 1992; The New London Group 2000). This reflects a restructuring of the economy and changes in the ways in which we perceive language and the importance we accord it (Chouliaraki and Fairclough 1999; Cope and Kalantzis 2000; Fairclough 1992). In an increasingly saturated market, language has become a commodity (Cameron 2005; Heller 2003) and carefully managing it is seen as a way of ensuring competitive advantage. Contemporary management practices in the ITES industry thus typically involve some ways of directing, controlling and monitoring the language that their workers use in interaction with customers (Cameron 2000; Kinnie et al. 2000; Taylor and Bain 1999). According to the Call Centre Association (CCA), the professional body for the ITES industry in the UK, **communication skills** are foremost among four skills required by workers, ranking above system, product and sales knowledge (CCA 2001) and are considered so important that they cannot be left to take care of themselves. A report by a management consultancy writes:

> Good quality interactions don't just happen; agents should be carefully coached in conversational skills as a priority. (CM 2004:16)

Although the extent of intervention in the linguistic behaviour of workers may vary across the ITES industry (Hutchinson et al. 2000; Taylor et al. 2002), the resources devoted to it are arguably unprecedented and it is probably fair to say that it constitutes one of the most important principles around which the work is organized.

The focus on **communication skills** in ITES workplaces manifests itself in various ways. It often starts in the recruitment process where priority is given to candidates who display the potential to provide good customer care (Belt 2002; Callaghan and Thompson 2002; Thompson and Callaghan 2002). It is also common to have some sort of training programme in place where agents are coached in how to talk to customers (Sturdy 2000). Many workplaces also choose to make use of customer service manuals which outline certain phrases that workers must use in interaction with customers (Cameron 2000; Kinnie et al. 2000; Taylor and Bain 1999). There also tends to be some sort of assessment system in operation by which workers' compliance with the linguistic regulation is monitored and assessed, either in real time or by recording the interaction for later assessment. The latter is typically conducted using a type of scorecard where workers' performance is ticked off following a set of predefined criteria, such as e.g. 'did the worker use the correct greeting?' or 'did the worker acknowledge the customer's problem?' The outcome of such call assessments may affect the worker's salary, bonuses and/or their possibilities for career advancement (Taylor and Bain 1999).

One important reason for this preoccupation with communication relates to the notion of **customer sovereignty** which has a crucial status in contemporary management paradigms (du Gay and Salaman 1992). Companies compete on service and aim at making customers feel that they are being personally cared for, something which is deemed particularly important in the ITES industry where traditional face-to-face interaction has been replaced by remote service provision. Strategies designed to compensate for the **en masse** service provided, aptly dubbed 'synthetic personalisation' (Fairclough 1989), are a central component of the way in which ITES workplaces understand and define **communication skills**. As one manager explained to us in an interview: the aim is to make the service interaction resemble 'a conversation between friends more than a business transaction between strangers'. Such **rapport** building, a concept often used in call centre communication material, typically involves asking service workers to engage in 'active listening' by giving verbal feedback in the form of 'mhm', 'aha', 'I see' and by acknowledging that they have understood the customer's problem and that they are going to help them, employing phrases such as 'I can certainly help with that'. They may also be told to empathize with the customer using phrases such as 'I understand that must be really difficult for you' and to engage in small talk by picking up on issues that are entirely unrelated to the transaction at hand. One service worker explained to us, for instance, that she and her colleagues were encouraged to say things like 'oh, how old is the baby?' if they heard a baby crying in the background while dealing with a customer's request (see also Thompson and Callaghan 2002).

While such ways of making the customer feel personally cared for are construed as crucial in many ITES workplaces, the industry is, it is widely agreed, simultaneously one of the most tightly controlled places to work in with little worker autonomy and a high degree of management involvement (Fernie and Metcalf 1998; Richardson et al. 2000; Taylor et al. 2002). Increased global competition puts the industry under constant pressure to rationalize operations, and this typically means implementing neo-Taylorist principles which predetermine every task of the worker and monitor their exact execution. Call centres are highly target- and measurement-driven and computer-generated performance reports regularly output the exact time each worker has spent on each task, i.e. talking to customers, updating customer records, being in a meeting or taking a toilet break. As one call centre worker interviewed by sociologist Marek Korczynski put it 'you get measured on how many times you scratch your shoulder' (2001:89–90).

The target culture that prevails in call centres extends, also to the linguistic behaviour of call centre agents, as most of the tasks that agents perform involve communicating with customers over the phone. In call assessments, a given number of calls are selected from the agent and their style of communication in those calls is then graded by comparing it to the prescribed style of communication. Thus, on call centre scorecards, workers may score points if they 'call the customer by their name at least twice in the interaction', deploy verbal feedback such as 'aha', 'mhm' and 'I see' or 'engage in small talk with the customer'. Because of the centrality of targets, the notion of what constitutes good **communication skills** in call centres inevitably comes to be defined in terms that require it to be quantifiable and measurable. The result is a decontextualized understanding of **communication skills** that does not allow for the complexities of spoken interaction.

In this chapter, we will scrutinize the notion of **communication skills** as it is understood in call centres and point to some of its problems and limitations. First, predetermining the spoken interaction of workers is always only going to be partially realizable given that conversations are locally managed phenomena (Nofsinger 1991). Thus, regulating spoken interaction cannot predict the conversational utterances of the co-speaker (i.e. the customer) which are likely to constrain what the speaker (i.e. the service worker) can reasonably say next. In some cases, this principle of speaker-hearer co-construction causes the service worker to deviate from the prescriptions laid out in the communication material. Ironically, this deviation often results in a 'better', or at least a less marked, service than had been the case if the prescriptions had been adhered to. Secondly, regulating spoken interaction may also be potentially counter-productive. Putting constraints on the use of 'negative language', for instance, as is common in some call centres, may confuse the caller by forcing the worker to communicate their inability to accomplish a certain task indirectly. We will support these two arguments by drawing on transcripts of real audio-recorded service interactions collected from an onshore call centre, Thistle Insurance, which is located in Scotland and is part of a large insurance compa-ny.[1] Since the data come from an onshore call centre, in contrast to what is the case in most chapters of this volume, it is necessary to briefly discuss some potential differences and similarities in the way in which on- and offshore call centres understand the notion of **communication skills**.

Communication Skills in On- and Offshore Call Centres

In offshore call centres, i.e. where agent and customer are located in different countries and the worker must communicate in a language which is usually not their first, training in communication is often said to be of a different nature and urgency. Training initiatives in offshore call centres in places such as India and the Philippines, e.g., may include elements of second language learning, such as phonology, intonation, grammar and vocabulary (Cowie 2007). 'Culture training' is also common practice in many offshore call centres (Elias this volume). By comparison, **communication skills** in onshore call centres, i.e. call centres where the agent and the customer are based in the same coun-try and share the same first language, tends to have less to do with phonological and grammatical correctness, as this is taken for granted, and more with issues belonging to the level of discourse, such as e.g. the ability of the worker to establish **rapport** with, and show empathy for the customer.

Despite such differences, however, there are considerable similarities between off- and onshore call centres, in relation to the notion of **communication skills**. The call centre industry is truly globalized and there are remarkable similarities between work practices and technologies used across countries (e.g. Bain et al. 2002; Buscatto 2002; Tsoukas and Vladimirou 2001). The establishment of call centres, whether on- or offshore, tends to rely on an operational prototype, a knowledge of how to do 'call centering', which can be infinitely reproduced across the globe. The similarities extend also to what sort of communication skills are favoured. Agents in offshore call centres are often taught to commu-nicate in a style that resembles one which prevails in the country where the client base is located. Frequent reliance on Western-based management consultants also tends to mean that much of what is taught to agents in onshore call centres is also being taught to agents in offshore call centres. Thus the belief that, for instance, creating **rapport** and showing empathy are crucial components of what constitutes good **communication skills** is shared by on- and offshore call centres (Hultgren 2008). It is **communication skills** understood in this way, i.e. as relating to the level of discourse, that we problematize in this chapter. So let us take a look at some of the problems entailed in the practice of regulating spoken interaction.

Regulating Spoken Interaction: Some Problems

The main problem with trying to implement a top-down approach to customer service by providing agents with rules about what to say and what not to say is that it disregards the fact that conversations must in the end be played out between the people who are engaged in them. Although this insight may appear obvious, it is difficult to allow for in scorecards, which disregard the presence of the customer and other relevant contextual factors. According to a scorecard used in Thistle Insurance, the call centre agent must 'acknowledge the caller's problem'. Rather than providing a solution to a customer's query straight away, they must first declare that they are willing to help and only thereafter proceed with the actual process of answering the query. The rule takes the following form

> [The agent] tells the customer they can help them and offers an apology if necessary, e.g. 'Let me see what's happened . . .', 'Let me see how I can help . . .', 'I do apologize for that, let me see what I can do . . .', 'I can certainly help with that'. (Thistle scorecard)

What happens in reality, however, is that the prescribed move 'acknowledge problem' is subject to conversational constraints, which would make it more conspicuous to abide by the rule than to flout it.

```
Caller right erhm I've just taken voluntary redundancy from my teaching post
  Agent  right okay
Caller and I'm just wondering what the sort of state of play is with my AVCs
    I've got my AVCs can I use them now or have I got to wait until I'm sixty
Agent  you've got to although you don't have to wait until you're sixty Mr Smith the main rule of
thumb with the AVC because it's linked to your teachers main pension scheme
```

In this example, the caller phrases his request as a direct question ('Can I use them [my AVCs] now or have I got to wait until I'm 60'). The agent responds to this in an entirely appropriate way, with a direct answer (replicated in bold above). Strictly speaking, the agent fails to comply with the scorecard because she does not acknowledge the caller's problem in the way prescribed by the communication material. Rather than contributing an acknowledgement, she contributes a straight answer. Her linguistic behaviour, however, is entirely appropriate and in line with the explicit assumption of the branch of discourse analysis known as conversation analysis, i.e. that many utterances are paired; a greeting normally follows a greeting and an answer tends to follow a question. The fact that many conversational contributions are constrained by what precedes them, in this case the customer's utterance, constitutes and obvious limitation to the practical usability of scorecards.

If the agent had prioritized adhering to the regulation, the outcome would arguably have sounded rather bizarre. Paradoxically, then, it is precisely because the agent deviates from the regulations that makes the excerpt reproduced above rather unremarkable. (There are also cases in which the agent seems to prioritize adherence to the prescriptions, an example of which we will examine below.) The agent's linguistic behaviour thus exceeds what she is credited with by the communication training material, which is based on the implicit assumption that agents are unable to speak in the way required. When good **communication skills** end up being defined in such reductionist and decontextualized ways, they are ill-suited to apply to what goes on in real interactions. When the sociolinguist Dell Hymes coined the term 'communicative competence' in 1972 he understood by this that successful communication is not simply about internalizing a set of rules and applying them in conversation. Rather, it is about the ability to make the right choices at any given point in a conversation.

At this point, authors of communication material may object that guidelines are not meant to be followed slavishly; that it is more about possessing the appropriate 'mindset and framework', as one consultant we interviewed told us. However, the overarching focus on targets and measurements in call centres carries a risk that, in reality, linguistic regulation material is accorded much more significance than it deserves. This became particularly clear when we spoke to the manager of a call centre in the financial sector in Hong Kong who, drawing a distinction between yes/no- and wh-questions, talked about which questions to use to which type of customers. At first she admitted that she was not able to 'say here and now which type of questions to use for which type of customers, it depends on the situation'. Shortly after, however, she revealed that 'you should use open questions for sophisticated [customers] and closed for more nervous ones'. On another occasion, she expressed a realization that agents should not use the caller's name in every sentence. That would, she admitted, 'be a nuisance'. She went on to say, however, that 'once in a while, say every five minutes, is good'. This illustrates a realization on the one hand that many rules are context-dependent and impossible to pin down to watertight regulation, and, on the other, a co-existing wish for these rules to be applicable and quantifiable at almost any cost. It is perhaps not surprising that given the extensive resources devoted to linguistic regulation practices in call centres, those who engage in it need to find some justification for it even if they at times seem to realize its inadequacies.

The idea that communication material has limited usability in practice is attested by agents we have interviewed. These often quote 'common sense' and 'experience' as more useful than actual communication training. Yet, call centre managements across the world continue to commit considerable resources to communication training and material. There is clearly a tension at work here between call centre workers and call centre managers in how they define 'good service' (Alferoff and Knights 2002). To managers, it tends to mean abiding by the targets whereas to agents, it has to do with freedom to provide the service, and the language, they feel is best. This tension is well documented in the sociological body of literature on call centres (Hutchinson et al. 2000; Frenkel et al. 1999; Korczynski 2001) where it is said to cause stress for the agents who are caught between these conflicting requirements. An agent sums it up like this:

> You're meeting the company needs, but it's not to say that you're actually meeting the customer's needs. In addition, you're just giving yourself that much more pressure, really. Umm, because you know yourself you're not giving the customer the service they would like, or that you would like to give them. At the same time, you are trying to meet the company's targets. Bit like a pig in the middle. (Alferoff and Knights 2002:196)

Moreover, there is not to our knowledge any empirical evidence that customers actually perceive of the language prescribed as service-related at all; in fact there is evidence to the contrary (Alferoff and Knights 2002; Finkelstein 1999).

Regulating spoken interaction also seems to be partly redundant from the point of view that a lot of what is prescribed appears to happen naturally in conversations anyway. We know from work in conversation analysis, for instance, whose enterprise is to document reoccurring structures in talk (e.g. Drew 2005), that some of the linguistic features which are prescribed in call centres also occur in talk which is not subject to regulation. For instance, in our communication material, agents are asked to verify whether the caller accepts the solution that has been proposed. They often do this by uttering an 'OK' with rising intonation towards the end of the call, a practice which bears a remarkable resemblance to a phenomenon observed by Schegloff and Sacks (1973) in ordinary, non-regulated, conversations. When speakers are about to close a conversation, they tend to signal this using an 'OK'. The 'active listening' rule, which asks agents to use feedback tokens such as 'mhm', 'aha', 'OK' and 'I see' to signal to the customer that they are paying attention, is another example. It is in no way empirically unsound but has been well documented by conversation analysts and others to occur in real interactions long before the advent of linguistic regulation (Schegloff 1982; Yngve 1970; Zimmerman and West 1975). A third example is the 'summary rule', which asks agents to summarize the gist of the call and possible future actions before closing it. This too is a phenomenon well known to occur in ordinary conversations (Garfinkel and Sacks 1970;

Heritage and Watson 1980; Murtagh 2005). Many of the prescribed linguistic features, then, are also found to occur in non-regulated conversations, which questions the necessity of at least some components of linguistic regulation.

In addition to the question of how practically implementable or necessary linguistic regulation is, there also seems to be cases which appear to create more problems than they solve. Because of the division of labour, a hallmark of the rationalization principles on which call centres build, it is not seldom the case that a customer's query cannot be resolved by the agent to whom they have been put through. Despite, or arguably because of, this, Thistle's communication material dictates that agents should 'present solutions' to the caller's problems. In view of the limited authorizations of the agents, however, such attempts to 'present solutions' may not be in congruence with what the customer actually asked for. They are therefore unlikely to satisfy the customer and may even serve to irritate them further. Moreover, another guideline in the communication material mandates that agents should avoid 'negative language' such as for instance 'I can't' and 'unfortunately'. This forces the agent to communicate their inability to solve the caller's problem in an obfuscate and indirect manner, which may confuse the caller. This is suggested in a call from Thistle partly reproduced below. It has been chosen because it is fairly typical of what goes on in our corpus of calls, and readers may have had similar experiences with call centres. The excerpt also serves to illustrate the organizational and operational pressures that constrain what agents can actually do; however skilled in communicating an agent is, that in itself cannot resolve the underlying problem of the agent's lack of authorization to provide what the caller wants.

The call in question involves an Independent Financial Adviser who calls Thistle on behalf of his client.[2] When the preliminaries (greetings and security checks) have been completed (not reproduced here[3]), it becomes apparent that the caller's main business is to resolve a problem that has arisen in the processing of his client's affairs. Two weeks after the caller's company asked Thistle to set up a new fund for the client, Thistle has not issued confirmation or collected premiums; the client is holding her financial advisers responsible for the delay, and the caller, representing the advisers, wants Thistle to provide written evidence of what the current situation is (and by implication, of Thistle's responsibility for it) in time for a meeting with the client which has been scheduled for the next day.

This request, however reasonable it seems to the caller in the circumstances, is problematic for the agent: what the caller is asking for could only be accomplished by deviating from Thistle's routine procedures, which the agent is not empowered to do. In the section of the transcript that is replicated here (from turn 37 where the caller begins to elucidate his problem to turn 64 where the underlying cause of the problem becomes apparent) the pattern of communication speaks to the problems which are created for the agent by the restrictions placed on what he can do and say.

36	Caller	if I gave you my email address //right- erh have you got=
37	Agent	//uh huh
38	Caller	=the facility to email me with what you've just told me it's just that- say if my colleague sees the client tomorrow right he's got SOMETHING which he can show her FROM This- tle which says YES this is what the situation is YES it's being completed otherwise it's all verbal
39	Agent	right that's- the letter you received dated the fifteenth is that not sufficient
40	Caller	well unfortunately no because it has two weeks ago is it not possible just for you to repeat what you said to me on an email
41	Agent	I would have to arrange for a- a full confirma- tion to be issued
42	Caller	<u>oh dear //God Almighty</u> <IN DISBELIEF>
43	Agent	//I can't guarantee that that will happen for tomorrow unfortunately
44	Caller	<FRUSTRATED OUTBREATH> right have you got an email address there for a manager
45	Agent	%right% we DO have an email address that you can email to
46	Caller	yeah but- does it just go into the system and not bothered with or will it be looked at straight away
47	Agent	it WILL be looked at straight away these are //quite of-=
48	Caller	//wh-
49	Agent	=throughout the day and depending on the vol- ume of emails that we receive they'll be actioned in order of receipt
50	Caller	right do you have a manager
51	Agent	I do yes
52	Caller	right c- has he got a personal email
53	Agent	%no% I don't have an email I can provide you with no not-
54	Caller	<FRUSTRATED OUTBREATH> <FRUSTRATED OUTBREATH> I- I- I know it sounds stupid right but we are being chased one HUNDRED percent by this client
55	Agent	//uh huh

56	Caller	//okay who: a:re believing that we: a:re fully at fault in what's HAPPENING i e NO premiums have been collected NO policy has been issued et cetera right
57	Agent	//okay
58	Caller	//my colleague's got to go SEE this lady tomorrow I would like to provide him with some sort of PHYSICAL evidence right that everything is proceeding QUITE normally okay //(xx)
59	Agent	//I CAN request that FOR you John I'm quite happy to do that but the only thing is I CAN'T at THIS point and that's at THIS PRECISE MOMENT guarantee that we'll have that for you for your meeting tomorrow
60	Caller	<INBREATH>
61	Agent	but I can CHECK for you
62	Caller	y- i- i- would it be possible to handwrite a FAX
63	Agent	unfortunately I am NOT authorised to DO that
64	Caller	oh dear God who IS authorised I don't beLIEVE this <LAUGHS IN DISBELIEF> all I want is somebody just to say you know yeah //(xxxxxxxxxx)
65	Agent	//I- I- can arrange that for you John (.) the only thing I'm s- explaining is at THIS point during THIS //telephone conversation
66	Caller	//now I- I- I- I understand what you're saying TO me right but you're also saying to me you can't guarantee SOMEthing to be given to us w-within plenty of time for MY colleague to go //speak to the lady tomorrow (. . .)
67	Agent	//during- DURING this conversation (. . .)

When the caller has established that there is a delay in the processing of his client's affairs (this part is not reproduced here), his next objective is to get written documentation which he can show to his client to persuade her that his own organization is not at fault (turns 36 and 38). From his point of view this is not an unreasonable or difficult request: all he is asking is that the agent should put the same information he has just given orally into writing. He is not asking the agent to misrepresent the situation or make new promises to the client on Thistle's behalf. The agent's problem, however, is the division of labour that is typical of companies like Thistle, in which a single customer's business will be processed by different parts of the organization, each specializing in a particular set of tasks and communicating with one another largely via standard formulas built into computer software. This is economically efficient for companies: each employee need only be trained in a limited range of tasks, and productivity is increased by having each employee do certain tasks repeatedly. But for customers it is frustrating that the only people they can talk to directly are unable to take responsibility for the entire transaction. Unlike the clerks who worked in traditional insurance offices, agents who are employed to handle customer calls can neither do everything necessary to solve a problem themselves nor resolve the problem there and then through direct interaction with colleagues. All they can do is log standard requests for action to be taken by another department. Customers may respond, as in this exchange, by trying to persuade the agent that the circumstances justify some deviation from the standard procedure.

The caller begins this part of the exchange with 'if I gave you my email address right erh have you got the facility to email me with what you've just told me' followed by a fairly lengthy explanation of why written documentation is so important for the caller. The agent, however, possibly in line with the guideline to avoid 'negative language' defers answering the question about whether he is able to send an email by asking a question of his own: 'the letter you received dated the fifteenth is that not sufficient'. The negative polarity of the question ('is that not sufficient' rather than 'is that sufficient') implies that the agent thinks it is or ought to be sufficient (Heritage 2002). The agent's contribution could be analysed as an orientation to Thistle's rule 'present solutions'. Realizing that he is unable to satisfy the caller's request, he attempts to provide an alternative solution, i.e. that the caller uses the letter of which he is already in possession. This solution, however, is not satisfactory to the caller because the letter in question is too old. The caller therefore chooses to disagree, mitigating his response in the manner one would predict: prefacing his 'no' with 'well unfortunately' and going on to elaborate a justification for the negative answer ('because it has two weeks ago'). He then makes a second attempt 'is it not possible just for you to repeat what you said to me on an email', which implies that in his view this ought to be possible. The agent once again avoids a bald refusal but communicates that he is unable to fulfil the request (turn 41). In line with the communication material, he suggests an alternative solution, i.e. that he reissues a full confirmation which, however, will require a longer processing time. As one might have predicted, this solution too is unsatisfactory to the by now audibly frustrated caller (turn 42) who is in need of the documentation there and then. In turn 43, the agent blatantly ignores the guidelines and uses both 'I can't' and 'unfortunately'.

At this point the caller's strategy changes, as he attempts what is known in call centres as 'escalation', that is, asking the agent to facilitate contact with someone higher up the chain of command. Customers who attempt this may hope that a supervisor or manager will be empowered to do something the rank-and-file agent cannot, or they may feel reluctant to subject a low-ranking employee to the full force of their displeasure. However, agents are generally instructed to deflect escalation requests in all but the most exceptional cases. As so often in call centres, agents must try to balance customers' demands with the expectations of their superiors, and may decide it is in their interests to put the latter above the former. In this case, too, the caller's bid to escalate eventually fails (turn 53).

The caller now tries a different strategy: appealing to the common ground between himself and the agent, who are both, after all, only doing their jobs. Prefacing his appeal with the self-belittling 'I know it sounds stupid', the caller explains that he and his colleagues too have a dissatisfied customer who is giving them a hard time, and then delivers an indirect request: 'I would like to provide him [the colleague who has to meet the dissatisfied customer] with some sort of PHYSICAL evidence right that everything is proceeding QUITE normally okay'. The agent's response displays a degree of compliance with the guidelines by saying what he *can* do: 'I CAN request that FOR you John I'm quite happy to do that'. He then, however, once again ignores the proscription against 'negative language': 'The only thing is I can't at THIS PRECISE MOMENT guarantee that we'll have that for you for your meeting tomorrow', but he then quickly returns to what he can do: 'but I can CHECK for you'. The caller makes one more attempt to get around Thistle's inflexible procedures, returning to the polite request formulation he used in the opening of this exchange about documentation, 'would it be possible to handwrite a FAX'. At this point, the agent overtly acknowledges what has been the real problem all along. He is not authorized to fulfil the request: 'unfortunately I am NOT authorized to DO that' and does this in a way that entirely disregards the proscription against 'negative language'. At turn 64 the customer exclaims his frustration outright, which prompts the agent to respond in terms of what he can do (turn 65) but modifies this by saying that he cannot do it during the current conversation, i.e. that he must get approval to deviate from routines from higher management. In the next turn, the customer expresses his confusion over what the agent can and cannot do ('now I- I- I- I understand what you're saying TO me right but you're also saying to me you can't guarantee SOMEthing to be given to us w- within plenty of time for MY colleague to go speak to the lady tomorrow'). It can be argued that this confusion stems from the agent's inability to communicate in direct terms what he is able and unable to do.

In this call, it seems rather clear that what causes the problem for the caller in the first place, is the lack of authorization for the agent to respond flexibly to his request. This is a far cry from locating the problem of call centres in the agent's (lack of) communication skills. What's more, rules mandating what the agent can and cannot say actually have the potential to cause more problems than they solve. 'Presenting solutions', as is advised in Thistle's communication material, when this obviously is not the *right* solution seems almost calculated to make many callers angrier. Similarly, proscriptions against 'negative language' places agents in the awkward position of being unable to communicate their inability to solve the customer's problem.

Conclusion

In the above, we have pointed to some problems with the widespread tendency in the ITES industry to intervene in the linguistic behaviour of employees. We have shown that there are limitations to the possibilities of implementing scorecards in practice and suggested that speakers' communicative competence provides an asset that would benefit from being further exploited rather than restricted. We also suggested that **communication skills** need to be considered together with the lack of authorizations faced by agents in the industry and which prevent them from solving many of the customers' requests. In some cases, we suggested, rules dictating what agents can and cannot say may even be more of a problem than a solution.

We do not want to give the impression that communication never matters. No doubt customers want to be met with a certain degree of courtesy. There is a problematic tendency in the ITES industry, however, to focus so extensively on communication that it risks distracting attention away from more fundamental problems. Elsewhere, Cameron (2000) speaks of a 'communication inflation', by which she refers to a tendency in the wider society to conflate almost every problem with a communication problem. Similarly, we would argue for the need to identify not only the communicative needs of customer-facing workers in the ITES industry, but to consider them within the constraints placed on what they can actually *do*. No matter how many resources are devoted to teaching agents to communicate well, it can never compensate for the structural problems that accompany such hyper-rationalized workplaces. Moreover, while there is a growing awareness of the inadequacies of 'cookie cutter' and simplistic culture training programmes in call centres (Lockwood and Elias this volume), the question remains of how training in communication is to be successfully implemented in a work environment that is so heavily regimented. It seems that as long as the number one foundational rationale of the ITES industry is targets, measurements and top-down control, there is a co-existing risk that workers are deprived of the linguistic autonomy that is a prerequisite of any such training to be effective.

Notes

[1] The data on which this chapter draws was collected as part of a larger project and also consists of observations and interviews with managers and agents and of communication training material, customer service manuals and scorecards collected at Thistle and other call centres.

[2.] Transcription Key

%right%	spoken quietly
HAS	spoken emphatically
that's-	incomplete utterance
:	lengthening of preceding syllable
< >	encloses description of prosodic/paralinguistic features
_____	indicates stretch of speech to which description in < > applies
//	onset of overlapping speech
=	turn continues on next line
( )	accuracy of transcription uncertain
xxx	inaudible (number of xs indicates approximate number of syllables)

[3.] For a more in-depth analysis of this call, readers are referred to Hultgren and Cameron (2010).

References

Alferoff, C. and David, K. (2002), Quality time and the 'beautiful call'. In Holtgrewe, U. Kerst, C. and Shire, K. (eds.) *Re-organising Service Work: Call Centres in Germany and Britain.* Aldershot: Ashgate, 183–203 .

Belt, V. (2002), Capitalising on femininity: Gender and the utilisation of social skills in telephone call centres. In Holtgrewe, U., Kerst, C. and Shire, K. (eds.) *Re-organising Service Work: Call Centres in Germany and Britain.* Aldershot: Ashgate, 123–145.

Buscatto, M. (2002), Les centres d'appels, usines modernes? Les rationalisations paradoxales de la relation téléphonique. *Sociologie du travail* 44(1), 99–117.

Callaghan, G. and Thompson, P. (2002), 'We recruit attitude': The selection and shaping of routine call centre labour. *Journal of Management Studies* 39(2), 233–254.

Cameron, D. (2000), *Good to Talk?: Living and Working in a Communication Culture.* London: Sage.

Cameron, D. (2005), Communication and commodification: Global economic change in sociolinguistic perspective. In Jacobs, G. and Erreygers, G. (eds.) *Language, Communication and the Economy.* Amsterdam: John Benjamins, 9–23.

CCA. (2001), *The State of the Centres: An Investigation of the Skills Level in the Industry and of Training Requirements.* CCA Research Institute.

Chouliaraki, L. and Fairclough, N. (1999), *Discourse in Late Modernity: Rethinking Critical Discourse Analysis.* Edinburgh: Edinburgh University Press.

CM. (2004), *The Truth about Staff Attrition and Absenteeism in Contact Centres: The Human Cost of Mass Production.* CM Insight Ltd.

Cope, B. and Kalantzis, M. (eds.) (2000), *Multiliteracies. Literacy Learning and the Design of Social Futures.* London and New York: Routledge.

Cowie, C. (2007), The accents of outsourcing: The meanings of 'neutral' in the Indian call centre industry. *World Englishes* 26(3), 316–330.

Drew, P. (2005), Conversation analysis. In Fitch, K. L. and Sanders, R. E. (eds.) *Handbook of Language and Social Interaction.* Mahwah, NJ: Lawrence Earlbaum, 71–102.

du Gay, P. and Salaman, G. (1992), The cult(ure) of the customer. *Journal of Management Studies* 29(5), 615–633.

Elias, N. This volume.

Fairclough, N. (1989), *Language and Power*. London: Longman.

Fairclough, N. (1992), *Discourse and Social Change*. Cambridge: Polity Press.

Fernie, S. and Metcalf, D. (1998), *(Not) Hanging on the Telephone: Payment Systems in the New Sweatshops*. Centre for Economic Performance, London School of Economics.

Finkelstein, J. (1999), Rich food: McDonald's and modern life. In Smart, B. (ed.) *Resisting McDonaldization*. Thousand Oaks, CA: Sage, 70–82 .

Frenkel, S., Korczynski, M., Shire, K. and Tam, M. (1999), *On the Front Line: Organization of Work in the Information Economy*. Ithaca, NY: Cornell University Press.

Garfinkel, H. and Sacks, H. (1970), The formal practices of practical actions. In McKinney, J. C. and Tiryakian, E. A. (eds.) *Theoretical Sociology*. New York, NY: Appleton-Century-Crofts, 338–366.

Heller, M. (2003), Globalization, the new economy, and the commodification of language and identity. *Journal of Sociolinguistics* 7(4), 473–492.

Heritage, J. (2002), The limits of questioning: Negative interrogatives and hostile question content. *Journal of Pragmatics* 34, 1427–1446.

Heritage, J. C. and Watson, R. (1980), Aspects of the properties of formulations in natural conversations: Some instances analysed. *Semiotica* 30(3), 245–262.

Hultgren, A. K. (2008), *Linguistic Regulation and Interactional Reality: A Sociolinguistic Study of Call Centre Service Transactions*. Oxford: University of Oxford dissertation.

Hultgren, A. K. and Cameron, D. (2010), 'How may I help you?' Questions, control and customer care in telephone call centre talk. In Freed, A. and Erhlich, S. (eds.) 'Why do you ask?' The function of questions in institutional discourse. Oxford: Oxford University Press, 322–342.

Hutchinson, S., Purcell, J. and Kinnie, N. (2000), Evolving high commitment management and the experience of the RAC call centre. *Human Resource Management Journal* 10(1), 63–78.

Hymes, D. (1972), On communicative competence. In Pride, J. B. and Holmes, J. (eds.) *Sociolinguistics*. Harmondsworth: Penguin Books, 269–293.

Kinnie, N., Hutchinson, S. and Purcell, J. (2000), 'Fun and surveillance': The paradox of high commitment management in call centres. *International Journal of Human Resource Management* 11(5), 967–985.

Korczynski, M. (2001), The contradictions of service work: Call centre as customer-oriented bureacracy. In Sturdy, A., Grugulis, I. and Willmott, H. (eds.) *Customer Service: Empowerment and Entrapment*. Basingstoke: Palgrave Macmillan, 79–101.

Lockwood, J. This volume.

Murtagh, G. M. (2005), Some initial reflections on conversational structures for instruction giving. In Baker, C. D., Emmison, M. and Firth, A. (eds.) *Calling for Help: Language and Social Interaction in Telephone Helplines*. Amsterdam: John Benjamins, 287–307.

New London Group, The. (2000), A pedagogy of multiliteracies designing social futures. In Cope, B. and Kalantzis, M. (eds.) *Multiliteracies. Literacy Learning and the Design of Social Futures* . London: Routledge, 9–37.

Nofsinger, R. E. (1991), *Everyday Conversation*. Thousand Oaks, CA: Sage.

Richardson, R., Belt, V. and Marshall, J. N. (2000), Taking calls to Newcastle: The regional implications of the growth in call centres. *Regional Studies* 34(4), 357–369.

Schegloff, E. A. (1982), Discourse as an interactional achievement: Some uses of 'uh huh' and other things that come between sentences. In Tannen, D. (ed.) *Analysing Discourse: Text and Talk.* Washington, DC: Georgetown University Press, 71–93.

Schegloff, E. A. and Sacks, H. (1999), Opening up closings. In Jaworski, A. and Coupland, N. (eds.) *The Discourse Reader.* London: Routledge, 263–274.

Sturdy, A. (2000), Training in service – importing and imparting customer service culture as an interactive process. *International Journal of Human Resource Management* 11(6), 1082–1103.

Taylor, P. and Bain, P. (1999), 'An assembly line in the head': Work and employee relations in the call centre. *Industrial Relations Journal* 30(2), 101–117.

Taylor, P., Hyman, J., Mulvey, G. and Bain, P. (2002), Work organization, control, and the experience of work in call centres. *Work, Employment and Society* 16(1), 133–150.

Thompson, P. and Callaghan, G. (2002), Skill formation in call centres. In Holtgrewe, U., Kerst, C. and Shire, K. (eds.) *Re-organising Service Work: Call Centres in Germany and Britain.* Aldershot: Ashgate, 105–122.

Tsoukas, H. and Vladimirou, E. (2001), What is organizational knowledge? *Journal of Management Studies* 38(7), 973–993.

Yngve, V. H. (1970), On getting a word in edgewise. In Chicago Linguistic Society (ed.) *Papers of the Sixth Regional Meeting of the Chicago Linguistics Society.* Chicago, IL: Chicago Linguistic Society, 567–577.

Zimmerman, D. and West, C. (1975), Sex roles, interruptions, and silences in conversation. In Thorne, B. and Henley, N. (eds.) *Language and Sex: Difference and Dominance.* Rowley, MA: Newbury House, 105–129.

Part II

Managing the Telephone Relationship with the Customer: Interpersonal Complexity

Chapter 5

'I was so angry. It was unbelievable . . .': A Comparison of Written and Spoken Customer Service Complaints

Jon S. Y. Hui

City University of Hong Kong, Hong Kong

Complaint letters and calls from customers are a fact of life in business. The way complaints are handled directly affects customers' satisfaction. Failure to achieve the desired result undermines the credibility and reputation of the company. Complaint texts are the realization of the complainers' attitude towards the complained company or organization. They are often loaded with interpersonal emotional lexis and expressions. Understanding the underlying interpersonal meanings of complaint texts is one step towards attenuating any negative effects. This study investigates interpersonal communication of both written and verbal complaint texts in business settings. In this chapter, I discuss the linguistic similarities and differences of interpersonal features in both the written and verbal texts. In all texts, non-delivery of services is the nature of the complaint. Results suggest that in both written and spoken texts, a discernible structure and common language features can be identified. The findings suggest that attitudinal meanings are hidden in the shadow of objective information, and strategies of audience alignment are used in order to achieve the intended communication goal of the complaint. These findings enhance the ongoing research of the language of complaints in call centre communication and are particularly useful in providing concrete insights into the development of industry-specific training material leading to an improvement in customer services.

Introduction

In business, many things can go unexpectedly wrong. Poor communication may lead to broken promises, and human oversight or inflexible systems may result in disappointing service outcomes. Inevitably, some customers feel strongly that they have been let down or ignored, and the service that they received is unsatisfactory. They vent their anger, disappointment and frustrations by lodging complaints through letters or calls to customer service centres. With the increasing implementation of e-services in the twenty-first century (Fluss 2005), customers are able to transmit their complaints almost instantly. They may even participate in internet complaint forums if unsatisfactory response is experienced (Harrison-Walker 2001). Research shows that complaints in the form of verbalized emotions affect customer loyalties and ultimately business prospects (Mattsson et al. 2004). An analysis of written and spoken complaint texts enables management to understand the building up of the customer's emotions and grievances, underlying values and expectations of customers. The results of the analysis inform organization management to adapt operational policies, adjust procedures and be more in-tune with customers' value system. Thus better customer satisfaction can hopefully be achieved.

Definition

Complaints are expressions of dissatisfaction, reactions to broken promises and the feeling of injustice. To complain is to vent anger because of an unhappy experience, to express disappointment due to an unfulfilled expectation or to say something is not right. Clyne (1994) distinguishes complaints into direct and indirect categories. Direct complaints usually are explicit, sometimes implicit, accusations (Clyne 1994), with the intent to hold someone or an organization responsible. A resolution is expected. On the other hand, indirect complaints are 'whinges' (Clyne 1994:49). They are usually in the form of sharing unhappy feelings and experience with the aim to seek support more than action. It is often a strategy to open conversations with strangers (Boxer 1996) and to build rapport and establish solidarity with others (Holmes and Riddiford 2009). However, whinges may develop into 'exercitive' complaints (Clyne 1994) if actions are undertaken to address the indirect complaints. A letter of complaint to companies and a phone call to customer service centres is usually associated with direct complaints. Customers who bothered to pick up a pen to write or pick up a phone to call, are exercising their power as consumers. They want someone to take responsibility and have their grievances addressed. A resolution is usually demanded, and expected.

Management Perspective

From the business management perspective, consumer complaint behaviour has been widely researched in the USA and Europe (Watkins and Liu 1996;

Davidow 2003; Phau and Sari 2004). This area of research, so far, tends to investigate the cause of the complaint. That is to say, it seeks to find out the reasons why the customer complains (Crosier and Erdogan 2001; Davidow 2003). In essence, customer dissatisfaction ignites when the product or services they receive do not match their expectation (Phau and Sari 2004). Some practitioners, instead of studying the cause of customer complaints, investigate the demographic and psychographic profile of complainers and non-complainers in order to discover various indicators that affect consumer complaint behaviour. One important benefit of knowing the profiles of the complainers, who they are and where they live, is that it helps companies and corporations to avoid 'inappropriate' product promotions and to reduce the risk of collateral damage in advertising campaigns (Crosier and Erdogan 2001). Different geographical and cultural dimensions perceive the act of complaint differently and this in turn affects their complaining behaviour (Watkins and Liu 1996). A comparison of the findings between developed and developing countries and across cultures could yield invaluable indicators for companies and corporations to adjust and adapt in the current globalized market. For instance, one of the findings from Phau and Sari (2004) is that in Indonesia, consumers in general adopt poor 'attitudes towards businesses'. In other words, customers usually have negative feelings about commercial organization's behaviour and their consumption of products and services. Also, complainers to the customer service department of companies in Indonesia hold a positive attitude towards the act of complaint and they tend to follow up on their unsatisfactory experience. Therefore, there is a high possibility of retaining the customer if the complaint is handled satisfactorily. In contrast, the non-complainers tend to warn their friends and families instead and exit quietly so there is very little chance to regain the loyalty of the non-complaining customers. These are indispensible indicators for local and multinational companies to take a proactive approach to complaints.

Understanding the profiles of complainers and their reactions to their bad purchase experience is important. However, organizational responses to these complaints are also vital for the management and maintenance of business. Indeed, response to complaints has been the subject of much research in the last decade. For instance, the way that a company handles complaints has been linked to customer loyalty (Mattsson et al. 2004; Homburg and Furst 2005) and profit (Johnston 2001). An organizational complaint handling approach can affect the company's future business. It is believed that the way a company responds to complaints has a direct influence on post-complaint customer behaviour. In other words, companies' responses to complaints have a direct link to how the consumers perceive the response and this in turn affects the follow-up action of the consumer. Inappropriate responses to complaints could set off a chain reaction including poor customer satisfaction, risk of repurchase reduction and bad publicity through word-of-mouth. Its effect is so pervasive that one bad complaint experience may ruin a well-established reputation of an organization as far as the complainer is concerned. This was shown in Homburg and Furst's (2005) study where they investigated the effects of complaint management on customer satisfaction and loyalty. Two distinctive approaches, mechanistic and organic, formed the framework of the research. The results indicate that companies may lose the loyalty of a customer if the complaint is not properly addressed even though the overall customer satisfaction was perceived as fine previously (Homburg and Furst 2005).

Other research (Davidow 2003), which reviewed complaint management handling under six different dimensions of organizational responses to complaints, namely, timeliness, facilitation, redress, apology, credibility and attentiveness, examined each of these dimensions' effects on customer post-complaint behaviour and suggested further work is needed on a mixed combination of dimensions in order to discover the best complaint management practices. Harrison-Walker's (2001) study provides further managerial responses to complaints in the twenty-first century. In her research, messages on an internet consumer complaint forum were analysed and discussed under headings including 'nature of the complaints', 'complaints to contact personnel', 'other attempts to resolve the problem', 'complaints to the internet complaint forum only', 'company responses to non-internet complaints', 'company responses to complaints on internet forum' and 'demographics of internet forum complainers'. The findings provide a wealth of recommendations to companies in complaint management by taking advantage of the internet. While Harrison-Walker's research investigates the content of complaint messages, its focus was mainly on the nature of the complaints, the behaviours of the complainers, the behaviours of the complained organization and the social background of the complainers, but the language used in complaint messages was not examined.

Investigating customer satisfaction and post-complaint behaviour may reveal the best complaint management practices (Johnston and Mehra 2002); examining factors that attribute to complaint behaviour could also identify managerial implications in business including company image and reputation, complaint settlement and pricing strategies (Phau and Sari 2004). However, to understand the intended and perceived meanings between the complaint texts writer and its audience, the language used has to be carefully examined.

Linguistic Perspective

The body of research reviewed so far includes factors attributed to complaint behaviour, customer satisfaction and loyalty as the result of complaint responses, and the relationship between post-complaint behaviour and the six organizational response dimensions to complaints. These studies complement each other in providing a better understanding of the effects of complaints on business. They represent the 'front end' (consumer complaint behaviour including complainer and non-complainer profiling) and the 'back end' (organizational responses to complaints) of the complaint process. In between there lies the realization of the complaint act through texts, in the form of letters or calls to customer service centres. In the following section, research on complaint texts is discussed.

The text of complaints can roughly be separated into spoken and written forms and the acts of complaint occur in a wide range of contexts. The contexts where spoken complaint text is investigated, range from direct complaints where people engaged in acrimonious argument (Dersley and Wootton 2000) to indirect complaints among acquaintances and friends (Boxer 1993); from complaints in everyday conversation among intimate family members (Laforest 2002) to complaints in customer service call centres where the interlocutors are usually total strangers (Reiter 2005; Forey and Lockwood 2007; Hood and Forey 2008 and others outlined in the present volume). The contexts where written complaint text is examined, include letters of complaint to a commercial service entity (Mattsson et al. 2004), complaint blogs in an e-complaint internet forum (Harrison-Walker 2001), and complaint letters to the editor of a humorous magazine (Lockyer and Pickering 2001).

Earlier research on the spoken form of complaints tends to address issues in the construction of social reality. For instance, Boxer (1993) studies the speech act of indirect complaints in relation to social distance. One of her conclusions suggests that people's 'complaint and response to complaint' pattern varies according to the social distance of the participants. The agreeability in a complaint/commiseration speech act sequence is directly proportional to the social distance of the interlocutors. That is to say, we are more agreeable to people who have a wider social distance than those who are closer to us. Drew (1998) examines the sequence of complaint narratives and describes it in terms of social conduct and relations. The complaining behaviour could be interpreted as a transgression. More recently, the spoken form of complaint in commercial context has gained attention. Reiter (2005) explores the pragmatic strategies used by the callers and the customer service representatives in a call centre by narrating their complaints and responding to the complaints, respectively. The study was based on a relatively small corpus, 15 telephone conversations, to a caregiver company call centre situated in the capital of Uruguay, Montevideo. The finding concludes that the callers' strategies tend to orient towards a closer relationship with the call takers. In contrast, the call takers' language is perceived to be distant and depersonalized.

Compared to the apparent imbalanced research attention to the spoken form of complaint in favour of non-commercial contexts, research on the written form of complaint appears almost solely in a commercial context. Lockyer and Pickering (2001) analysed letters of a complaining nature to the editor of a humorous magazine. They were particularly interested in the language employed in negotiation between ethical and comic discourse. Other research analysed letters of complaint focus on the effect of verbalized emotions in complaint letters on loyalty to the service provider (Mattsson et al. 2004). Lexical items in the letters are coded with emotions, such as positive emotion, anger, sadness, fear and pressure, and they are measured and correlated with the objects of complaint, such as technical, invoice, accessibility and programming. Mattsson et al. (2004) found that the show of anger relates negatively to customer loyalty but sadness correlates positively. Examination of the nature of these lexical items and the development of the writer's emotion could provide invaluable clues to handling complaint incidents which in turn improve customer satisfaction and loyalty, and ultimately business prospects of an organization.

Complaint texts have also been widely adapted in education and research applications. Letters of complaint have been used as teaching and learning tools to address ethical issues (Jurkeiwicz et al. 2004), and as diagnostic tools for students' linguistic and sociocultural competence (Coffin 2003). Tanaka et al. (2000) used incidence of complaints to solicit apologies from Japanese and English speakers in comparing cross-cultural communication differences. Spoken forms of complaint have also been included as instruments in the study of interlanguage pragmatics (Tatsuki 1999).

The body of literature reviewed so far indicates that research in the business management perspective has mostly been limited to the examination of consumer complaint behaviour, complainer and non-complainer profiling and organizational response to complaints. On the other hand, research into the linguistic aspects of complaint texts mainly focuses on social reality construction, interlanguage and cross-cultural pragmatics in a non-commercial context. In comparison, research that focuses on the linguistic aspect of complaint texts in a commercial context and the interpersonal meanings in business communication, is somewhat neglected. The current study attempts to fill this research gap and aims to expand the knowledge about interpersonal meanings in business communication research through the analysis of two complaint texts.

Research Framework

The quantitative approach (e.g. Mattsson et al. 2004) and qualitative approach (e.g. Dersley and Wootton 2000) have been applied in the study of complaint texts. Some studies took advantage of both (e.g. Boxer 1993; Laforest 2002). A conversation analysis framework seems to be popular in analysing the spoken form of a complaint (e.g. Drew 1998; Edwards 2005) though an interactional sociolinguistics approach has also been employed (e.g. Reiter 2005; Hood and Forey 2005). The study of complaint texts essentially aims at decoding the complainer's intent through analysis of the interpersonal textual meanings. One relevant framework that can be applied to tease out the interpersonal meanings of texts is **appraisal**.

The **Appraisal** system emerged from the Systemic Functional Linguistic tradition (Martin 2000; Halliday and Matthiessen 2004). The system critically examines the writer or speaker's choice of lexis in expressing opinions, in other words, their evaluative stance on topics bound by the discourse contexts. The preference for lexical choices reflects the expressed and created meanings of the writer or speaker in particular contexts (Thompson and Hunston 2000). These meanings can be analysed according to three categories in the basic system: **engagement**, **attitude** and **graduation** (Martin and Rose 2003, 2007; Martin and White 2005).

A brief survey reveals that the interpersonal meanings of many genres have been investigated through the evaluation of texts. These range from narratives (Cortazzi and Jin 2000) to political speeches (Butt et al. 2004; Lazar and Lazar 2004); and from editorial (Martin 2004) to academic writing (Hood 2004). Recently, researchers have incorporated **appraisal**, along with corpus linguistics, when analysing written text (Miller 2006) and websites (Kaltenbacher 2006). However, very few have focused on business correspondence. One such example is Hood and Forey (2008). They explored the dynamic flow of emotions in customer call centre communications. The current study adds to the small but growing body of work which applies **appraisal** to the language in the workplace. Two forms of complaint texts, written (Text One) and spoken (Text Two), were examined under this framework. The data set is limited, but by taking a detailed look at two texts we are able to gain a more in-depth discussion of specific choices within sample texts. In addition, a qualitative study of authentic texts may provide insights which can then be explored in a more corpus-driven study.

Within **appraisal**, **engagement** examines the writer or speaker's degree of commitment and their positioning in regard to the text referenced. The category is divided into two mutually exclusive subcategories: **monogloss** and **heterogloss**. **Attitude** deals with feelings. Further subcategories **affect**, **judgment** and **appreciation** are established covering three semantic regions: emotions, ethics and aesthetics (value of things) respectively (Martin and White 2005; Martin and Rose 2007). **Affect** reflects emotional reactions of the writer (people's feelings). For example in [1], the feeling of helplessness, e.g. frustrated and disappointed in dealing with a delivery service company:

[1] (Text One, line 20)
I continue to feel highly **frustrated** and deeply **disappointed** . . .
(- affect)

Judgment identifies the resources that evaluate people's character (people's behaviour). For example in [2], a comment by a customer of an insurance staff:

[2] (Text Two, turn 63)
. . . there's somebody got a case of **incompetence** (- judgment)

Table 1   Examples of **graduation**

Force	raise	[4] (Text Two, turn 53) It was **very** clear
	lower	[5] (Text One, line 23) . . . if you **could** give . . .
Focus	sharpen	[6] (Text Two, turn 72) . . . drawn down the **right** amount . . .
	soften	[7] (Text One, line 11) . . . had . . . been left **some** where . . .

Appreciation concerns with resources that indicate our attitudes towards things (value of things). For example in [3], a customer's evaluation of a letter sent by his insurance company:

[3] (Text Two, turn 67)
    . . . it's just a **stereotypical** letter

Graduation is the grading of meaning within **appraisal**. **Force** and **Focus** are the subcategories of **graduation**; the evaluated resources can be either **raised** or **lowered** (**force**), and either **sharpened** or **softened** (**focus**) (Martin and White 2005; Hood 2006). Examples of these categories are given in Table 1 above.

Methodology

This chapter draws on the **appraisal** framework modelled by Martin (2000) and Martin and White (2005). Texts are evaluated under **attitude** and **graduation** categories because the complaints tend to relate to the feelings of the writer and the speaker. Due to the limited space in the current research, **engagement** is not included although it is clearly a valuable resource.

Both inscribed and invoked attitudinal lexis and expression are analysed in order to account for attitudinal responses of the audience. Attitudinal lexis and expression can be directly inscribed, or implicitly expressed as a token representing attitude, as outlined below in example 9 (Martin and Rose 2007).

Inscribed attitudes are lexis that explicitly reflect the evaluative position of the writer or speaker. For example in [8], a customer's feeling (shock and horror) towards the poor service of an internet ordering and delivery company.

[8] (Text One, line 17)
I am shocked and horrified by your poor service!

Attitudes could also be expressed implicitly as a token that invokes attitudinal lexis or expression. Lexical Metaphor is a case in point. For example in [9], a customer retold his stressful experience; and does not necessarily mean his wife travels through the ceiling, but rather she is very upset.

[9] (Text Two, turn 55)
. . . they send me a termination which **sends my wife through the ceiling and** . . .

Identifying **judgment** and **appreciation** can be confusing at times. In Text Two turn 63, '. . . somebody got a case of incompetence . . .', it is obvious that the reference is to someone's ability therefore it is categorized under **judgment**. However, there exist incidences where either **judgment** or **appreciation** can be applied to a single item. For instance in [10],

[10] Text Two, turn 57
. . . I don't know what **the incompetence** is at all?

It is unclear whether the 'incompetence' is referring to the ability of the insurance staff, or to the act of sending unnecessary termination letters regularly causing stress to customers. Under the context of complaint texts, the complaint tends to be directed towards the collective action of the company rather than individuals, therefore in cases such as this within the present context, the item is labelled as **appreciation**.

These attitudinal meanings are often subjected to amplification. Martin and White (2005) refer to this as turn up or turn down the volume. The expression of attitude can be strengthened, heightened or lowered, sharpened or softened in focus, within **appraisal**, this strengthening or weakening of evaluative lexis is categorized through the **graduation** system. In the call centre talk, often the items are being amplified through the **graduation** system. For example in [11], the frustration of the customer is being intensified by the lexico-grammatical choice of 'highly': Martin and White (2005) refer to such choices as turning up or turning down the volume. Whereas focus is related to narrowing down or widening the scope of the lexical item, for example in Text One the writer uses an inscribed choice of graduation 'poor service', where the choice of 'poor' is narrowing down and focusing on a particular type of 'service' the customer experienced.

[11] Text One, line 20
I continue to feel **highly** frustrated . . .

Under **graduation**, the network outlined by Hood (2004) is employed to complement the framework introduced by Martin and White (2005). The category 'graduation evoke attitude' identifies items that render **attitude** through the GRADUATION system. These are being treated as implicitly expressed **attitude** items.

The Data

Two complaints were analysed. The first (Text One) is a complaint letter (via email) from a customer to the Director of Customer Services in an internet order retail and delivery service company. The writer is a female British national, a native speaker of English. She ordered and pre-paid for an item from this company to be delivered in the UK. The item did not turn up on the date specified. The letter was written after several unsatisfactory calls to the delivery service company. In fact, up to the date that this letter was written, the item had still not been delivered to the destination.

The second (Text Two) is a telephone exchange between a customer and the Customer Service Representative (CSR) from an insurance company out-sourced call centre in the Philippines. The customer, a male US national, has repeatedly received termination letters of his policy because of non-payment, notwithstanding that he had earlier written a letter authorizing the insurance company to make automatic direct debits from his bank account to ensure reg-ular payment. He called the service support phone line to clarify the situation and complain about the insurance company's inefficiency. Like the author of Text One, the complainer of Text Two is also a native speaker of English.

Since the focus of this study is how interpersonal meanings are expressed and transmitted through complaint texts, the analysis of Text Two mainly focuses on the caller's dialogue. This research recognizes the interactive nature of tele-phone conversations and how utterances are influenced by the one preceding it. Therefore, the interactional sequences are considered from time to time in order to accurately gauge the intended meaning of lexical and phrasal choices.

Results and Discussion

This study only focuses on **attitude** and **graduation** categories within **appraisal**. Lexical items and phrasal expressions are further identified as **affect**, **judgment** and **appreciation** under the **attitude** category, and **force** and **focus** under the **graduation** category.

Distribution of Attitude Items

a) Text One – The Complaint Letter

The complaint letter is addressed to the director of customer services. It was written by a female customer to complain about a pre-paid item for her sister's birthday which the internet-order company failed to deliver on that day. Despite numerous phone calls and emails to the customer service department, the item still had not been delivered when the letter was written. The letter consists of a subject line, six paragraphs and a signature block. The first three paragraphs narrate the background details of the order, the actions carried out by the company and the subsequent correspondence between them. Paragraphs four and five describe her disappointment with the company, and a somewhat courteous closing in the sixth paragraph but included a demand for an apology (Table 2).

Out of three hundred and sixty words in Text One, there are fifty-seven items that can be identified as expressions of attitude, close to 16% of the total word count. These expressions of attitude items slot into two categories and five sub-categories. Examples of each sub-category are shown below. Their percentage of occurrence is charted in Figure 1 and the full analysed result is presented in Appendix A.

i. Inscribed **attitude**

There are nineteen occurrences of explicitly expressed attitude items of which fifteen are **affect** and four are **appreciation**.

Table 2   Structure of Text One

	Line	Function/Topic
	1–2	Salutation and subject line
Paragraph 1	3–5	Background information to the order. A brief summary of the
Paragraph 2	6–11	actions that have been carried out by the company and the subse-
Paragraph 3	12–16	quent correspondence between them
Paragraph 4	17–19	Describe her feelings towards the company
Paragraph 5	20–21	
Paragraph 6	22–24	Closing
	25–26	Signature block

Text 1 Frequency

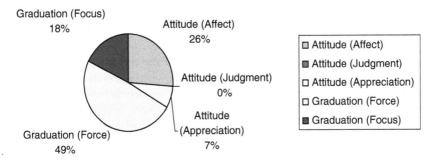

FIGURE 1   Attitude Items Frequency Chart (Text One)

For example:

[12] Text One, line 3
I am writing in sheer **frustration – affect**

[13] Text One, line 2
Re: **Unbelievably poor service – appreciation**

ii. Graduation evoke **attitude**
There are thirty-eight lexical items or phrases that can be classified as **Graduation** evoke **attitude** items: twenty-eight items under the **force** category and ten under the **focus** category.

For example,

[14] (Text One, line 3)
I am writing in **sheer** frustration – **force (intensification)**

[15] (Text One, line 7)
After **a number of** emails – **force (quantification)**

[16] (Text One, line 13)
one of your representatives – **focus (specification)**

Among the fifty-seven expressions of attitude items in Text One, about one-third are inscribed, whereas **graduation** evoke **attitude** occupies nearly two thirds. There is no **judgment** in this text probably because complaints are usually addressed to the company or an organization. **Judgment** being the evaluation of people and their behaviour, it is not surprising that it is lacking in the context of a commercial correspondence.

Figure 1 shows the frequency occurrence of both inscribed and invoked attitude items. The percentage represents the occurrence of a particular item in proportion to the total number of attitude items in the text.

Figure 2 below shows that the majority of the inscribed attitude expressions are in the latter part of the letter. In fact, over 63% are in the fourth, fifth and sixth paragraphs. In contrast, nearly 74% of the implicit expressions of **attitude**, and **graduation** evoking **attitude** items, are in the first part of the complaint letter. Most of them appear in the first, second and third paragraphs. There is a clear imbalance of explicitly and implicitly expressed attitude items in the first, second and third paragraphs where **graduation** evoking **attitude** items are four times greater than the inscribed ones. This pattern, together with the distribution pattern of Text Two, will be further discussed in a later section.

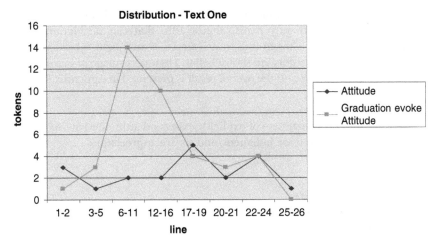

FIGURE 2 Distribution of Inscribed and Invoked attitude items (Text One)

Text Two – The Complaint Call

In Text Two, a customer called the customer service centre of his insurance company to complain about receiving termination letters regularly because of unpaid premiums but in fact the insurance company was authorized to direct debit the amount from the insurer's bank account monthly for the policy premium. Unlike written text where there are paragraphs to mark the information groupings, spoken text is one long stretch of text. The demarcation of text is then based on its functions and topics.

The conversation between the customer and the CSR in Text Two can be divided into four stages according to the functions that they serve and within the third stage, it can be subdivided further into three text chunks based on the generic stages which are clearly identified within the grammar (see Martin and Rose 2008 for a detailed discussion of generic stages). The structure is illustrated in Table 3 below.

Table 3 Structure of Text Two

Turn	Function/Generic stage
turn 1–18	greetings, establishing and confirming contacts
turn 19–50	identifying the problem and actions
turn 51–77	re-iterates and emphasizes the problem
51–57	the Nov. 16 letter
58–64	the amount
65–77	the Nov. 30 letter
turn 78–79	the closing

The total word count of the caller in Text Two is five hundred and twenty four. Among them, there are fifty items, almost 10% that can be identified as expressions of attitude. They fit into three categories and eight sub-categories. Examples of each sub-category are shown below. Their percentage of occurrence are presented in Figure 2 and the overall result is presented in Appendix B.

iii. Inscribed **attitude**

There are twenty occurrences of explicitly expressed attitude items, of which eleven are **affect**, three are **judgment**, and six are **appreciation**.

For example:

[17] (Text Two, turn 24)
. . . we sent a letter in to customer services in reference to this practice this's causing **stress – affect**

[18] (Text Two, turn 63)
. . . there's somebody got **a case of incompetence – judgment**

[19] (Text Two, turn 71)
I just don't want to have to go to my lawyers about all these **goof ups – appreciation**

iv. Token of **attitude**

There is one incidence of Token of **attitude** in the form of lexical metaphor:

[20] (Text Two, turn 55)
. . . every time something happens they send me a termination which **sends my wife through the ceiling** . . .

v **Graduation** evoking **attitude**

There are thirty lexis or phrases that can be classified as **graduation** evoking **attitude** items, twenty items under the **force** category and ten under the **focus** category:

For example,

[21] (Text Two, turn 53)
It was **very** clear – **force (intensification)**

[22] (Text Two, turn 55)
I have **tons** of letters here – **force (quantification)**

[23] (Text Two, turn 72)
. . . when no one has drawn down the **right** amount from the bank account – **focus (specification)**

[24] (Text Two, 63)
I'm willing to do that – focus (fulfilment)

Similar to the complaint letter Text One, although not as significant, the occurrence of implicit expressions of **attitude** in Text Two again out numbers explicit expression of **attitude** items. The ratio is 60 to 40% respectively. Figure 3 shows the occurrence frequency of both inscribed and invoked attitude items.

In Text Two, in order to show the ratio and the distribution of the inscribed and implicitly expressed attitude items, the complaint text is divided into six discreet sections according to its functions and the topics. As we can see from the distribution in Figure 4, 80% of these items are between turn 51 and 77. The disproportional balance of the two categories, inscribed attitude and graduation evoking is generally more or less evenly spread throughout the

Text 2 Frequency

Graduation (Focus)
20%

Attitude (Affect)
22%

Attitude (Judgment)
6%

Attitude (Appreciation)
12%

Graduation (Force)
40%

□ Attitude (Affect)
■ Attitude (Judgment)
□ Attitude (Appreciation)
□ Graduation (Force)
■ Graduation (Focus)

FIGURE 3 Attitude Items Frequency Chart (Text Two)

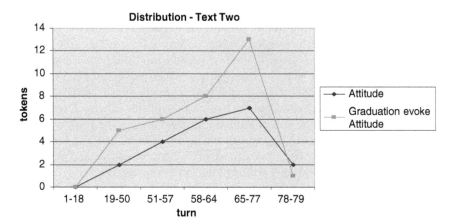

Distribution - Text Two

tokens / turn

— Attitude
-■- Graduation evoke Attitude

FIGURE 4 Distribution of Inscribed and Invoked attitude items (Text Two)

sections as shown in Figure 4. Interpersonal meaning is much lower at the beginning, peaks between turn 65 to 77, and drops back at the closing.

Studies in written and spoken forms of English suggest that the two forms differ in vocabulary, lexical density, nominalization, grammatical intricacy and modality (Halliday 1989, 2001; Maybin and Mercer 1996). Other obvious differences include false starts, hesitations, pauses and self-corrections in speech compared to the use of punctuation, sentences and paragraph organization in writing. The two analysed complaint texts in the current study exhibit these grammatical and delivery differences. However, there exist common features between the two forms.

Three interesting features common to both complaint texts are: (i) prosody of complaints, (ii) ideational features invoking interpersonal meaning (iii) alignment of audience, emerged in the findings. In what follows, these features are discussed further.

Prosody of Complaints

Texts are often constructed to serve a number of purposes. One obvious purpose would be to help the reader more easily understand the intended message better. Systemic Functional Linguistics differentiates three 'meanings' within a message, namely ideational, interpersonal and textual. They are associated with particulate, prosodic and periodic structures (Martin and White 2005).

In order to study the prosody of complaints, the prosodic structure of a text needs to be examined, as interpersonal meanings are often not packaged in isolation but are cumulated and expressed throughout the stretch of the discourse (Halliday 1979). Therefore studying the text's prosodic structure can help to reveal the intended interpersonal meanings of the writer or the speaker.

Judging from the distribution of the **attitude** items, it seems that the interpersonal distribution of the two texts is very different. In Text One, the 'facts' are laid out in a logical sequence in the first, second and third paragraphs. The generic structure agrees with the complaint letter writing genre (Guffey and Almonte 2006; Watson 2000). There is a bundle of **graduation** evoking **attitude** items in Text One in the first half of the letter with explicitly expressed emotion items erupting towards the end of the letter as illustrated in the prosodic progression pattern in Figure 5. In contrast, the distribution in Text Two seems to climb steadily towards the last topical group of exchanges and the ratio between **attitude** and **graduation** evoking **attitude** item fairly constant (Figure 4). There seems to be no prosodic pattern correlation between them from a macro point of view.

However, a closer examination reveals that each wave of emotion, is introduced by a hypertheme and this predicts the flow of the pattern found in the

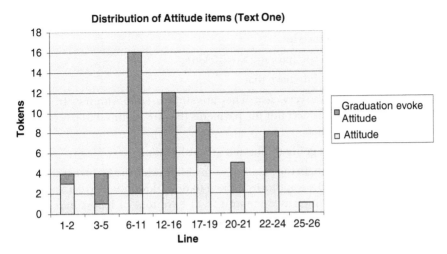

FIGURE 5 Prosodic progression pattern – Text One

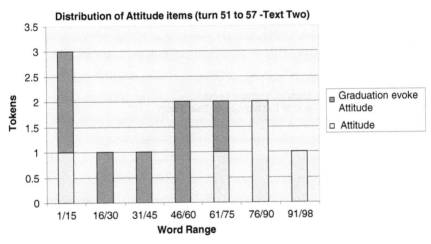

FIGURE 6 Prosodic progression pattern – First Topic Text Two

complaint letter. In Text 2, it begins with some facts, and then moves into an explosion of emotions signposted by **attitudinal** items as, for example [25], in turn 51 to 57. The **graduation** evoking **attitude** items group in the first half of the exchange and the inscribed Attitude items are more prominent in the latter half of the wave. This prosodic progression pattern is captured in Figure 6.

[25] (Text Two, turn 51 to 57)

turn	speaker	Transcript
51	caller	Do you have my Nov 16 letter?
52	CSR	Yes I do have that
53	caller	It was very clear. They are authorized to withdraw from the bank account the payments that are required to pay for this policy
54	CSR	I'm going to put that as a justification
55	caller	yeah. In the past they were withdrawing the incorrect amount and we authorized them to draw down the correct amount, the increased amount . . . I have tons of letters here, back and forwards . . . on termination . . . every time something happens they send me a termination which sends my wife through the ceiling and myself causes us distress . . . you can understand that?]
56	CSR	[Uh huh I]
57	caller	[. . . I don't know what the incompetence is at all!?

Similar pattern exists in turn 58 to 64 and turn 65 to 77. The trend becomes clearer when the pattern in Figure 5 is compared to Figure 7. In Figure 7, the cumulative attitude items of the three topical emotion waves are added together

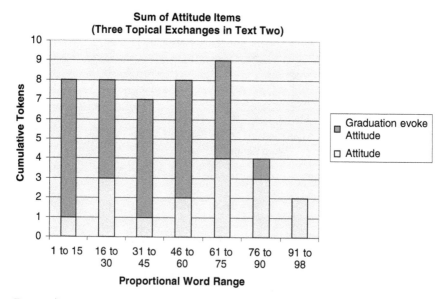

FIGURE 7 Prosodic progression pattern – Three topics combined (Text Two)

relative to the proportional sequential order that it appears in the spoken text. It is interesting to observe that the prosodic progression of both the written and spoken forms of complaint tend to follow the 'facts' then 'comment' pattern.

Ideational Disguises Interpersonal

While it has been recommended that the body of a complaint letter should 'present information' (Watson 2000: 37) and 'state the facts logically, objectively and unemotionally' (Guffey and Almonte 2006:128), it is observed that seemingly neutral lexical items are loaded with attitudinal meaning through the graduation system. In other words, in trying to remain objective and factual, the complainants realize interpersonal meanings in the discourse by resorting to intensified or lowered, sharpened or softened ideational meanings of the chosen expression. Both informative and emotional functions of the language are thus fulfilled. The second and third paragraphs of Text One exemplify this phenomenon. For example, in the following excerpt [26] from the third paragraph,

[26] (Text One, line 12 to 13)
I have spent hours chasing staff in your customer 'care' department to rectify the situation and at the end of April, after a **long** international phone call . . . (Force – Intensified)

In the process of providing the case's background information, the writer describing had to 'chase' staff 'rectify the situation', which is then compounded by the additive conjunction elaborating further 'and at the end of April' here the writer is clearly using graduation to demonstrate the protracted amount of time the delivery has taken. After this clause the writer does not simply choose to say that she had made a phone call but it was a 'long international phone call'. Here without any inscribed attitude the writer is clearly venting her frustration on a number of levels, and that this frustration is being construed by choices of Graduation evoking attitude. In so doing, plain data has been raised and turned into attitudinal items through the Graduation system.

Similarly in the second paragraph of Text One [27], plain description 'with direct access', the word 'direct' sharpened the attitudinal item.

[27] (Text One, line 9)
My sister lived, at that time, in a terraced house, with **direct** access onto the street . . . (Focus – Sharpened)

This sharpening of focus aims to narrow the opportunity for any rebuttal on behalf of the retail company.

Anger, Sympathy and Solidarity

Anger seems to be the most common and comprehensible emotion that people express when lodging a complaint. This is because of their strong feelings of injustice and their situational issues. In both texts, there are many examples of angry comments.

[28] (Text One, line 2)
Re: Unbelievably (Graduation – Force; neg affect) Poor Service (neg appreciation)

[29] (Text Two, turn 63)
. . . I'm not yelling (graduation-force) at you sir. Please understand (pos affect) that Mr. Kel someone's goofing up (neg judgment) here and putting me through stress (neg affect) . . .

Emotions are running high in these texts. Indeed, the informant of the complaint letter (Text One), when asked about the letter after it had been posted reportedly sighed: 'I was so angry. It was unbelievable . . .'. However, underneath these angry feelings other emotions seem to be at work.

The purpose of writing a complaint letter or making a complaint call is to 'correct' the 'wrong', or the 'disservice' rendered by a company or an individual. Gaining the audience's understanding, support and agreement of the problem which ultimately leads to the need for corrective action is the goal. In other words, aligning the audience so they sympathize with your situation is one step closer for them to be on your side. Martin and White (2005) provide analytical tools to explain and understand how solidarity is construed through choices in the lexico-grammar. The findings from the analysis of the 2 complaint texts suggest the writer and speaker are attempting to gain solidarity, even sympathy from the audience, and it is this motivation to engage with their interlocutor that motivates certain choices in the lexico-grammar. Martin and White (2005) refer to the use of concessive conjunctions e.g. but, while; projecting clauses e.g. I feel (projecting clause) that my sister . . . (projected clause); modality e.g. would, might, possibly; if clauses are all features which add alternative voices to the text, and by doing so open up a space for negotiation. In both Text One and Two, certain lexico-grammatical choices of words to express engagement and in some cases solidarity is created through evoking empathy and positioning the writer / speaker as a victim of helplessness, as shown in examples 30 and 31.

[30] (Text One, line 20–21)
Three months later, I continue to feel highly frustrated and deeply disappointed that my sister's gift has not arrived.

[31] (Text Two, turn 72)

Mr. Kel this has been going on for a year and a half almost two years and I've written down all these errors made by the insurance company. I've talked to numerous different representatives to straighten it up and even then it turns out you send me the same type of stereotypical letter notifying me of termination . . .

In both 30 and 31 we can see that the writer is using the length of time taken to position the intended reader in as a 'sympathetic' listener. The construal of Solidarity (Martin and White 2005) is even more evident in Text Two after turn 50. At turn 50, the call could have been completed since the problem had been identified, the CSR had promised to do something about it, and someone from the insurance company had agreed to inform the customer of the decision. Thus, the transactional nature of the call is completed at this point, everything has been taken care of and there is no need to continue.

[32] (Text Two, turn 34, 46–51)

turn	Speaker	Transcript
34	CSR	I'm going to put this to our reinstatement department
:	:	:
46	CSR	You've got it correctly right now sir
47	Caller	Ok thank you
48	CSR	So I'm going to make a request here. It will be looked upon by that department
49	Caller	Uh huh
50	CSR	So you are going to hear whatever the decision is in this case
51	Caller	Do you have my Nov 16 letter?

However, in turn 51 as shown in [32], the caller mentioned again the subject of a letter he sent to the company a few months earlier to seek an opportunity not only to vent anger, but also to seek the CSR's sympathy and to establish solidarity by telling the seemingly horrific story of his experience in dealing with the company, and the helplessness he felt with his encounters during recent months. In fact, towards the end of this turn, the caller explicitly looked for an agreement from the CSR by asking whether he 'understands' his suffering [33]. Here it is clear that the customer is using a projecting clause 'you can understand', 'please understand', where the agency of the mental process of knowing / understanding is projected on to 'you' the CSR. Even though the two clauses appear to be an interrogative 'you can understand that?' and an imperative 'please understand' the customer here is making a statement which he wishes the CSR to agree with. The mental projection purely serves to deflect proposition on to the interlocutor.

[33] (Text Two, turn 55)
. . . I have tons of letters here, back and forwards . . . on termination . . . every time something happens they send me a termination which sends my wife through the ceiling and myself causes us distress . . . **you can understand that?** . . .

[34] (Text Two, turn 63)
Please understand Mr. Kel someone's goofing up here and putting me through stress . . .

In addition [34], the caller is almost pleading for the CSR's understanding of the kind of suffering he and his wife have endured. In Text One, we have a similar situation where the sender wrote about her suffering and is almost pleading with the company representative.

[35] (Text One, line 22 to 24)
I would be grateful if the situation could finally be resolved and if you could give my sister, Jane Smith, and I an apology and a detailed explanation of why we have received months of torment and frustration due to your company's incompetent service?

Such lexicogrammatical choices demonstrate the attempts of the writer or the speaker to align their audience's views closer to their own position. By sharing how much they have suffered, and loading their side of the story with affective items, the customers seem to align their audience to their side, gain sympathy and attempt to establish solidarity. It is like saying 'if you were in my position, you would have done the same – written the same complaint letter or made the same complaint call'. The hope is that this solidarity building language will lead to a quick resolution in their favour.

Conclusion

Complaints occur when customers perceive that the delivery of services is unsatisfactory, and they demand redress. The act is realized through a complaint text – complaint letters or complaint calls to the customer service call centre. Misjudgment in handling complaint responses could lead to low customer satisfaction and serious consequences. Indeed, there is a strong link between company financial performance and complaint management (Johnston 2001). Discourse analysis techniques are instruments to dissect and expose interpersonal meanings of complaint texts. By applying an **appraisal** analysis to one written and one spoken complaint text in this study, it is suggested whether spoken or written, complaint texts follow 'facts' then 'comment' patterns. The emotions in the 'factual' part of the complaint tend to be embedded in seemingly neutral ideational lexis and expressions but are rendered through the evaluation grading system by invoking attitude. The complainers not only express anger, but emotions of sympathy and solidarity are also detected in the text. The probable purpose is to align the audience to their position and point of view by creating solidarity, so the complainers may achieve their goal to efficiently resolve their problem once and for all. While there are differences in spoken and written text in terms of construction, delivery and lexical choices (Halliday 1989; Maybin and Mercer 1996), this study detected evidence of some structural and language features common to both spoken and written complaint texts.

This present study argues that linguistic analysis plays an important role in the business context especially in the area of customer relationship management. Understanding the complaint text at the functional level helps management to gauge the expectations of the customers, adjust operational policies and form complaint response procedures accordingly. CSRs can be trained to recognize the prosody of complaint calls and signs of invoked attitude. The knowledge will enable them to anticipate the emotional peaks of calls and employ strategies to ameliorate the complaint impact and hence raise customer satisfaction, maintaining customer loyalty and ultimately improving business prospects.

The present research examined only one spoken and one written complaint text. Three salient features which are common to both forms, prosodic structure of complaints, hidden interpersonal meanings and creating audience solidarity, have been singled out in this study because of their relevance to the management of complaints. However, more studies in written and spoken complaint text are needed in order to support, adjust and modify the current findings. In addition, the inclusion of online complaint texts, which tend to have time, space and format constraints, would appropriately extend and expand this area of research in future, as the ever growing number of companies and corporations take advantage of the world wide web to implement and improve their e-resources (Fluss 2005).

Although the scope of this study is limited, it offers a glimpse of the complexity of complaint discourse. More studies in this area of business communication would certainly help to explore and expose interpersonal meanings in the realm of discourse and business management.

Appendix A

Text One	Attitude			Graduation	
	Affect	Judgment	Appreciation	Force	Focus
salutation	Dear				
subject (line 1–2)	unbelievably		poor service	poor service	
1st para. (3–5)	frustration			from the emails attached	
				sheer frustration	
				in February	
2nd para. (6–11)	'. . . safe . . .'			on 12 February	somewhere
	'. . . no safe . . .'			on 16 February	no notification
				on 16 February	no outbuilding
				a number of emails	no access
				an international call	direct access
				on 16 February	no safe place
				at that time	
				an 80cm laundry basket	
3rd para. (12–16)	'. . . care . . .'		a failed delivery	hours	one of your representatives
				at the end of April	someone
				a long international phone call	no laundry basket
				both	no notification

4ᵗʰ para. (17–19)	Shocked Horrified no confidence in your service no confidence in your ability	poor service	on 6 May on that day a number of times poor service frequently recommend at this moment in time
5ᵗʰ para. (20–21)	highly frustrated Deeply disappointed		three months highly frustrated deeply disappointed
6ᵗʰ para. (22–24)	Torment Frustration Grateful	incompetent service	all details months if you could detailed explanation
Closing (25–26)	Regards		

Appendix B

Text Two	Attitude			Graduation	
	Affect	Judgment	Appreciation	Force	Focus
turn 1–18					
turn 19–50	Stress thank you			every month on November 16th one amount the higher amount direct payment	
turn 51–57	sends my wife through the ceiling Distress		very clear	my Nov 16th letter very clear in the past tons of letters back and forwards every time	
turn 58–64	Yelling Please Stress	goofing ups a case of incompetence	the incompetence*	that amount one thousand what two seven	I'm willing to do that! someone's somebody

turn 65–77	thank you	commonsense	stereotypical letter	The November 30th	that amount
	Appreciate		goof ups*	very much	the correct amount
					the payment directly
			errors	all these	no mention
					any amount
					numerous different representatives
			stereotypical letter	for a year and a half	no one
				almost 2 years	the right amount
				all these	someone
				these termination letters	
turn 78–79	thank you			very much	
	a blessed weekend				

---

*In Exchange 65, '. . . somebody got a case of incompetence . . .', it is obvious that the reference is to someone's ability: **judgment**. On the other hand, **judgment** and **appreciation**. For example in Exchange 59, it is unclear whether the 'incompetence' is referring to the ability of the insurance staff, or to the act of sending unnecessary termination letters regularly causing stress to customers. In incidences such as this, the item is underlined and counted only once under **appreciation**.

References

Boxer, D. (1993), Social distance and speech behavior: The case of indirect complaints. *Journal of Pragmatics* 19(2), 103–125.

Boxer, D. (1996), Ethnographic interviewing as a research tool in speech act analysis: The case of complaints. In Gass, S. and Neu, J. (eds.) *Speech Acts across Cultures*. Berlin: Mouton de Gruyter, 217–239.

Butt, D. G., Lukin, A. and Matthiessen, C. M. I. M. (2004), Grammar – the first covert operation of war. *Discourse and Society* 15(2–3), 267–290.

Clyne, M. (1994), *Intercultural Communication at Work: Cultural Values in Discourse.* Cambridge: Cambridge University Press.

Coffin, C. (2003). Exploring different dimensions of language use. *ELT J.* 57(1), 11–18.

Cortazzi, M. and Jin, L. (2000), Evaluating evaluation in narrative. In Thompson, G. and Hunston, S. (eds.) *Evaluation in Text.* Oxford: Oxford University Press, 102–119.

Crosier, K. and Erdogan, B. Z. (2001), Advertising complainants: Who and where are they? *Journal of Marketing Communications* 7(2), 109–120.

Davidow, M. (2003), Organizational responses to customer complaints: What works and what doesn't. *Journal of Service Research* 5(3), 225–250.

Dersley, I. and Wootton, A. (2000), Complaint sequences within antagonistic argument. *Research on Language and Social Interaction* 33(4), 375–406.

Drew, P. (1998), Complaints about transgressions and misconduct. *Research on Language and Social Interaction* 31(3), 295.

Edwards, D. (2005), Moaning, whinging and laughing: The subjective side of complaints. *Discourse Studies* 7(1), 5–29.

Fluss, D. (2005), *The Real-time Contact Center.* New York: AMACOM.

Forey, G. and Lockwood, J. (2007), 'I'd love to put someone in jail for this': An initial investigation of English in the business processing outsourcing (BPO) industry. *English for Specific Purposes* 26(3), 308–326.

Guffey, M. E. and Almonte, R. (2006), *Essentials of Business Communication* (5th ed.). Canada: Thomson Nelson.

Halliday, M. A. K. (1989), *Spoken and Written Language.* Oxford: Oxford University Press.

Halliday, M. A. K. and Matthiessen, C. M. I. M. (2004), *An Introduction to Functional Grammar* (3rd edn.). London: Hodder Arnold.

Harrison-Walker, L. (2001), E-complaining: A content analysis of an internet complaint forum. *Journal of Services Marketing* 15(4), 397.

Holmes, J. and Riddiford, N. (in press), Complaints. In Cummings, L. (ed.) *Encylopedia of Pragmatics.* London: Routledge.

Homburg, C. and Fürst, A. (2005), How organizational complaint handling drives customer loyalty: An analysis of the mechanistic and the organic approach. *Journal of Marketing* 69(3), 95–114.

Hood, S. (2004), Managing attitude in undergraduation academic writing: A focus on the introductions to research reports. In Ravelli, L. and Ellis, R. (eds.) *Analysing Academic Writing: Contextualised Frameworks.* London: Continuum, pp. 24–44.

Hood, S. and Forey, G. (2008), The interpersonal dynamics of call-centre interactions: Co-constructing the rise and fall of emotion. *Discourse and Communication* 2(4), 389–409.

Johnston, R. (2001), Linking complaint management to profit. *International Journal of Service Industry Management* 12(1), 60.

Johnston, R. and Mehra, S. (2002), Best-practice complaint management. *Academy of Management Executive* 16(4), 145–154.

Jurkiewicz, C. L., Giacalone, R. A. and Knouse, S. B. (2004), Transforming personal experience into a pedagogical tool: Ethical complaints. *Journal of Business Ethics* 53(3), 283–295.

Kaltenbacher, M. (2006), Culture related linguistic differences in tourist websites: The emotive and the factual. A corpus analysis within the framework of appraisal. In Thompson, G. and Hunston, S. (eds.) *System and Corpus: Exploring Connections.* London: Equinox, pp. 269–292.

Laforest, M. (2002), Scenes of family life: Complaining in everyday conversation. *Journal of Pragmatics* 34(10–11), 1595–1620.

Lazar, A. and Lazar, M. (2004), The discourse of the new world order: 'out-casting' the double face of threat. *Discourse and Society* 15(2–3), 223–242.

Lockyer, S. and Pickering, M. (2001), Dear shit-shovellers: Humour, censure and the discourse of complaint. *Discourse Society* 12(5), 633–651.

Martin, J. R. (2000), Beyond exchange: Appraisal systems in English. In Thompson, G. and Hunston, S. (eds.) *Evaluation in Text.* Oxford: Oxford University Press, 142–175.

Martin, J. R. (2004), Mourning: How we get aligned. *Discourse and Society* 15(2–3), 321–344.

Martin, J. R. and Rose, D. (2003), *Working with Discourse.* London: Continuum.

Martin, J. R. and Rose, D. (2007), *Working with Discourse: Meaning Beyond the Clause* (2nd edn). London: Continuum.

Martin, J. R. and Rose, D. (2008), *Genre Relations: Mapping Culture.* London: Equinox.

Martin, J. R. and White, P. (2005), *Language of Evaluation.* London: Continuum.

Mattsson, J., Lemmink, J. and McColl, R. (2004), The effect of verbalized emotions on loyalty in written complaints. *Total Quality Management and Business Excellence* 15(7), 941–958.

Maybin, J. and Mercer, N. (eds.) (1996). *Using English: From Conversation to Canon.* London: Routledge.

Miller, D. R. (2006), From concordance to text: Appraising 'giving' in Alma Mater donation request. In Thompson, G. and Hunston, S. (eds.) *System and Corpus: Exploring Connections.* London: Equinox, pp. 248–268.

Phau, I. and Sari, R. P. (2004), Engaging in complaint behaviour: An Indonesian perspective. *Marketing Intelligence and Planning* 22(4), 407–426.

Reiter, R. M. (2005), Complaint calls to a caregiver service company: The case of desahogo. *Intercultural Pragmatics* 2(4), 481–514.

Tanaka, N., Spencer-Oatey, H. and Cray, E. (2000), 'It's not my fault!': Japanese and English responses to unfounded accusations. In Spencer-Oatey, H. (ed.) *Culturally Speaking: Managing Rapport through Talk across Cultures.* London: Continuum, 75–97.

Tatsuki, D. H. (2000), If my complaints could passions move: An interlanguage study of aggression. *Journal of Pragmatics* 32(7), 1003–1017.

Thompson, G. and Hunston, S. (eds.) (2000). *Evaluation in Text.* Oxford: Oxford University Press.

Watkins, H. S. and Liu, R. (1996), Collectivism, individualism and in-group membership: Implications for consumer complaining behaviours in multicultural contexts. *Journal of International Consumer Marketing* 8(3/4), 69.

Watson, D. (2000), *Communication in the Workplace.* Sydney: Prentice Hall.

Chapter 6

Naming and Negotiating Relationships in Call Centre Talk

Susan Hood

University of Technology, Sydney, Australia

Much of the research interest in the discourse of call centre interactions focuses on interpersonal meaning, that is on how speakers relate to each other, on positions of power and identity, and on emotions such as positive or negative satisfaction. Much of the research to date relies on surveys of perceptions and to a lesser extent on observational, ethnographic data. While the retrospectively oriented interpretations of participants provide some insight into customer-CSR relations, they tell us little about the actual roles played by the speakers in interaction, how meanings unfold in talk to generate the potential for perceived satisfactory or unsatisfactory outcomes. The analyses underpinning this discussion focus on what speakers actually say, and specifically on how speakers name and reference each other in the talk. The aim is to better understand the ways in which choices in naming function to construct, to maintain or to shift relationships between customers and CSRs across the duration of a call. While naming practices might be culturally or institutionally proscribed to a greater or lesser extent, shifts in naming choices are also seen to result from contingent decisions to do with the management of the talk towards satisfactory outcomes.

Introduction

Call centres have become an increasingly familiar aspect of global business in the late capitalist world, contributing in significant ways to changed employment contexts in many provider countries with consequent reverberations in social and cultural life and extending into many aspects of the lives of global consumers. Not surprisingly the industry attracts research interest from a diverse range of disciplines including business management, sociology, cultural studies and linguistics, and much of this interest focuses in one way or another on issues of relationships and interaction, or what we might refer to as interpersonal meaning.

Research from a sociological perspective includes studies on relations within call centres as workplaces and among the workforce (e.g. Knights and McCabe

2001; Mulholland 2004; Taylor and Bain 2003, 2007; Taylor et al. 2002). Taylor and Bain (2003) for example, explore the role of humour and joking practices among employees in call centres, and Knights and McCabe (2001) focus on issues of gender in relationships of management to employees (cf. Cameron 2000). There is also interesting work emerging from the field of identity studies, which we might interpret as a concern for relationships of self to culture (Das, Dharwadkar and Brandes 2008; Shome 2006).

Within the industry itself there is a significant focus on the issue of customer relations from a quality assurance perspective. Telephone mediated customer service interactions through call centres are usually understood as highly routinized and scripted exchanges of information (via reference to computerized databases) to resolve customer concerns and problems. Typically calls are monitored and measured against a matrix of criteria including duration and outcomes, but also routinized customer orientations of various kinds (Bolton and Houlihan 2005; Taylor et al. 2002). The focus within the industry is dominantly on the role played by the customer service representative (CSR), sometimes with an implicit assumption that relationships with the customer can be managed satisfactorily, if not controlled, by the CSR.

Interest in perceptions of quality in call centre customer relations is also evident in the organizational management research literature, where the customer is likely to be a key source of data. Studies may be based on quantitative designs involving large surveys of customers' perceptions. Dean (2007), for example, relies on surveys of customers to explore constructs such as 'employees' customer orientation' and 'customer loyalty'. Quantitative studies of this kind sometimes suggest generalizable strategies for improving customer relations. The implication here may also be that the CSR is the key variable in achieving quality.

Customer perception is also the focus for Bolton and Houlihan (2005), although they take a very different methodological approach from the large-scale customer survey methods noted above. Bolton and Houlihan's study is based on a collection of spontaneous anecdotal reflections from a diverse collection of people who have interacted as call centre customers. This study is just one dimension of a larger project that includes a relatively long-term ethnographic study involving insider participant observation, interviews and case studies of several call centres. Bolton and Houlihan (2005) counter simplistic assumptions of predictable inequality between customer and call centre representative – an inequality that favours the customer – and refer instead to the customer as 'mythical sovereign'. They interpret the relationship as complex, involving the customer in roles of both **functional transactant** and **moral agent**. They point out that

> many routine service encounters are minor episodes that are carried out in a perfunctory manner involving (. . .) **functional transactants** who are happy to complete the transaction in the simplest, most straightforward manner possible. For them, efficiency and routinization is a demand met – and service

'superfluity' is an irritant rather than a re-enchantment. The customer senti-
ment in this case is 'let's not pretend this is something it is not'. (696)

Yet, within a context of routinized and scripted interactions, many service workers reported their role as one of 'working with people' and 'helping people',
interpreting the relationship with the customer as between 'human beings' and
as a 'socially relevant activity' (697). Bolton and Houlihan argue that

> [c]all-centre workers and their customers, though aware of the material
> demands made of them, re-interpret the restrictions of routinized service
> encounters depending upon context and different motivations. (. . .) Whilst
> they have little influence over the setting of the stage on which they must play
> out the encounter, both parties are, nevertheless, an active and controlling
> force. Both the customer and service provider are people who relate to each
> other, socially and morally. (2005:697– 698)

While the retrospectively oriented interpretations of customers (or call centre
workers) provide some insight into aspects of customer-CSR relations, these
data tell us little about the actual roles played by the speakers in interaction,
how meanings unfold in talk to generate the potential for perceived satisfactory
or unsatisfactory perceptions of outcomes. In understanding the nature of
customer-CSR relations it is vital that we also consider what speakers say, and in
doing so it is wise to work on an assumption that what people say they say, and
what they actually say are not the same thing. Perhaps because of difficulties in
accessing linguistic data of genuine customer-CSR interactions there is as yet
relatively little published research that explores the issue of relationships from
a linguistic perspective, and less from a linguistic perspective that considers the
flow of discourse.

In this chapter I report on an aspect of a larger project of studies on call
centre interactions. The studies draw on sets of transcribed and scrubbed
(personal and company identifying information removed) inbound customer
service calls to call centres in the Philippines predominantly from customers in
the USA (see e.g. Forey and Lockwood 2007; Hood and Forey 2008). The concern in this study is to add a complementary linguistic perspective to surveys
and case studies (e.g. Bolton and Houlihan 2005), to explore the question: in
what sense and by what means 'the customer and service provider are people
who relate to each other' (Bolton and Houlihan 2005: 697). It should be noted,
however, that while this study draws on data from actual interactions it, too,
is limited, most notably in a lack of analysis of original sound recordings
and hence data of voice quality (see van Leeuwen 1999 and Wan this volume).
Analyses are also restricted in this chapter to a small number of features
pertinent to the construal of interpersonal relations with a focus on resources
for naming and referencing the other in the talk, and their expression as vocative structures.

The theory informing the analyses and interpretations of the data is that of Systemic Functional Linguistics. As such the study is premised on an understanding that interpersonal relations enacted in the talk are reflective of the context of the talk, but at the same time they are constitutive of the context (Halliday 1994; Martin 1992). In other words the way we talk is constructive of our social relations. The aim of this chapter is to better understand the ways in which different choices in naming the other can function to construct, maintain or shift relationships between customers and CSRs across the duration of a call. In particular I explore how naming choices can be made variously available to either speaker in the unfolding discourse, and how choices can be opened up or constrained not only by expectations or practiced institutional scripts brought to the interaction, but also as a result of contingent decisions in managing the flow of talk towards a satisfactory outcome.

Of particular relevance to the analyses undertaken in this chapter is the foundational work by Poynton (1985/1989, 1990) on naming and relating. Poynton identifies, for example, the principle of reciprocity in naming as signalling relationships of power, or unequal social status (Martin 2000), and the principles of proliferation and of contraction as signalling relationships of high contact or familiarity. On the question of power Martin (1992, 2000) argues the need to factor out power along multiple dimensions of genre and register each of which implicates language in different ways. This framework for analysis of power will be further explained and exemplified with extracts from the data. While drawing on a different theoretical base, the work also connects with a long history of studies from the field of pragmatics concerned with interaction (e.g. Brown and Levinson 1987; Gumperz 1982).

Choosing to Name Each Other Differently

The short extract [1] is introduced as an example of an inbound customer service call that proceeds routinely, unproblematically and to a quick and mutually satisfactory conclusion. We can take this call as a point of reference against which to compare other instances of interaction. Here, as in other transcripts in the chapter, R is the customer service representative and C is the customer.

[1]
R: Thank you for calling [company name] technical support and product information. This is Joe. May I get your first and last name or reference number?
C: Yeah, the number is ****–****
R: Just give me just a moment – ****–**** . . .
C: umh . . .
R: I am just checking that . . .

C: Yes . . .

R: Ok, this [make and item name], how do you wish to proceed with the repair?

C: Displace . . .

R: Ok, I see [make and item name] displacement was offered and . . . you would go ahead with the re-placement . . .

C: That would be lovely, ok?

R: Ok, thank you very much for calling [company name]. Have a good day.

C: Thank you

R: Bye bye.

In [1] the CSR introduces himself in a routinized and scripted opening by using only his first name. He then asks the customer for her full name or a reference number. In this case the customer offers a reference number and not her name. The offer of a number rather than a name has the potential to restrict naming options available to the CSR in subsequent turns in this episode of talk. While the CSR is likely to have computer access to the customer's name via the reference number, an immediate response using her name in a vocative construction, as in:

Just give me just a moment, **Mary/ Ms Smith**

cannot be anticipated by the customer on the basis of the talk to this point, and so is potentially disjunctive. The CSR could, of course, have chosen to make use of perceived gender based on voice quality to construct a vocative, such as:

Just give me just a moment, **maam**

or, as in this case, to choose a non-vocative construction. As the analyses in this study reveal, choices such as these offer varied potentials in the construction of interpersonal relationships. In the case of extract [1], the call proceeds with the CSR referring to himself as 'I' and 'me' and to the customer as 'you' and 'your' while the customer makes no use of any pronominal reference to self or other. These choices can be interpreted as minimizing the interpersonal orientation of the call in favour of a focus on the efficient exchange of information.

Some of the options for naming discussed above are evident in extract [2]. The CSR chooses to use the caller's name in a vocative construction, **Ok, Ms Smith**. In choosing to name the customer the CSR in [2] (in contrast to [1]) is explicitly encoding a relationship of unequal social status. In this case the vocative use of title and surname reflects and constructs a relationship of unfamiliarity or a degree of social distance. This relationship is reinforced in a subsequent turn in the vocative **maam**.

[2]
R: Thanks for calling customer services. This is Chris. May I have your policy number please?
C: Yes, that's ******
R: Thank you. One moment please.
     (Pause)
R: Your first name?
C: Mary Smith
R: Ok, Ms Smith. Please verify your address and social security number.
C: ******
R: Thank you. What can I do for you, maam?

Here it is not simply that the CSR refers to the customer by surname or as **maam** that is significant, but that the naming options taken up by the CSR in [2] are not reciprocated by the customer. The lack of reciprocity in the linguistic choices results in the construction of a kind of interpersonal inequality in the talk (Poynton 1990, 1994).

I avoid rushing to use the term 'power' here in that it can too readily be interpreted as a singular construct. From a linguistic perspective we need to see power as multi-faceted dimensions of inequality, to be factored out along aspects of genre and of register. From the perspective of genre, power has to do with who controls the talk from stage to stage as the genre unfolds. From the perspective of register, we can factor out power further along dimensions of field, mode and tenor. In relation to field the question of power has to do with who controls the knowledge or the information; in relation to mode we ask who is dominant in putting forward their message, for example, who talks louder in an actual or metaphorical sense; and in relation to tenor, our concern is in markings of in/equality in social status through naming reference and deference (Martin 1992). The talk therefore constitutes a complex set of relationships, in which power may be distributed differently. If we leave aside the issue of relations with respect to mode, we can say that in the stage of the interaction represented in extract [2], the CSR is in control of the genre as his questioning role positions the customer as respondent; we say that the customer is in control of the field, as she is the provider of the information; and we can say that the customer is in the position of superior social status in terms of tenor, a relationship constructed not solely in the naming choices made by one or other speaker, but by both. This factoring out of power relations will of course shift at different points in the discourse.

While it is important to acknowledge that constraints are likely to be imposed on the CSR through scripting and monitoring practices (Taylor et al. 2002), nonetheless each speaker has options in how to mean in terms of their social relations. As later examples make evident, the speakers do at times vary from this jointly constructed pattern of difference and deference in naming, and often appear to do so for strategic purposes, or in constructing a shift in genre or register. The lack of reciprocity identified in the examples above is therefore understood to be a consequence of linguistic choices on the part of both speakers.

A linguistic analysis of the construction of relationships as social status can be approached from a quantitative and synoptic perspective. For example, the naming choices of speakers can be analysed, quantified and compared across a whole interaction or, more commonly, across a corpus of interactions (cf. Friginal 2008). On this basis we could describe the relative frequency of a particular choice in the data as a whole, or per turn, according to gender of CSR and so on. If, for example, extract [3] were indicative of a larger corpus of call data, marked differences in frequency of use of the title **maam** as a vocative would be evident. The CSR uses this vocative in every turn (100%), while the caller not at all (0%).

[3]
R: Thank you. What can I do for you, **maam**?
C: OK you sent me a letter saying that you're missing a payment, due for November. You took all those payments out. I don't know why they're trying to charge me again?
R: OK well the reason for that, **maam**, if you double check your bank record, it would show there that we didn't really receive the premium payment for the month of November because there were some billing problems with the posting of the payments.
C: With the what?
R: with the posting of the payment. We didn't really receive the money from your bank. You can verify that with the bank, **maam**.

Quantitative analyses can also identify and compare speaker preferences for particular naming options, perhaps at different stages in the interaction. We could consider, for example, speaker variation in vocatives in closing turns, as illustrated in [4] where the caller uses the CSR's first name and the CSR refers to the customer as **maam**.

[4]
C: OK, **Kim**, thank you for your time and your help.
R: OK thank you, **maam**. You're welcome.

Such analyses provide strong evidence of inequality in social status, but they do not allow us to track the extent to which, the points at which, or the ways in which social status shifts in the discourse. For that we need a complementary dynamic or logogenetic perspective whereby we analyse in detail the patterns of meaning in individual interactions. Before offering such a dynamic perspective there is a further consideration of meaning potential to be taken into account.

Naming Choices across Languages

To this point linguistic choices in naming have been considered within a single language, in this case, English. However, we can also consider linguistic choice in a broader cultural sense, that is, in terms of a speaker's potential to mean in one language or another. While a commonsense notion of translation may suggest that wordings are taken from one language and transformed into wordings in the other, what is at stake is not just wordings but meanings (see, e.g., Caffarel et al. 2004). The starting point is then what is meant in the first language, and how that meaning can be meant in the second language, or in fact, whether that meaning can be meant in the second language. In this study the CSRs are all speakers of Tagalog (although not necessarily as first language) and of Filipino English and they are interacting with speakers of North American English. While the intercultural nature of the communication is not a major focus of this study, its potential significance is noted here in respect to an interpretation of one pattern of choice, that is, the frequent use of the vocative 'maam' on the part of the Filipino CSRs.

Taking the construction of social status as our focus, it is noted that Tagalog has multiple and complex means for signalling such status in talk. These include the use of clitic particles that attach to all verb forms (see Martin 1990) meaning that relative social status is repeatedly marked morphologically in interactions. Clitic particles or verb forms to mark social status are not resources available in English, though other resources are, including choices in vocatives. Deferring in social status terms can be achieved in English in the choice of a specific title and surname such as **Mrs Smith**, or in a more generic form of **maam** or **sir**. Other contextual variables of genre and register would then come into play to promote or constrain the extent of such explicit marking. This provides at least a potential explanation for what seems to this author, (as a native speaker of Australian and not North American English) to be a marked frequency of use of **maam/sir** vocatives on the part of the Filipino English-speaking CSRs. The heavy reliance on these vocatives could be explained as the speaker taking up resources available in English to do the kind of high frequency explicit marking of social status required in Tagalog. More research would be needed to support this hypothesis, for example, research that investigates equivalent calls in other locations including those between native speakers of English. The question also then arises as to the meaning potential of **maam/sir** vocatives for the speaker of other varieties of English. It is also important to note that there are shifts in the frequency of vocatives at points where there is a shift in genre and a move away from institutionally predicted topics for talk, as is discussed in a later section.

Naming Strategically

In this section I shift focus from a quantitative or generalized account of differences in naming to a more dynamic orientation, to highlight the constructedness of relationships in the flow of talk. Of particular interest are points in the talk where the naming choices change, and the linguistic (meaning) contexts within which such changes occur. The aim is to explore when and why speakers choose to relate differently in the talk.

Text [5] is an extract from one of a small percentage of interactions in this study that did not proceed smoothly towards a satisfactory resolution of the caller's problem. There is evidence of heightened negative emotion in this phase of talk on the part of the caller, both in multiple instances of explicit attitude – **goofing up, stress, incompetence** (Hood and Forey 2008), and in references to loudness in voice quality – **I'm not yelling at you** (cf. Wan 2007).

[5]
C: I'm willing to do that. They have authorization to pay the premium from my account . . . I mean why's someone not drawing the correct amount . . . because I don't send money to you, you are automatically supposed to withdraw the payments from the account.
(?)
C: I'm not yelling at you, **sir**. Please understand that, **Mr. King,** someone's goofing up here and putting me through stress. . . . There's somebody got a case of incompetence. I've never sent the payment directly from my house in the mail to . . . you can automatically draw it out of the bank account and the money is always there.
R: (Silence) Let me see . . .
C: In fact, excuse me, do you have a copy of the November 30th letter you sent me of termination?
R: Yes, **sir**.

In extract [5] there is a marked change in naming on the part of the caller. Prior to this phase in the call the CSR has referred multiple times to the caller as **sir**. The customer on his part has not reciprocated in this respect, resulting in the construction of an unequal relation in social status. The beginning of extract [5] reveals that there has been some breakdown in communication. The customer's request for clarification of the problem is not met by the CSR with more information, but rather with an apparent (untranscribed) admonition of the customer for raising his voice. The shifts in naming occur at this point.[1] The caller refers in quick succession to the CSR as **sir** and **Mr King**.

The shift in naming on the part of the customer is interpreted as a means of shifting the interpersonal dynamic of the interaction. At this point in the exchange the customer is demanding answers. He is taking control of the genre, and in raising his voice he asserts control of the mode. The customer has also been constructed up to this point in the interaction as superior in social status (in unreciprocated **sir** vocatives). However, as the source of the information required by the customer, the CSR is in control of the field. A critical point is reached in the exchange when the field focus shifts from the problem with finances (e.g. **authorization to pay the premium from my account**) to the attitude of the caller (**I'm not yelling at you**). This represents a breakdown in communication for both speakers. The caller's strategy for repair is to shift one or more of the other relationships of inequality towards a more equal footing. He chooses to do so with a shift in social status. (A shift in loudness and hence mode may also be evident in the sound files but such data is not available to the researcher.) In reciprocating with vocatives of **sir**, and title plus surname in **Mr King**, the customer works to restore an equality in social status, albeit one of social distance, facilitating a return to a shared focus on the ideational aspect of the interaction, on the issue of finances. The reciprocity in marking social status can be interpreted in this context as a strategic move to re-establish a relationship of co-professionals, or what Bolton and Houlihan (2005) refer to as 'functional transactants'.

In theory the caller could have moved the relationship in another direction. He could, for example, have called the CSR by his first name, a name which is typically proffered by CSRs in the opening turns of the calls in the data. This would have constituted a strategic move towards greater familiarity rather than one towards equalizing social status. However, such a move was not an option for the customer in this call as is revealed in the opening phase of this call in [6]. Tracking back, we find that the customer has misheard the CSR and the exchange finished with the caller only having access to what he understands to be the CSR's surname.

> [6]
> R: Customer services this is Kel, how can I help you?
> C: Ah, good morning, L**** J**** from [location] calling. Who am I talking to?
> R: Kel. K-E-L
> C: Pardon me?
> R: Kel. K-E-L
> C: Kal?
> R: Kel, K-E-L
> C: Kel – King?
> R: that's right
> C: OK. I'm calling in reference to my policy, my life insurance policy.

Naming as Responsive to Genre and Field

The data also reveal instances where shifts in patterns of naming are implicated in a shift in genre as well as field. The extracts [7[1]] to [7[7]] are taken from a long call of almost 2,000 words. Beyond the initial greeting by the CSR and elicitation of personal details from the customer, the primary purpose of the call is revealed in [7¹] namely seeking an explanation for the unexpected deduction of two payments from the customer's account.

[7¹]

R: Thank you. What can I do for you, maam?

C: Ok, you sent me a letter saying that you're missing a payment, due for November. You took all those payments out. I don't know why they're trying to charge me again?

Upon its apparent resolution, the customer initiates a second phase of interaction on a related but different topic – how much she has in her insurance policy.

[7²]

C: Ok, yes, while I have you, what is my status with my insurance?

When this is resolved she initiates a third stage of interaction to do with the implications of not repaying a loan against her policy.

[7³]

C: Ok. Let me ask you this. If I . . . because you know I had always, when I took it out years ago, (. . .). . . so if I leave the loan like it is, that will eat it up?

Each of the phase openings [7¹] to [7³] functions as a request for information, and the phases themselves construe fields of technical information, as for example:

[7¹]: letter, payment, charge, bank record, premium payment, billing problems, bank statements, policy, draft, system, update, real draft.

[7²]: status, insurance, active, policy, coverage, cash value, $25,000, loan, 1,556:47, death benefit

[7³]: left over, loan, $25,000, $1500, benefit, $23,500

In these phases of discourse, the CSR is constructed as expert in the field and the source of information, but at the same time as unequal in social status, in the high frequency of **maam** vocatives that are unreciprocated by the customer.

In a fourth and longest phase of the whole call, begun in [7⁴], the customer shifts the genre to one of seeking sympathetic advice rather than seeking information. The exchange is set up to seek alignment around a moral issue of familial care and displays features identified by Eggins and Slade (1997) as obligatory stages of the genre of gossip, namely third person focus, substantive behaviour and pejorative evaluation. Eggins and Slade (1997:278) define gossip as:

> Talk which involves pejorative judgement of an absent other. More specifically the focus is on talk which is meant to be confidential (or at least not reported back to a third party), and is about an absent person who is known to at least one of the participants.

The caller proceeds to ask for advice in that context. The genre implicates the CSR is a very different role from that in the preceding talk. He is no longer positioned primarily as an expert in technical knowledge, but something approaching an agent on a personal help-line.

[7⁴]

C: So let me ask you this, baby, whilst I have you on the phone, I'm having some great problems . . . what do you think. . . . I have this one daughter . . . and originally that's how . . . you know . . . she was going to bury me and all that business . . . and I've been having a lot of problems, and I was going to change it over to someone else to take care of me . . . excuse me I have to sneeze (sneezes)

R: Bless you

C: Thank you. And it's like she treats me like an animal now that I'm living and people say to me 'what will she do when you pass away? She'll just throw you anywhere and take the money.' Now how do you feel? And then some people say 'when you're gone, you're gone'. How do you feel about that, sugar? If that was you, you know, would you leave someone. . .? I would like to be put away as the good person I was . . . that I am, you know what I'm saying?

The field also shifts from a technical construal of insurance issues to a more familiar and personal one of family, funerals and feelings, construed in lexical choices such as:

[7⁴]: great problems, one daughter, bury, lot of problems, take care, treats me like an animal, living, people, pass away, throw you anywhere, take the money, feel, gone, leave, put away, good person, daughter, good burial, pass away, funeral home, left over, daughter, the most expensive cask.

In [7⁴] corresponding to the shift in genre and field, there is a marked shift in the construction of social status. In the previous phases, the CSR had used the

maam vocative in almost every turn. However in [7^4] there are only two instances of use in a long phase. Differentiating social status in this context could potentially have required the CSR to counter the caller's control of the genre, that is, to reject his positioning as sympathetic advisor.

A similar phase follows, commencing with the extract in [7^5], where again the social function of the discourse is to seek sympathetic advice, and again the field is that of family matters, this time insurance for a very elderly mother. Again there is a notable scarcity of use of the **maam** vocative throughout this phase.

[7^5]

C: And would you have any suggestions for my, ma . . . she's 95. I can't get no insurance on her, so I've been saving it in the bank.

Then in [7^6], the beginning of a new phase, the caller returns the interaction to the technical field of the loan begun in [7^4], and to the genre of exchanging information. Here the **maam** vocative returns in the majority of CSR turns.

[7^6]

C: Yes, ok, now what about the loan? What did you say? What do I need to do? How does that work?

R: Well you don't need to do anything, **maam**, I'm doing it for you right now.

Finally in [7^7], the caller raises one last query about withdrawing money. From this opening turn the phase continues as an exchange of information on the name and telephone number of an agent.

[7^7]

C: Alright, baby . . . Ok I guess that's that, let me see. No, you don't have any policies where you can take out everything. It has to be in effect for like what about 2 or 3 years before the benefit . . .

While all phases of the interaction indicated by the opening turns in [7^1] to [7^7], construe aspects of the field of banking and insurance, there are marked shifts in institutional orientation from the practices of the professional world on the one hand to the domestic world of family and making funeral plans on other. These field shifts correspond significantly with differences in the ways in which power as social status is negotiated in the talk. It is noted too that the shifts in field also correspond to shifts in genre from negotiating information to negotiating shared values and of services.

Naming as a Resource for Solidarity

In the introduction I made reference to the work of Poynton (1994) on naming and how it relates to power and to familiarity. I also refer to Martin's (1992) discussion of the factoring out power in terms of different dimensions of language. While power is reflected in non-reciprocal choices in language (including naming), familiarity and in that sense solidarity is reflected in the principle of **proliferation**. Where naming choices proliferate the relationship is construed as more familiar and the solidarity as stronger. Where naming choices are constrained the relationship is construed as less familiar and the solidarity as weaker. In the brief extracts in [7¹] to [7⁷] there is already some evidence of the tendency for this caller to proliferate naming choices. The proliferation is very evident in the closing stage of the call, as highlighted in [7⁸]. This level of proliferation is, however, an uncommon and unreciprocated choice.[2]

[7⁸]

C: **Chris**, and I thank you so much **baby**, **Chris**, thank you, **honey.**
R: You have a good one ok?
C: You too, **baby**, And you said you're going to send me a draft in March, not February, not in February, in March on oh about the 15th.
R: That's right.
C: Oh alright, **baby**, and that will be $28 twice.
R: That's correct.
C: For March and November.
R: Uh ha.
C: Alright, **honey**, and thank you, **Chris**. Ok, **sweetie**. Bye bye.
R: Bye bye.

Knowing Names as a Source of Power

Earlier in the chapter I briefly discussed the issue of who gets to know whose name in what forms and how this information can impact on the potential for marking social status in the interaction. Knowing or not knowing names is itself an indicator of familiarity and contact, or lack thereof. It is reflective of a kind of social distance. And the giving and withholding of this knowledge about names is an issue of power as control of information, as expertise. The issue of names as information is highlighted in [8]. Specific information about names is sought by the customer in an attempt to find a successful resolution to a problem. Names are, however, not things to be given out lightly.

[8]

C: Ok. Your name is?
R: My name is Adele.

C: Adele what?

R: Y for yell, U for uniform, B for boy, O for Oscar, C for Charles, O for Oscar

C: Ok. Your supervisor's name?

R: We're not allowed to give out that information, maam.

C: What are my hours to talk to this supervisor. You're a big [kind of business] company . . . Who's this R**** B****? Ok, he's on your paper work . . . 'Please send a carbon copy'.

R: Let me just check that one, maam. One moment please. I'm seeing R**** B****, the servicing agent.

C: Then I need his telephone number. I will call him myself.

While the CSR represents herself as in a position of inferior institutional status to her supervisor (**we're *not allowed to* give out that information**), she none the less asserts control of the information in relation to the customer. She is the primary knower in the talk at this point. Given the complex ways in which names impact of relationships it is not surprising to find names and naming at the core of many problematic episodes in calls that do not proceed smoothly (cf. Hood and Forey 2008). Extract [9] provides another example.

[9]

C: Ok , is B**** P**** in your office?

R: No, maam.

C: I'm told that she is.

R: I'm not familiar with her, maam.

C: OK, do you have by any chance a customer service or somebody that can look her extension up for me?

R: Um I don't have an extension for her, maam, in our office for B**** . . . I don't know . . .

C: I am told by J**** who I just talked to (number) that this is where R**** is . . .

R: No, maam, it isn't . . . it's not . . .

C: You know, this is **very pathetic** as far as knowing that you cannot get your hands on something . . . that you're **like a tennis ball being hit from one court to another** . . .

The withholding of names, or the inability to make contact with a named person is often a source of frustration for the customer as is evident in [9] (**very pathetic; like a tennis ball being hit from one court to another**). The customer interprets this as a hindrance to the successful resolution to their problem, although as we see in [10], knowing a name is no guarantee of access to that named person.

[10]

C: I'm calling to ah . . . in contact with Brian, I got a separate number for *****.

R: As far as what is concerned, sir?

C: Excuse me?

R: As far as what? It's you know . . . calling regards to what?

C: To speak with Brian?

R: Brian?

C: Yes . . .

R: . . . ah . . . I don't know any Brian. Do you have a case number?

C: No.

The issue that is highlighted in these problematic exchanges is one of disjunctive expectations, not just on an individual to individual level but in the broader context of the industry. The customer seeks to build a relationship of continued contact and of familiarity with one CSR in relation to an issue that is ongoing for them over more than one call. This necessitates knowing names. In contrast the relationship of CSR to customer is of one to very many and it is an arbitrary one. The CSR appreciates that names of other representatives are mostly irrelevant in the context of this industry.[3]

Conclusion

Naming issues are frequently foregrounded in problematic episodes of talk. From the customer's point of view an inability to know or to access a name is often the focus for expressions of frustration and dissatisfaction. However, a repertoire of ways to name is also an important resource in repairing dysfunctional relationships that are created in the talk, and for getting the interaction back on track. We have also seen the significance of naming in the construction of relationships of solidarity, relationships of the kind that Bolton and Houlihan (2005) refer to as demonstrating a 'moral commitment'.

Call centre customer service interactions frequently begin with an exchange of names. In the data analysed in this study the CSR typically proffers a first name only, as an institutional requirement (any first name will do). Depending on the nature of the company business, customer identification may be sought, and if so often involves the customer providing their full name. Each speaker may therefore be differently resourced in respect to the options they have for naming each other. This potential to name is also constrained by institutional expectations and by cultural expectations. Nonetheless, the speakers in the data in this study do shift their naming practices strategically and in respect to shifts in the genre and to register in the talk. Resources for naming differently are one important means by which the speakers negotiate a complex of relationships of solidarity of institutional and social status, and of expertise in interaction.

In this chapter I have explored not just the question of how speakers name differently but more importantly the contexts in which they do so and the potential implications of their choices. There is of course much more to be analysed in terms of the construction of interpersonal relations in the talk, but it is intended in this chapter to illustrate the potential for linguistic analyses of what is actually said in interaction, especially linguistic analyses that show how meanings unfold dynamically in talk, to complement other approaches to understanding customer relations.

Notes

[1.] Other shifts in referencing are also evident here, for example, in reference to *somebody* at this point the speaker is committing less meaning potential in terms of who is being blamed. Pronominal and other resources for referencing, while also important, are not included in the analyses in this chapter.

[2.] In interview data in similar contexts CSRs noted that older callers sometimes seem to want to just have a chat and to talk to someone.

[3.] CSRs may select different names and/or personas at different times. Only in a minority of 'premiership' contexts would there be a designated CSR–client relationship.

References

Bernstein, B. (2000), *Pedagogy, Symbolic Control, and Identity: Theory, Research, Critique (Revised edition)*. London: Taylor and Francis.

Bolton, S. C. and Houlihan, M. (2005), The (mis)representation of customer service. *Work, Employment and Society* 19(4), 685–703.

Bourdieu, P. (1973), Cultural reproduction and social reproduction. In Brown, R. (ed.) *Papers in the Sociology of Education: Knowledge, Education and Cultural Change*. London: Taylor and Francis, 71–112.

Brown, P. and Levinson, S. (1987), *Politeness: Some Universals in Language Use*. Studies in Interactional Sociolinguistics 4. Cambridge, England: Cambridge University Press.

Caffarel, A., Martin, J. R. and Matthiessen, C. M. I. M. (eds.) (2004), *Language Typology: A Functional Perspective*. Amsterdam: Benjamins.

Cameron, D. (2000), Styling the worker: Gender and the commidification of language in the globalized service economy. *Journal of Sociolinguistics* 4 (3), 323–347.

Dean, A. M. (2007), The Impact of the Customer Orientation of Call Center Employees on Customers' Affective Commitment and Loyalty. *Journal of Service Research* 10(2), 161–173.

Das, D., Dharwadkar, R. and Brandes, P. (2008), The importance of being 'Indian': Identity centrality and work outcomes in an off-shored call center in India. *Human Relations* 61(11), 1499–1530.

Friginal, E. (2008), Linguistic variation in the discourse of outsourced call centres. *Discourse Studies* 10(6), 715–736.

Forey, G. and Lockwood, J. (2007), 'I'd love to put someone in jail for this': An initial investigation of English in the Business Processing Outsourcing (BPO) Industry. *English for Specific Purposes Journal* 26(3), 308–326.

Gumperz, J. J. (1982), *Discourse Strategies*. Cambridge: Cambridge University Press.

Halliday, M. A. K. (1994), *An Introduction to Functional Grammar*. London: Edward Arnold.

Hood, S. and Forey, G. (2008), The interpersonal dynamics of call-centre interactions: Co-constructing the rise and fall of emotion. *Discourse and Communication* 2 (4), 389–409.

Knights, D. and McCabe, D. (2001), 'A Different World': Shifting masculinities in the   transition to call centres. *Organization* 8(4), 619–645.

Martin, J. R. (1990), Interpersonal grammatization: Mood and modality in Tagalog. *Philippine Journal of Linguistics* 21.1 (Special Issue on the Silver Anniversary of the Language Study Centre of Philippine Normal College 1964–1989 – Part 2), 2–51.

Martin, J. R. (1992), *English Text: System and Structure*. Amsterdam: John Benjamins.

Martin, J. R. (2000), Beyond exchange: Appraisal systems in English. In Hunston, S. and   Thompson, G. (eds.) *Evaluation in Text: Authorial Stance and the Construction of Discourse*. Oxford: Oxford University Press, 142–175.

Mulholland, K. (2004), Workplace resistance in an Irish call centre: slammin', scammin' smokin' and leavin'. *Work, Employment and Society* 18(4), 709– 724.

Poynton, C. (1985/1989), *Language and Gender: Making the Difference*. Geelong, Victoria: Deakin University Press. Republished 1989 Oxford: Oxford University Press.

Poynton, C. (1990), *Address and the Semiotics of Social Relations: A Systemic Functional Account of Address Forms and Practices in Australian English*. Unpublished Ph.D. Thesis, Department of Linguistics, University of Sydney.

Shome, R. (2006), Thinking through the diaspora: Call centers, India, and a new politics of hybridity. *International Journal of Cultural Studies* 9(1), 105–124.

Taylor, P. and Bain, P. (2003), 'Subterranean Worksick Blues': Humour as Subversion in Two Call Centres. *Organization Studies* 24(9), 1487–1509.

Taylor, P. and Bain, P. (2007), Reflections on the Call Centre – A Reply to Blucksmann. *Work, Employment and Society* 21(2), 349–362.

Taylor, P., Hyman, J., Mulvey, G. and Bain, P. (2002), Work organization, control and the experience of work in call centres. *Work, Employment and Society* 16(1), 133–150.

Van Leeuwen, T. (1999), *Speech, Music, Sound*. London: Palgrave Macmillan.

Wan, Y. N. (2007), *How Voice Quality Features Create Meaning Potentials and Form Alignments in Telephone Conflicts*. Paper presented at Semiotic Margins Conference, Sydney, December, 2007.

Chapter 7

Call Centre Discourse: Graduation in Relation to Voice Quality and Attitudinal Profile

Jenny Yau Ni Wan

Hong Kong Polytechnic University, Hong Kong

Recently, offshore outsourcing has become an integral part of many multinational companies. One back office role which has been outsourced to Asia is the English customer service call centre. The means of communication between the two parties, the Customer Service Representative (CSR) and customer, is only through telephonic verbal conversation. Gestures, body language and other resources usually encountered in a face-to-face service encounter are absent. The interpersonal relationship developed through the verbal exchange becomes extremely important. To understand the construction of interpersonal meanings, we employ analyses of Appraisal and Voice Quality. In this study, 100 English telephone conversations (approximately 52,600 words) have been collected from the Philippines and transcribed in Hong Kong during 2005 to 2007. From these data a sample of problematic conversations between the Filipino CSR and American customers have been extracted, and analysed for interpersonal meaning; the findings are discussed in the present paper. In particular, in this paper I will focus on interpersonal meaning, and specifically Appraisal in what appears to be communication problems. The findings from this study will support the training and services offered by this developing industry.

Background

The call centre industry is a significant new type of customer service work and is rapidly increasing in size, range of sectors and number of employees within the industry (Cross, Barry and Garaven 2008; Datamonitor 1998). In the last 15 years, 3.3 million US service industry jobs and $136 billion in wages have been outsourced to Asian countries such as India, China and the Philippines (c.f. Downey and Fenton 2007; O'Neill 2003). The Philippines will continue to be one of the dominant offshore players with a market potential of $110 Billion in 2010 (Sanez 2007). At the same time, this industry also faces many challenges. In the press we often hear of problems related to call centre operations.

Devoid of gesture and eye contact, the Customer Service Representative (CSR) and customer communicate with each other only through telephonic verbal conversation. Communication breakdowns often occur due to this limited mode of exchange. Hence, the interpersonal relationship construed through the verbal, i.e. sound exchanges is critical to the success of the call.

Various studies have been conducted focusing on business and management research into call centres, such as customer relationship management (c.f. Irish 2000), recruitment criteria (c.f. Arzbabacher et al. 2000), job design and motivation methods (c.f. Taylor et al. 2002), division of labour (c.f. Broek 2002) and emotional labour (c.f. Erickson and Wharton 1997). Very little attention has been paid to linguistic analyses of these calls (Adolphs et al. 2004; Cameron 2000a and 2000b; Forey and Lockwood 2007; Hood and Forey 2008; Lockwood, Forey and Price 2008). Cameron's (2000a) study discusses some sociolinguistic characteristics of the speech style prescribed to CSRs when interacting with customers, stating that the vocal 'styling' prescribed for the CSR in UK call centres directly relates to gender issues. Cameron (200a) collected data from several centres located in various parts of the UK Data took the form of notes on observations, tapes/transcripts of interviews and copies of written material. Cameron's findings suggest that there was a femininsing of speech, i.e. in training and performance characteristics of 'feminine speech' were modelled in the discourse. In a later study, Cameron (2000b) analyses, in more depth, the communication factories inside the call centre. She argues standardizing scripts leads to a 'communication factory' where the call centre communication service provided is unified and standard, and there is an emphasis to the notion of 'efficiency'. Although the efficiency, i.e. handling more calls, will be enhanced by using standard script, it also limits the flexibility and possible varieties of calls. Lockwood, Forey and Price (2008) and Hood and Forey (2008) point out that current market forces have exerted pressure on the language to correspond to a standardized variety of English. There is a tendency in recent papers to focus on interpersonal feature of the calls. For example, Adolphs et al. (2004) investigate the communication in health care encounters, focusing on a corpus linguistic analysis of the British National Health Service Direct (NHS Direct) telephone interactions conducted in the UK This study is a conversational analysis of the use of modal verbs such as **can, could, may,** personal pronouns '**you**' and '**your**' which were centred around possibility, probability and inclination or obligation of the caller or the CSR, they also focused on politeness markers. Adlophs et al.'s (2004) study investigated the language strategies in health industries, and there are similarities relevant to the discussion in the present chapter, where data were collected from a health insurance company. Many of the recent studies on language in the call centres have limitations with respect to their sample size and method of data collection. Only a limited number of studies outlined above draw on authentic data from the call itself, as the sensitive nature of calls and access to data are extremely difficult. A few applied linguistic studies which discuss the language of call centre communication in terms of interaction and linguistic features; in particular, the voice quality features (Adolphs et al. 2004; Cameron 2000a; Cameron 2000b). However, the multimodal features of voice quality are, I argue, crucial to the call. The multimodal features of voice quality are, I argue, crucial to the call.

Theoretical Framework

In this chapter, I draw on aspects of social semiotic theories (van Leeuwen 1999) to explore the interpersonal development of call centre discourse through an analysis of the semantics of both verbiage (what was actually said with relation to the lexico-grammatical choice in the transcribed text) and sound. Three major theoretical areas of interpersonal meaning which inform the present study are those of Appraisal theory (Martin and White 2005), Graduation network (Hood 2004 and 2006) and the semantics of voice quality (van Leeuwen 1999); all follow Systemic Functional Linguistics (SFL) as a theoretical framework.

Appraisal (Martin and White 2005) is a resource that allows the analyst to deconstruct attitudinal/evaluative meanings in a text, i.e. language choices that inscribed or evoke the authors' viewpoint. There are three main categories for expressing and negotiating attitudes – Affect, Judgment and Appreciation (Martin 2000; Martin and White 2005; Martin and Rose 2007: 28). According to Martin and Rose (2007), Affect is to do with emotion, people's feelings which can be positive (e.g. I'm *glad*) or negative (e.g. I'm *dissatisfied*); Judgment relates to the way in which the speaker/writer evaluates the behaviour and character of people in terms of their ability (e.g. She is *capable* of handling this problem); their tenacity (e.g. That CSR is *diligent*); or their normality (e.g. Things in your company are *strange*) and their ethical standard (e.g. Their behaviour is *immoral*); Appreciation which refers to how writers evaluate the value of things, e.g. calls/service (e.g. This is a *ridiculous* case).

In the present study, Appraisal theory is applied to understand the different viewpoints and interpersonal language employed in call centre interactions. The lexico-grammatical choices that constructed interpersonal relationship are identified, in the transcribed transcripts. Affect, Judgment and Appreciation

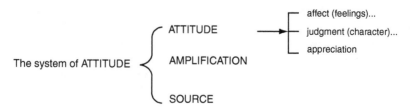

FIGURE 1   The system of ATTITUDE (Martin and Rose 2007:28)

are all gradable resources, we can grade them up or down according to how strongly we evaluate emotion, people and things. The grading of meanings is represented in Appraisal theory as Graduation. There are two main areas of Graduation, i.e. **Force** and **Focus** (Martin and Rose 2005). Graduation construes the speakers' values by raising or lowering their impersonal impact. Force is related to turning up and down the volume of their utterances, and Focus refers to the blurring or sharpening the semantic categorizations (White 1998). Examples of Force are, e.g. I have complained *many times*; I have waited for *almost a month*. Examples of Focus are, e.g. The reason is *probably* due to postal delay; You *may* receive the letter by this week.

Within the field of Appraisal Analysis the starting point for analysing Graduation in a text is quite different. For example Martin and White (2005) discuss Graduation from the starting point of Engagement while Hood (2004 and 2006) analyses Graduation from the starting point of Attitude (see Figure 2). In addition, Hood (2006) extends the realm of Focus to apply not just to the Focus of entities (as in Martin and White 2005) but as also including the focus of process meanings and propositional meaning (see Figure 2). A process meaning can be focused in term of 'Fulfillment' and interpreted as positive or negative completion, e.g. *I tried to talk to you* (meaning less than Fulfillment). A proposition can be graded in Focus through resourced modulation, such as possibility, as Fulfillment: realization, for example, *just possible that* and *very possible that* (Hood 2006).

Most studies drawing on Appraisal analysis, discuss Appraisal in relation to the lexical and grammatical choices – the verbiage, i.e., the study of attitudinal meaning in the written and spoken texts, such as children narratives in story telling and news (c.f. Martin 2004; Page 2003; Painter 2003). It is clearly very important in call centre communication to study the spoken discourse, not only for what is said, i.e. to study the verbiage, but also in terms of the sound quality, i.e., how the verbiage is presented in sound. Martin and White (2005:37) state that Force as a Graduation resource 'can be realized through intensification, comparative and superlative morphology, repetition, and various graphological and phononlogical features'. Call centre conversation is an exchange of voices between the customer and CSR often from two distant locations through an electronic telephonic conversation. Only through the study of both the verbiage and sound quality are we able to generate a clearer overview of how the call centre discourse is constructed and how the interpersonal is developed. Voice quality is a part of the semiotic resources of sound, creating different meaning potential in different context (van Leeuwen 1999). For example, in a room if someone shouts very loud and in a tense manner they get a very different reaction than if they simply converse at a normal level of loudness. Both the choice of verbiage and voice quality can be used to construe emotional and attitudinal meanings. In this regard, I combine the verbiage, emotion conveyed by words, with sounds from voice quality – emotion carried by sounds to explore interpersonal meaning in call centre conversations.

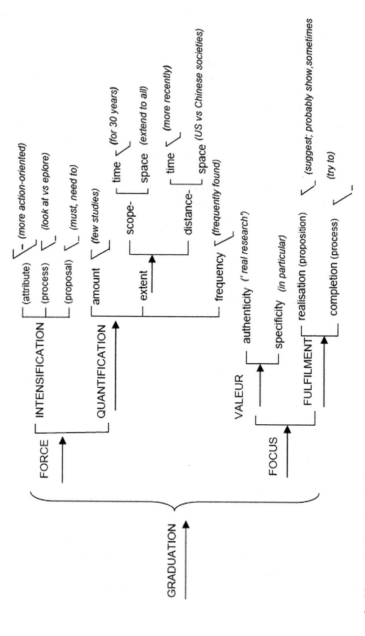

FIGURE 2   Network of options in Graduation showing instances of the grading of experiential meaning (Hood 2006:39)

In order to understand voice quality and how it construes meaning we need a systematic way to model the different choices which are possible for the speaker. Following a systemic functional approach, van Leeuwen (1999) proposed a model for the analysis of sound quality and timbre. He considers aspects of the materiality of sound as meaning-making semantic resources. Van Leeuwen argues that 'Sound quality "affects" us and is able to create meaning potentials' (van Leeuwen 1999:127). He identifies a number of key features of voice quality including (i) tension; (ii) loudness; (iii) pitch register (high/low); (iv) roughness; (v) breathiness; (vi) vibrato and (vii) nasality, as shown in Figure. In Figure 3 the system network proposed by van Leeuwen demonstrates that as speakers we have a choice of either being tense or lax, loud or soft, speaking high or low, etc. The square brackets demonstrate that there is a binary choice between the two categories presented. The curly bracket illustrates that all of these features may be simultaneously selected, so a speaker may use a particular voice quality, relative to their normal voice, which is both tense, loud and high.

Van Leeuwen (1999) when presenting his sound quality framework included a discussion of a wide range of sounds, such as music from movies and songs, human voice and even sound from musical instruments and bare hands. Van Leeuwen's (1999) framework is employed in the present study as a starting point to look at the human voice quality in call centre discourse. The choices outlined in Figure 3 for sound quality are adopted as a method of analysis to examine the voice quality features used by the customer service representatives and customers during points of communication breakdown in authentic customer service calls.

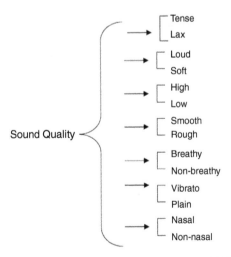

FIGURE 3   Systems network of voice quality (van Leeuwen 2007:151)

Data and Method

This chapter examines the attitudinal profile of voice quality features and appraisal resources in a small sample of calls. I have chosen to examine in depth the interpersonal development in a collection of 20 calls from an inbound insurance company in the Philippines. These 20 calls were part of a larger study from within the Call Centre Communication Research study at The Hong Kong Polytechnic University. In order to fully understand the choices made the present chapter adopts a qualitative study, focusing specifically on Graduation, one of the categories in Appraisal analysis, and features of voice quality in call centre conversations. The aim is to investigate how sound quality and lexico-grammatical choices relate to the attitudinal profile. In addition, I discuss how voice quality and graduation construct the prosodic patterns leading to interpersonal meaning and a communication breakdown in call centre discourse.

Findings: Graduation Analysis

The Graduation items are frequently located in the call centre discourse conversations. By employing Hood's (2006) network of options in Graduation (see Figure 2 for reference), the Graduation items in the data can be classified into five classes named Intensity (Force), Quantity (Force), Enhancement (Force), Valuer (Focus) and Fulfillment (Focus) which are listed in the following table:

Table 1 Graduation examples in call centre texts

Graduation category (Force/Focus)	Subcategories	Examples in the texts
Force	Intensity	*again, still, just, ever, anything, anybody, else, have to/ had to, shouldn't, need to, must already, etc.*
	Quantity	*every month, over a week ago, for five weeks ago, specific date, in the past, today, tones of, every time, right now, by now, now, now recent, for many times, only, actually, not the first time, several years now, one moment, one billing cycle, something, the last time , etc.*
	Enhancement	*frequently, increased, immediately, ect.*
Focus	Valuer	*here, your anniversary date etc.*
	Fulfillment	*authorized/authorization, actualy, let me explain, seems, can, may, guess, probably, would, minght, etc.*

When examining the Graduation resources in terms of how these choices function in the discourse in the texts, it is apparent that customers frequently employ Graduation as Force to express meanings of Intensity and Quantity when complaining (see Hood and Forey 2008). Their examples of Intensity include **again, still, ever, anybody, shouldn't, must,** etc. and the instances of Quantity to create the extent, proximity in time and space are **over a week ago, in the past, tones of, every time, recent, many times, many years** and so on. The customer intends to complain by emphasizing the degree and seriousness of the problem.

However, when I further studied the Graduation choices of the CSR, the findings showed a range of different choices being made by the CSR, and a different construction of events being postulated by the CSR. The CSR frequently employs Graduation items (Focus) to minimize dimension of intensity and quantity created by the customers in order to solve the problems. The choices of Focus lexical items used were e.g. **actually, let me explain, seems, can, may, probably, would.** In addition, the CSR also employs quantity (Force) including **one moment, the last time, (send you) by now, immediately** in order to diminish the Graduation level and heightened amplifiable created by the customers.

Between Customer and CSR

Figure 4 demonstrates how the customers tend to construe a higher level of Graduation or exaggerate the degree of their disappointments by using the Intensity and Quantity resources. The lexico-grammatical choices of the CSR, however, work in an opposite way (shown by the arrows in the figure), the CSR

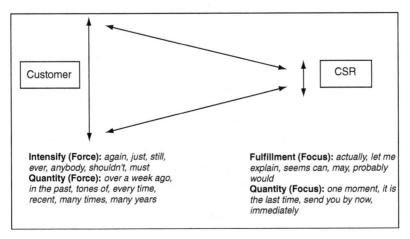

FIGURE 4 The use of Graduation resources Force and Focus in call centre discourse

tries to reduce the intensity and minimize the problem. This phenomenon is due to differences in the underlining motivation and goals of the interlocutors. The work of the CSR is always restricted in terms of the average handling (AHT) time limits of each call. This affects their interactions with the customers. Deery et al. (2002) states that such interactions require a high workload, and cause a great deal of pressure for the CSR. In most call centres there is a constant effort to increase the number of calls taken per employee, i.e. to reduce the AHT and reduce both customer call time and to wrap-up the call in a short a time as possible (Taylor 1998; Taylor and Bain 1999; Taylor and Bain 2007). However, in opposition to the efforts of the CSR to narrow the scope and reduce the length of the call, the customer often up-scales the degree of the seriousness by complaining and thus increasing the AHT. The CSR thus has to down-scale the Graduation level, to accomplish the task and to meet the expected target AHT for the call.

These findings, based on Hood's (2006) work in Graduation, support findings outlined by Hood and Forey (2008). Thus it seems that the scaling for Force and Focus in call centre interactions provides a space for negotiation between CSR and customers. However, when looking at the interpersonal features of the call and the emotional profile of the talk, it is useful to extend the analysis to beyond just the verbiage. In this chapter I suggest that the paralinguistic feature of voice quality plays a key role in the construction of the interpersonal. In order to understand the role of voice quality in the call, the variety of choices available in relation to variation or choices of voice quality need to be identified, resources employed by the different speakers need to be recorded and how voice quality works in the interaction needs to be explored further.

Findings: Voice Quality Features

Voice quality has been discussed in applied linguistic terms for many years, Crystal (1969) defines voice quality as a main source of our ability to recognize personal identity vocally. As pointed out by Crystal (1969) many associate voice quality with personal or interpersonal meaning. In this section I present a clearer definition of what is meant by voice quality along with the initial finding of five key areas of voice quality which were seen to be important within the call centre discourse. Descriptions of voice quality have traditionally consisted of qualitative terms to describe as warm, rough, creaky, breathy, dull, etc. Voice quality features can be viewed as a paralinguistic, non-verbal and multimodal resources which convey meaning (Martin 2007; Leijssen 2006). Work is now ongoing to address a few of these voice qualities on a physiologic and acoustic level (Titze and Story 2002:3). A number of studies establish a strong association between voice quality and interpersonal meaning (c.f. Stokoe and Edwards 2007; Leijssen 2006). This association is particularly noticeable when there is a change in voice quality feature which results in a change of interpersonal meaning (Buchbinder 2008). After listening and analysing a number of texts, focusing specifically on voice quality and its role in construing the interpersonal meaning, a number of key extracts were identified as being important points in the text where voice quality is seen to clearly flag interpersonal meaning. From the data analysed five voice quality features emerged as areas worthy of deeper investigation:

1) rhythm associated with loudness
2) rhythm associated with tension
3) soft voice graded by repetition
4) plain voice for grading down the gratitude
5) breathiness in call centre work

Each of these five points will be discussed in detail below. Please note that all the voice qualities featured in this analysis refer to the relative shift of the voice quality features in the conversation. In the present study, relative shift is the term used to designate when one speaker's voice changes to a particular degree compared with the remaining utterances by the identified speakers.

The purpose of voice quality analysis is not to make a glossary or dictionary for voice, the findings from the present study allows us to understand how voice quality features help to construe interpersonal meaning within a particular context. In the following examples found in Tables 2–6, C stands for customer, R refers to Customer Service Representative. Voice quality features are marked in bold and Graduation items are categorized by italics.

Rhythm Associated with Loudness

Loudness and softness are closely associated with social distance (van Leeuwen 1999). Loudness is a crucial perceptive factor necessary for the information to be transmitted (Möller 2000). Loud voice can function as carrying further, claiming more territory and negotiating more space for the speaker (van Leeuwen 1999). As shown in Table 2, lines 175 and 176 provide examples of faster speed and loudness found in the data.

In line 174, the CSR (R1) is describing the action which the customer (C1) needs to perform. The customer (C1) interrupts in line 175, by saying 'what happens what happens if you guys draw money out' in louder, faster rhythm. The pace here is faster than in previous turns, and C1's voice also becomes louder. In the call centre discourse, rhythm differences are frequently noted between CSRs and customers. In the call centre data, I observed that faster rhythm is often associated with loudness and this association functions to obtain the speakership, where the speaker is self-selecting themselves and taking the turn (Sacks, Schegloff and Jefferson 1974). As pointed out by Sacks et al. (1974) the first rule of turn taking is when one speaker asks a question or directly names the next speaker. Self-selection is a marked choice and indicates specific features of status and power within the exchange. In the above example, when

Table 2   Graduation and voice Quality analysis: Rhythm associated with loudness

Examples in the Transcription 001	Voice Quality (Bold)	Graduation Category (Underlined)
169. C1: because **I asked**, do I **need to** sign the form, do I	Nasal, Loud, Tense	+ Force (Intensity)
170. **need to** write a letter and the lady **I spoke with,**	High, Tense, Fast	+ Focus (Fulfillment)
171. her name is Kelt		
172. R1: Mm hm		
173. C1: **they know,** she <u>would do</u> it for me and **that's all**	Soft, low	
174. R1: That's right (attitude) what you <u>need to</u> do [is	Loud	+Force (Quantity)
175. C1: [what		+Force (Intensity)
176. **happens what happens if you guys draw money**		
177. **out** <u>again</u>? With the, that's unacceptable (attitude)	Faster, Loud	+Force (Intensity)
178. R1: **We won't draw** <u>any</u> money out, maam, <u>now</u> that	Loud, Tense	+Force (Intensity)
179. your request is <u>already</u> placed on the system		+Force (Quantity)
		+Force (Quantity)

the customer speaks fast and loud, the CSR immediately gives up her speakership in line 174. The customer is very keen to occupy the speakership and claim more territory to sound more persuasive and more powerful (van Leeuwen 1999). It is also an Engagement resource in Appraisal analysis that expands the space by closing down the other voice and taking the speakership (see Martin and White (2005) for a detailed discussion of Engagement). Thus in this example there are choices related to tenor which signal power and social distance, first being the dominance of speakership by the customer, which is simultaneously realized through a noticeable shift in voice quality.

Rhythm Associated with Tense

There is a common understanding that the customer and CSR may speak slower in order to achieve a clearer transmission of information in telephone communication, especially when there is an absence of visual cues. However, when a customer intends to emphasize a particular ideational meaning, they may also employ slow rhythm, sometimes, even prolonging and stretching-out the syllables or words. The pronunciation of a particular syllable and word becomes more elongated than usual, such as '**I-was-not-aware-of** it' in line 17 in Table 3. C2 here pronounces each word very clearly and as independent units, with each unit being extended beyond the word length given in previous turns by the speakers.

Table 3 Graduation and Voice quality analysis: Rhythm associated with tense

Examples in the Transcription 002	Voice Quality (Bold)	Graduation Category (Underlined)
16. R2: The policy **has lapsed**, Elle?	Loud and high	
17. C2: Yes, but (Engagement: concession) **I was-not-aware** of it. And I	Tense and increase in length	
18. **got-this-notice** <u>yesterday</u>	Tense and increase in length	+ Force (Quantity)
19. **and is there-***anyway***,** what is that I have to do: I, I had this a <u>long</u>	Tense and increase in length	+ Force (Intensity)
20. time and **I-was-not-aware-that** I have to pay <u>anymore</u> money on	Tense and increase in length	+ Force (Intensity)
21. it?		

Tension occurs when you tense the muscles of your throat, the voice becomes higher, sharper and brighter. The sound that results from tensing is not only tense, it also construes tension in the shared meaning (van Leeuwen 1999). Table 3, lines 17 to 21, illustrates some examples of slow rhythm and tension found in the data.

When the tension is associated with an increase in length, for example, 'I-was-not-aware-that I have to pay any more money on it' in line 20, this can construe particular meanings in context, as this voice quality is used to create negative affect such as a defensive, sarcastic or self-protective retort to the CSR. In this instance the customer is emphasizing that she, the customer, was not to blame. As a result, the choice of a slow rhythm with tension in the voice quality graded up the negative affect of this particular turn. In this example, the slow rhythm and tension both grade up the FORCE in relation to Graduation resources.

Soft Voice Graded by Repetition (Grade up)

In the call centre data, it is possible to identify a softness of features in the arguments, as shown in lines 46 and 47, in Table 4. There is a common perception that when customers complain, they shout, speak loudly or use a high pitch. However, this is not always the case. They can employ other resources to express their frustration and disagreement, for instance, employing qualities of a soft voice, is clearly a marked choice for some speakers. The loud and soft voice qualities work differently. If the conversation becomes overheated, 'hot anger' (Scherer 1986; Wehrle et al. 2000) is created. A speaker then dominates by what is considered to be an **'active emotion'** (Wallbott 1998:887). For instance in line 44, the CSR (R1) raises the volume of the voice to speak loudly to the customer in order to create a counter expectancy, i.e. 'but you already, was informed you'. However, the customer (C1) chooses to employ softness instead of loudness in her turn to continue to express her anger, this choice

Table 4   Graduation and Voice quality: Soft voice graded by repetition

Examples in the Transcription 001	Voice Quality (Bold)	Graduation Category (Underlined)
44. R1: [**but you** *already*, was informed, you were informed about the	Loud	+ Counter expectancy
45. premium renewal [*last October*		+ Force (Quantity)
46. C1: [**No. I haven't signed** *anything*. **no I**	Soft	+ Force (Intensity)
47. **haven't signed** *anything*, **I haven't say** *anything*, except	Soft	+ Force (Intensity)
48. (concession) I recieved the letter		

contrasts with the CSR's choice, and clearly construes frustration on behalf of the customer in a different manner. I have termed such a choice as 'cold anger' which is a marked contrast to the raised and faster speed of the discourse so far (Scherer 1986; Banse and Scherer 1996). In the data shown in Table 4, C1 is a female speaker. Sometimes, when a speaker is disappointed or angry, they may choose a soft voice. This choice, 'cold anger', can sound more convincing and powerful than if the speaker were expressing their emotion directly through loudness and an increase in speed.

   Another resource which is crucial for interpreting the interpersonal meaning construed in the short text above is repetition. Martin and White (2005) mention that intensification, as one resource of Force, can be realized via repetition or repeating the same lexical item, or by the assembling of lists of terms which are closely related semantically. For instance, in Table 4 line 46–47, the customer (C1) repeats, 'No, I haven't signed anything, no I haven't signed anything, I haven't said anything'. The customer holds the turn for a longer period which makes her argument sound more emphatic and less-negotiable. Levels are accumulated and longer turns have been created. This kind of repetition of the same lexical item or similar meaning can be categorized as Force: Intensity in this particular call centre conversation.

   In the analysed data, when softness is combined with repetition, this combination helps to construe a particular kind of interpersonal meaning which impacts the interaction in a negative passive aggressive manner and the result is cold anger. This combination also helps to upgrade the level of inscribed or implicit attitude for the speakers in factual complaints in relation to the Graduation resources in the Appraisal analysis.

Plain Voice for Grading Down the Gratitude

Plain refers to sounds that are unwavering, not trembling and unmoved (van Leeuwen 1999). However, when a customer uses plain voice, which means the speaker expressed their view through limited positive emotion, one simple

Table 5 Graduation and Voice quality analysis: Plain voice for grading down the gratitude

Examples in the Transcription 005	Voice Quality (Bold)	Graduation Category (Underlined)
158. C5: This is not right, **hahaha**, he's just going through a divorce? And	Laugh	+Force (Intensity)
158. here has no money, em, now who's supposed to pay this taxes?	Fast	+Focus (Valuer) +Force (Quantity)
159. My husband here?		+Force (Valuer)
160. R5: (**breathy**) ok, hold on just a second. [10 seconds] ok maam I	Breathy	+Force (Intensity)
161. did verify that one in and since Carl is the owner Central he		
162. is the owner I mean **he will be the one who's going to shoulder**	Slower and plain	+Force (Intensity)
163. **the taxes. Carl is the owner so he should be the who's one**	Slower and plain	
164. **going** to pay for the taxes	Slower and soft	
[9 seconds]		
165. C5: **thank you very much**	Plain	+Force (Intensity)
166. R5: you are welcome, maam		

example is when someone says **thank you** in a monotone manner, devoid of intonation, this can be seen to construe irony or frustration call centre interactions. Such lack of intonation is a marked choice used to grade down the satisfaction level. In Table 5, the customer uses a plain voice to say **thank you very much** to the CSR in line 165 at the end of the interaction. The 'thank you very much' in the current data is a flat tone which sounds monotone. The expression is totally devoid of real gratitude.

Generally, gratitude carries positive interpersonal meaning in normal semantic properties. However, in the above example, the meaning potential of the monotone gratitude 'thank you very much' is seen as a superficial and insincere construal of the speaker's viewpoint. This is seen as a sarcastic phrase, what the speaker really means is that the CSR has not provided real help and really does not deserve to be thanked. In fact, it is another way for the customers to show they are still disappointed and dissatisfied. A normal and fruitful 'thank you' is categorized as positive Force level. However, a plain voice **thank you very much** in this example encounters the Intensity of negative Force in the Graduation system. This analysis reveals that when a plain voice combines with appreciation, the level of positive inscribed attitude between speakers will be graded down.

Breathiness in Call Centre Discourse

Breathiness is an extraneous sound which mixes in with the tone of the voice itself (van Leeuwen 1999). Breathiness is a voice quality resource that can be frequently noticed in the call centre interactions. The breathiness is realized as air voice form (such as sigh) or inserted along a sentence. Breathiness in the following example refers to sigh or air voice.

The point to be made in this text is that the customer (C1) is very eager to know whether the company will continue to draw money from her bank account or not. She asks several times in the text through different forms of questions,

Table 6　Graduation and Voice quality analysis: Breathiness in call centre discourse

Examples in the Transcription 005	Voice Quality (Bold)	Graduation Category (Underlined)
95: C1: [you will withdraw my money of the end of <u>next month</u>	Loud and High	+Force (Intensity)
96: R1: Yup, no money will be withdrawn. The have stopped that <u>already</u>.	Loud and Tense	+Force (Intensity)
97.　We won't get <u>any</u> further premium anymore. <u>What I'm trying to</u>	Loud, Tense and slower speed	+Force (Intensity)
98.　<u>say is that</u> the payment that you have paid for March, <u>85 dollars 66</u>		+Force (Fulfilment)
99.　<u>cents</u> that has made you paid up to April 10[. . .]<u>now</u> you will be		+Force (Quantity)
100.　covered]		
101. C1: my] old policy policy		
102: R1: Yes, you <u>now</u> you will be [covered		+Force (Valuer)
103: C1:　　　　　　　[until April 10, right		
104: R1: That's right, you will be covered even after <u>April 10 until May</u>		+Force (Quantity)
105: C1: So my expiration would be on [May 10		
106: R1:　　　　　　　[May 10		
107: **C1: Yes, and <u>no more</u> payment?**	High, Loud, Tense	+Force (Intensity)
108: R1: No more payment but if you receive bill, just disregard the bill		+Force (Intensity)
109: C1: But is the 85 dollars is covered until April 10		
110: R1: until May 10, yes maam		
111: C1: until May 10?		
112: R1: yes, it's a 30-day grace from <u>April 10 up to May</u>		+Force (Intensity)
113: C1: OK		
114: R1: OK?	Loud	
115: C1: And ar and no more withdraw from my　　[account	Breathy Increase in length.	+Force (Intensity)
116: R1: (deep breath) **[there-will-be-no-more]**	very slow, soft	
117: C1: in March, in April and May, [right		
118: R1:　　　　　　　[that's right		

e.g. in Line 95, 'you will withdraw my money at the end of next month?' In line 107, 'Yes, and no more payment?' Finally in line 115, she asks for the third time, 'and ar and no more withdrawn from my account?, the CSR (R1) feels frustrated and languid. She takes a deep breath afterwards in line 116, and says 'there will be no more payment'.

Breathiness in this example acts as letting off steam and releasing pressure and stress. It is also an alternative for building up anger for the CSR. When there is an unresolved problem, pressure and intensity will build up. In a normal situation, the tension can be released through verbiage which carries attitudinal meaning. However, the CSR is a professional who needs to manage and restrict personal emotions due to concepts, such as emotional labour, in order to maintain a professional image (c.f. Hochschild 1979 and 1983; Shuler and Sypher 2000; Tracy 2000). Thus, they choose to release the tension through breathiness which carries inscribed meaning.

In the space allowed I have been able to highlight five key features which have emerged from the data as key resources used by the customer to construe a particular meaning. The change in voice quality is a relative shift of the individual choices of voice, and is clearly marked in the construction of interpersonal meaning.

Conclusion

In this chapter, I have started to combine the theories of Appraisal analysis (Martin and White 2005), to extend the Graduation category outlined by Hood (2006) and to relate Appraisal analysis, included Graduation more directly to voice quality as introduced by van Leeuwen (1999). In Figure 1, I outline the system of Attitude in Appraisal analysis (Martin and Rose 2007). There are 3 main categories, Affect, Judgment and Appreciation, to express and negotiate attitudes. As outlined above complaints tend to be presented as factual information, and the Appraisal items invoking frustration are frequently Graduation items (see Hood and Forey 2008).

A CSR is often required to sustain high levels of interpersonal interaction with the customer (Deery et al. 2002), and this must be sustained through resources of voice quality and choices in the lexico-grammar, devoid of visual modes of interaction. In the present study, I demonstrate how voice quality and verbiage relate to the attitudinal profile of the discourse by identifying the voice quality features in the data; illustrating how they function in the attitudinal work; and further interpreting their meaning potentials with reference to the Graduation. The findings from the data provide evidence that the interpersonal meaning is not only made through verbiage but also voice quality. If we only consider the verbiage without paying attention to the sound, the interpersonal meaning of the customer and the CSR exchanged would not be comprehensive. However, a great deal more work such as identifying common patterns of complaint calls through an analysis of verbiage and voice quality features, systemizing voice quality findings, merging of voice quality into Appraisal theory needs to be carried out to further provide a more robust theoretical framework capable of dealing with voice quality. In addition, one of the significant future research directions would be to develop the validation of voice quality analysis. Bateman (2008) calls for multimodal meaning to be interpreted through a more rigorous validation process than has been so far evident. Greater rigour will diminish subjectivity and increase credibility. Finally, these findings should contribute to updating the CSR's training material and supporting services offered by the call centre industry.

Note

[1] This study is based on a Departmental Research project called Call Centre Communication Research (CCCR) of the Department of English at the Hong Kong Polytechnic University.
Link: http://www.engl.polyu.edu.hk/call_centre/default.html.
An earlier version of this article was published as Wan, Y. N. (2008). 'The exchange of interpersonal language in call centre conversations', in Nørgaard, Nina (ed.) *Systemic Functional Linguistics in Use, Odense Working Papers in Language and Communication* 29, 825–839.

References

A. C. C. U. Group (2001), *On the Line: The Future of Australia's Call Centre Industry*. Sydney: Australian Council of Trade Unions.

Adolphs, S., Brown, B., Carter, R., Crawford, P. and Sahota, O. (2004), Applying corpus linguistics in a health care context, *Journal of Applied Linguistics* 1(1), 9–28.

Arzbabacher, S., Holtrgewe, U. and Kerst, C. (2000, December), Call centres: Constructing Flexibility. Paper presented at Are Regimented Forms of Work Organization Inevitable? Call Centres and the Change of Innovative Work Organization of Service Work in Eurpose, University of Duisberg.

Banse, R. and Scherer, K. R. (1996), Acoustic profiles in vocal emotion expression. *Journal of Personality and Social Psychology* 70, 614–636.

Broek, V. D (2004), 'We have the values': Customers, control and corporate ideology in call centre operations. *New Technology, Work and Employment* 19(1), 1–13.

Buchbinder, M. H. (2008), 'You're still sick!' Framing, footing, and participation in children's medical play. *Discourse Studies* 10, 139–159.

Cameron, D. (2000a), 'Styling the worker: Gender and the commodification of language in the globalized service economy', *Journal of Sociolinguistics* 4(3), 323–347.

Cameron, D. (2000b), Good to talk? Living and Working in a Communication Culture. London: Sage.

Cross, C., Barry, G. and Garaven, T. (2008), The Psychological Contract in Call Centres: An Employee Perspective. *Journal of Industrial Relations* 50(2), 229–242.

Datamonitor. (1998), Call Centres in Europe 1996–2001: Vertical Market Opportunities. London: Datamonitor.

Deery, S., Iverson, R. and Walsh, J. (2002), Work Relationships in telephone call centres: Understanding emotional exhaustion and employee withdrawal, *Journal of Management Studies* 39(4), 471–495.

Downey, J. and Fenton, N. (2007), Global Capital, Local Resistance?: Trade Unions, National Newspapers and the Symbolic Contestation of 'Offshoring' in the UK, *Current Sociology* 55(5), 651–673.

Erickson, R. J. and Wharton, A. S. (1997), Inauthenticity and depression: Assessing the consequences of interactive service work. *Work and Occupations*, 24(2, May), 188–213.

Forey, G. and Lockwood, J. (2007), I'd love to put someone in jail for this: English in the Business Processing Outsourcing (BPO) Industry, *English for Specific Purposes* 26/3,308–326.

Halliday, M. A. K. (1994), *An Introduction to Functional Grammar.* 2nd edn. London: Edward Arnold.

Halliday, M. A. K. and Matthiessen, C. M. I. M. (2004), *An Introduction to Functional Grammar.* (3rd edn) London: Arnold.

Hochschild, A. R. (1979), Emotion work, feeling rules, and social structure, *American Journal of Sociology* 85, 551–575.

Hochschild, A. R. (1983), *The Managed Heart: The Communication of Human Feeling.* Berkeley: University of California Press.

Hood, S. (2004), *Appraisal Research: Taking a Stance in Academic Writing.* PhD. Thesis. Faculty of Education, University of Technology, Sydney.

Hood, S. (2006), 'The persuasive power of prosodies: Reading values in academic Writing', *Journal of English for Academic Purposes* 5, 37–49.

Hood, S. and Forey, G. (2008), Co-constructing emotion: The interpersonal dynamics of call-centre interactions, *Discourse and Communication* 2(4), 389–409.

Irish, C. (2000), Web-enabled call centre, *BT Technol J,* 18(2), 65–71.

Leijssen, M. (2006), Validation of the Body in Psychotherapy. *Journal of Humanistic Psychology* 46, 12–146.

Lockwood, J., Forey, G. and Price, P. (2008), Englishes in the Philippine Business Processing Outsourcing Industry: Issues, opportunities and initial findings. in Bautista, M.   L. S and Bolton, K. (eds.) *Philippine English: Linguistic and Literary Perspectives.* Hong Kong: Hong Kong University Press, 157–172.

Martin, J. R. (2000), Beyond Exchange: APPRAISAL systems in English. In Hunston, S. and Thompson, G. (eds.) *Evaluation in Tex: Authorial Stance and the Construction of Discourse* (pp. 142–175). United States: Oxford University Press Inc., New York.

Martin, J. R. (2004), Mourning: How we get aligned, *Discourse and Society* 15(2–3), 321–344.

Martin, J. R. (2007), *Multimodality – some issues.* Paper presented at the Semiotic Margins: Reclaiming meaning, Department of Linguistics, University of Sydney, Australia.

Martin, J. R. and Rose, D. (2007), *Working with Discourse: Meaning beyond the Clause.* London: Continuum.

Martin, J. R. and White, P. R. R. (2005), *The Language of Evaluation: Appraisal in English.* Great Britain: Antony Rowe Ltd, Chippenham and Eastbourne.

Möller, S. (2000), *Assessment and Prediction of Speech Quality in Telecommunications.* Kluwer Academic Publishers, Boston, MA. 41.

O'Neill, D. A. (2003), Offshore Outsourcing Takes Hold, *Mortgage Banking, December,* 38–43.

Painter, C. (2003), Developing attitude: An ontogenetic perspective on APPRAISAL, *Text* 23(2), 183–209.

Page, R. E. (2003), An analysis of APPRAISAL in childbirth narratives with special consideration of gender and storytelling style, *Text* 23(2), 211–237.

Sacks, H., Schegloff, E. A. and Jefferson, G. (1974), A simplest systematics for the organization of turn-taking for conversation. *Language* 50(4), 696–735.

Sanez, O. (2007), Driving Breakthrough Growth in BPO/IT-Services. Business Processing Association. Philippines. Retrieved 22 June 07 from http://www.bpap.org/bpap/research/SanezBPAPgoals.pdf.

Scherer, K. R. (1986), Vocal affect expression: A review and a model for future research. *Psychological Bulletin* 99, 143–165.

Shuler, S. and Sypher, B. D. (2000), Seeking emotional labor: When managing the heart enhances the work experience, *Management Communication Quarterly* 14, 50–89.

Stokoe, E. and Edwards, D. (2007), Black this, black that: Racial insults and reported speech in neighbour complaints and police interrogations, *Discourse & Society* 18, 337–372.

Taylor, S. (1998), Emotional Labour and the new workplace in Thompson, P. and Warhust, C. (eds.) *Workplace of the Future.* London: Macmillan, 84–103.

Taylor, P. and Bain, P. (1999), An assembly line in the head: Work and employee relations in the call centre, *Industrial Relations Journal* 30(2), 101–117.

Taylor, P. and Bain, P. (2007), Reflections on the call centre – a reply to Glucksmann. *Work, Employment and Society* 21(2), 349–362.

Taylor, P., Mulvey, G., Hyman, J. and Bain, P. (2002), Work Organization, Control and the Experience of Work in Call Centres. *Work, Employment and Society* 16(1), 133–150.

Titze, I. R. and Story, B. H. (2002), Voice quality: What is most characteristic about 'you'. *Echoes* 12(4), 3–4.

Tracy, S. J. (2000), Becoming a character for commerce: Emotion labor, self-subordination, and discursive construction of identity in a total institution, *Management Communication Quarterly* 14, 90–128.

Van Leeuwen, T. (1999), *Speech, Music, Sound.* London: Palgrave Macmillan.

Wallbott, H. G. (1998), Bodily expression of emotion. *European Journal of Social Psychology* 28, 879–896.

Wehrle, T., Kaiser, S., Schmidt, S., Scherer, K. R. (2000), Studying the Dynamics of Emotional Expressing Using Synthesized Facial Muscle Movements. *Journal of Personality and Social Psychology* 28(1), 105–119.

White, P. R. R. (1998), '*Telling Media Tales: The News Story As Rhetoric.*' Unpublished Ph. D. dissertation, University of Sydney, Sydney.

Chapter 8

Researching and Understanding Accent Shifts in Indian Call Centre Agents

Claire Cowie
University of Edinburgh, UK

Lalita Murty
University of York, UK

*This chapter investigates the use of American accent features among Indian call centre agents. The performances of 10 agents are compared on the following tests: a simulated call with an American-accented 'customer' and an extempore speech. Some agents show variable use of a highly salient American accent feature, namely the production of an approximant /r/ after a vowel, and others show no use of this feature at all. We aim to describe and explain this variable use, based on the assumption that performances in these tests reflect to some degree how these agents behave in a call centre setting. Three possible scenarios are investigated: (1) the agent does not use the American accent feature at all (2) the agent does make use of 'American' postvocalic /r/, but the feature is present only in selected words or phrases, or scripted segments of talk and is therefore not produced in response to the caller's usage (3) the use of the American postvocalic /r/ is distributed throughout the call and therefore more likely to mirror the caller's usage. This last scenario suggests that the agent controls the sociolinguistics of a variety that is not typically considered part of the repertoire of an English speaker in India. In all cases agents' control of the American feature is compared to their control of a feature /w/ which is indicative of standardness **within** an Indian context. We find that at least three out of ten agents show use of the American feature which goes beyond single words and phrases. We further find that this linguistic behaviour is not linked to standardness from an Indian perspective: a number of relatively 'standard' speakers in our study did not use the American feature at all. We suggest that this potential for accent accommodation be further researched in relation to external factors such as call centre experience, attitude to American posing and Indian identity.*

Introduction

Trainers, coaches and managers in the call centre industry constantly have to deal with the wide range of linguistic skills that agents demonstrate in telephone interactions. Not all agents are able (or willing) to adjust their speech in encounters with customers, and of those that do make adjustments, these may or may not make a difference to the success of the transaction. Analysis of call centre communication has, in the main, focused on lexical and discourse choices made by the agent (Forey and Lockwood 2007). The present chapter looks at phonological or accent choices.

There is widespread debate in call centre training about how to train for 'accent': should agents be trained to use an American accent (for American customers), if indeed this is possible, or should they be trained to 'neutralize' the features of their own accent (see Cowie 2007, Cowie 2010)? Our position here is that even if agents are explicitly trained or asked by management to use an American accent (usually such instructions are inexplicit – see Poster 2007), it is unlikely that accent training actually results in changes in an agent's speech patterns because communication-related training is usually so brief. In India 3 weeks of 'soft skills training' is typical, but this period is constantly being squeezed.

We speculate that where Indian agents do use American accents, or partial American accents on the telephone, that this may be due to a natural process of 'accommodation', in which one party adjusts their speech to their interlocutor to reduce the social distance between them. Such behaviour could be attributed to 'acting' ability (after all, we see actors adopting an accent wholesale on the screen), but few agents transform themselves so entirely, and we are more interested in the small scale adjustments that more ordinary agents make, which are not accompanied by narratives of complete identity change. Accommodation theory suggests that most speakers are acting out a role, in a limited way, in any conversation. The fact that accent adjustments on the part of call centre agents tend to be partial rather than wholesale has led to, at worst, customer complaints about 'fake accents', and, at best, within the industry, common recognition of that hybrid entity, the 'call centre accent'.

This chapter investigates the use of an American accent feature among Indian call centre agents. The performances of ten agents on an accent and customer care training programme are compared on the following tests: a simulated call with an American-accented 'customer' and an extempore speech. A number of these agents clearly use American accent features on the mock call (MC). We find an approximant [ɹ] after a vowel in words such as **star** and **card** (henceforth 'American postvocalic /r/'); 'flapping', the pronunciation of words like **better** with a flap /ɾ/ instead of /t/ in the middle so that it sounds like 'bedder', and a front vowel æ rather than the usual Indian English back vowel in words like **class**.

No agent uses all of these features all of the time in their interaction with the American customer. What we want to investigate in this chapter is the respect in which this usage is partial. Ideally, we would examine the distribution of all of these American accent features, but in this chapter we concentrate on the production of the postvocalic American /r/. The selection of this feature is discussed in greater detail below in section 4. Three possible scenarios are investigated:

(1) The agent does not use the American postvocalic /r/ at all.
(2) The agent does make use of American postvocalic /r/, but the feature is present only in selected and oft repeated words or phrases (e.g. computer), or scripted segments of talk (such as **may I have your service tag number please; to help us serve you better**) and is therefore unlikely to be produced in response to the caller's accent.
(3) The use of the American postvocalic /r/ is distributed throughout the call and therefore more likely to mirror the caller's usage.

Scenario number 2 suggests that the agent has very limited control of the feature, and is not changing their accent as such. It may be this behaviour which is associated with the terms 'fake accent' and 'call centre accent'. On the other hand these terms may refer to more extensive use of American accent features (Scenario 3), but concurrently with Indian accent features, resulting in a 'hybrid' accent. Scenario 3, the more distributed use of the American accent feature, we believe corresponds to what we have termed 'accommodation': the ability to shift one's accent closer to that of one's interlocutor. Such a pattern implies that the agent controls the sociolinguistics of a variety that is not typically considered part of the repertoire of an English speaker in India. Until now, accommodation theory has not had to contend with new forms of dialect contact brought about by call centres. Accommodation theory in linguistics and social psychology and its relevance to this study is described in greater detail in section 2 below.

For the control test, the free speech (FS), we would not expect to find American accent features at all. If the agent is really converging towards the 'customer' (as in scenario 3) then there should be no such convergence in the FS. If the use of American accent features is only symbolic (as in the case of 2) then the agent should not feel a need for these indicators in the FS, and certain words and scripted segments which might receive American pronunciation on a call are less likely to appear in the FS anyway. However the data is not that 'clean', and we do see **some** American postvocalic /r/ in the FS, which we will discuss.

For each agent we also measured their variable use of a well-known feature of Indian English in the MC and FS, namely the use of a labiodental approximant /ʋ/ where L1 varieties use /w/. Where this is used, words like *which* and *always* sound more like 'vich' and 'alvays' (although technically /w/ is not replaced by fricative /v/). The /w/ variant is more likely to be used by educated speakers in more formal contexts (see section 4 below). Monitoring use of this Indian feature means that we can investigate whether agents who command a more standard (or more L1 like) English are also more likely to converge towards an American accent.

'Accommodation' in Sociolinguistics and Social Psychology

In the sense that it is used here, linguistic accommodation (as described in Speech Accommodation Theory or Communication Accommodation Theory) refers to the process whereby a speaker shifts their language variety towards another variety (convergence) or away from another variety (divergence) (Giles 2001:193). Some writers emphasize that the speaker shifts towards or away from the variety that they *believe* is characteristic of their recipient (Coupland 1984:49). Accommodation has been studied for phonological features, but also in prosodic phenomena such as intonation and speech rate and non-verbal phenomena such as gaze and smiling.

A strategy of convergence may reflect the speaker's need to achieve greater communication efficiency (Coupland 1984:49) or to gain approval, integrate socially or identify with the recipient (Giles 2001:194). This strategy may, for the listener, increase the speaker's (1) attractiveness, (2) supportiveness and predictability, (3) level of personal involvement, (4) intelligibility and comprehensibility and (5) ability to gain the listener's compliance (Giles 2001: 194). The cost to the speaker in terms of the threat to his or her own identity is likely to be lower than the anticipated reward (Coupland 1984: 49).

The classic study of accommodation in phonological features or accent is Coupland's Welsh travel agent who converges towards her socioeconomically diverse clients (Coupland 1984). For example, Sue is more likely to produce an /n/ instead of a velar nasal /ŋ/ (doin' and goin') when speaking to clients from a lower economic bracket, and more likely to produce a velar nasal /ŋ/ (doing and going) when speaking to clients from a higher economic bracket. This is sometimes referred to feature-for-feature matching and is shown in this study to take place in a range of phonological features which are characteristic of the regional dialect. The correspondence between Sue's use of the standard /ŋ/ feature and her clients' use of it is as follows (Coupland 1984: 56):

Occupational class:	I	II	III	IV	V	VI
Clients:	0	9.4	41.8	68.9	73.8	100
Sue:	58.3	53.8	55.7	75	83.8	85.7

These overall scores can however obscure the way that Sue may style-shift **within** an interaction depending on whether she is playing the role of a sympathetic friend or an efficient and business-like travel agent (Coupland 1984: 68).

In any social encounter, there is always the possibility of both parties accommodating, and it is the power differential that will determine directionality. By and large, it is convergence on the part of the service provider in the direction of the customer that is associated with commercial encounters, given the power that customers exert in commercial settings (Giles 2001: 194). The relevance to call centre transactions is obvious, and if Giles and colleagues are right about positive listener evaluation, call centre managers should be very interested in convergence. In our study we are assuming that if there is any accommodation in the MC, that the agent will be converging towards the customer. It is worth noting however that Christine Krafft, in her study of call centre agents in Cape Town, found that at least one South African agent (speaking to a Canadian customer) explicitly drew attention to her local identity both in terms of her accent and in metalinguistic commentary, an interactional strategy which Krafft considered to be a case of divergence (Krafft 2008).

In Coupland (1984), the sociolects that the Welsh travel agent is converging towards are **already** in her repertoire. Coupland notes that little is known about 'cross-national accent accommodation', even in passive situations where subjects are evaluating a speaker in a matched-guise test. 'Individuals' accent repertoires, he says, 'are typically considered to be subsets of (nationally bounded) speech-community repertoires' (1984:52). Even since this time accent accommodation has not been extensively examined in situations where one of the relevant sociolects is *not* in the agent's everyday repertoire, such as that brought about by call centres. Suzy Orr's work in a Glaswegian call centre has shown that agents can also converge to varieties that they would not be expected to normally control such as Southern British English (Orr 2003). Orr investigated two phonological variables: the use of a glottal stop /ʔ/ for /t/ and the vowel quality of words such as PRICE and PRIZE. In the first case agents showed convergence towards a caller using /t/, which is also the standard variant for those agents. Agents **also** showed convergence towards callers' vowel qualities, even when the callers' vowel qualities had no place in the agents' repertoires. Interestingly, Orr points out that convergence took place even when customers were obviously dissatisfied, and for this reason we should take care in ascribing motivations for convergence such as social identification to call centre agents and call centre contexts.

Orr's Glaswegian agents are still in the same country as their interlocutors. If it *is* the case that Indian agents can shift their accents towards those of their American customers, this is a very novel and unusual case of accommodation. Existing studies of 'cross-national accent accommodation' (to use Coupland's term) describe the linguistic behaviour of longtime sojourners in another country, for example Americans living in Britain for some time decreasing the level of 'flapping' in words such as **heating** (Shockey 1984), or Irish students of French acquiring a non-standard French variant such as deletion of negative particle *ne* (Regan 2004). Sharma (2005) studies Indian immigrants to the USA (settled between 2 and 40 years) and finds that the use of American variants such as postvocalic /r/, velar /l/ in words like **call** and the aspiration of voiceless plosives /p/, /t/ and /k/ depends more on speakers' attitudinal stance than their proficiency level. Adamson and Regan's study of Cambodian and Vietnamese immigrants to the USA (settled from 2 to 96 months) shows that speakers in this group acquire some of the sociolinguistics of the variable (ing) which can be pronounced /in/ or /iŋ/ (Adamson and Regan 1991).

Similarly to Sharma's Indian immigrants, the Indian agents in the present study could be described as L2 speakers of English, or at least speakers of English as an additional language. However, they are not immersed in a country context surrounded by the L1 target accent. Immigrant accents are the products of long-term processes of accommodation (Giles 2001: 194), not the brief (although repetitive) telephone encounters associated with call centres. There is now a large and growing body of work (summarized and developed in Jenkins 2007) on the recognition and evaluation of native and non-native accents by English language learners in a wide range of countries. Jenkins' most recent survey includes responses from Austria, Brazil, China, Finland, Germany, Greece, Japan, Poland, Spain, Sweden and Taiwan (2007:154). Clearly different native speaker accents on the global stage are familiar to many but it is not obvious which L2 speakers in what countries are likely to be able to control the features of an American accent.

The unanswered question is: how and where do Indian call centre agents such as the ones in this study gain sufficient exposure to American English to be able to control the features of that accent? None of the agents in this study had travelled to the USA. Much is made of the influence of American media in India, but it is hard to measure the level of exposure among the relevant agent group. Poster (2007) draws attention to the way that the highly visible non-resident Indian (NRI) population has to some extent provided a role for American accents within India, and even encouraged agents to use American accent features outside of calls. But maybe we should consider the obvious: agents who spend at least 8 hours a day on calls to American customers (usually for periods of up to 2 years) are in fact receiving a dramatic amount of exposure to the accent. In section 6 we briefly consider whether members of the agent group in this study show differences related to their level of call centre experience.

The Data

The ten speakers in this study were randomly sampled from a 'batch' of around twenty trainees being trained by an Indian-owned call centre training company in Bangalore in 2004. The trainees had been recruited by an international computer firm and were being trained for an American customer base. This was a typical arrangement and any recruits were usually sent for the course regardless of previous experience, training or skills. The training manual which dealt with language provided minimal information about two American accent features (postvocalic /r/ and flapping). It contained more material on 'neutralizing' features such as the de-aspiration of voiceless stops /p/, /t/, /k/. These are ascribed to 'MTI' (Mother Tongue Influence) although most features labelled MTI tend to be features of General Indian English and not linked to specific L1s. The overt policy of the training company (expressed by documents and by staff) was that agents should learn to neutralize their accent, and there was considerable ambivalence about trainees acquiring American accent features.

Local staff who acted as 'phonetics trainers' never corrected agents in the direction of American accent in class, although non-local staff with American accents were recruited to give trainees practice in dealing with American customers (see Cowie 2007, Cowie 2010).

The two tests (MC and FS) take place 2 weeks into a 3-week training course. The customer on the MC is played in all cases by 'Amy', a woman in her early twenties who grew up in the USA as a child of Indian immigrant parents. We have not analysed Amy's speech for variability, but we are sufficiently confident that Amy uses US variants consistently. For both tests the class acts as the broader audience and the phonetics trainer (sometimes accompanied by a representative of the employer) assigns a score to the agent. In the MC Amy goes to some length to put the agent under stress by claiming not to understand the agent and frequently finding his or her troubleshooting efforts to hypothetical computer problems unsuccessful. Even though the FS is also evaluated, the agent is addressing his or her peers and the atmosphere tends to be more relaxed with more laughter and interaction. All of the agents have some tertiary education, usually an undergraduate degree in engineering, business or commerce.

All were in their early twenties, with the exception of Ravindra in his late twenties. Akshata, Jasmine, Sanju and Vijay had US call centre experience. Ashwin and Ravindra had worked in call centres but not for the US market. Gargi, Kartikeyan, Kiran and Sharan had no previous call centre experience. Most agents came from Bangalore or outside of Bangalore with either Kannada or Tamil as their mother tongue. Kartikeyan is from neighbouring Tamil Nadu and Kiran and Sanju are from Kerala. Unsurprisingly the jobs on offer in Bangalore have drawn others from further afield: Gargi is from Bhutan and Jasmine from Bihar.

Selection of Phonological Variables

Postvocalic American Approximant [ɹ] and Indian ø

We were clear that the American variant for one of our variables should **not** occur in Indian English, or indeed in British English (which could possibly act as an alternative standard target for these agents). This way we would be able to say with certainty that the agent was converging towards the American-accented customer. Our position is that American postvocalic approximant /r/ does not occur in Indian English, but this is not to say that the treatment of postvocalic /r/ in the literature on Indian English is not complex.

Indian English has been described as variably rhotic by Bansal (1990:222) and Kachru (1994:514) who claim that only a small minority of RP-influenced media personalities do not have postvocalic /r/. Gargesh (2004) however regards Indian English as mostly non-rhotic and suggests that any postvocalic /r/ in Indian English is trilled, and even these realizations may be a case of spelling pronunciation (2004:998). Wiltshire and Harnsberger's review of

General Indian English concludes that 'r-ful' varieties have an /r/ that is a flap or a trill (2006:93). For Sharma, 'Indian English varieties may either be non-rhotic or may have a partially devoiced, trilled /r/ and so Indian English on the whole cannot be assumed to be non-rhotic. However, trilled /r/ in the in rhotic dialects does not resemble the approximant /r/ of American English' (2005:209). Sharma warns that rules for rhoticity may differ for speakers with Dravidian as opposed to Indo-Aryan L1s, but Wiltshire and Harnsberger's comparison of Gujarati and Tamil speakers of English finds that neither group have much post-vocalic /r/ (15% for Tamil speakers and 17% for Gujarati speakers). This may be because they are dealing with relatively highly educated speakers.

In our data trilled postvocalic /r/ is not noticeable although closer analysis may reveal an occasional flap in this position. We are reasonably confident that when we do hear a postvocalic /r/ it is an approximant which can only be associated with an American accent.

Each possible environment for postvocalic /r/ was coded as not-realized <ø> or realized <r>. We did not differentiate between word-final postvocalic /r/ as in *star* and postvocalic /r/ in a consonant cluster as in *hard*. Environments for unstressed /r/ e.g. **er** were excluded, as were environments for linking /r/ e.g. **are in, your end**. There is little mention of this in the literature, but Indian English definitely seems to have linking /r/.

/ʋ/ and /w/ in Indian English

For the second variable we wanted to single out a feature which would reflect the standardness of agents' speech from a purely Indian perspective. The pronunciation of /v/ and /w/ in Indian English seemed a good candidate as it was clearly variable in the speech of our agents, and it is more amenable to auditory analysis than other variable features of Indian English such as de-aspiration. Some accounts of Indian English simply observe that /v/ and /w/ are not distinguished in the speech of some South Asian speakers (Kachru 1994:515). For Bansal again it is a small group of L1-like speakers who maintain the distinction (1990:225), which does suggest that the distinction may be partially there for a larger and less elite but nevertheless educated group. In fact it is not the case that /v/ and /w/ are switched around, but that both tend to be substituted by a sound that is in between: labiodental approximant /ʋ/ (Wiltshire and Harnsberger 2006:100), and this is why a 'v' tends to sound like /w/ in words like **very**, and 'w' tends to sound like /v/ in words like **with**.

The patterns for the realization of English 'w' and 'v' are not exactly the same in all positions. So at the beginning of a word beginning with 'w' we might find /w/ or /ʋ/, and at the beginning of a word with 'v' we might find /v/ or /ʋ/. When 'w' is in the middle of the word as in *power* we might find /w/, /ʋ/ or also ø. When 'v' is in the middle of the word as in **develop** we might find /v/ or /ʋ/. When 'w' is word-final as in **show** this is not pronounced in L1 varieties anyway, so we do not count these cases. When 'v' is at the end of a word as in **love** this may be realized by speakers of Indian English as /v/ or /ʋ/, but some very basilectal or low proficiency speakers may have ø here. This is a very stigmatized form which hardly appears in our data at all.

We measured the extent to which the 'standard' variants /v/ and /w/ are realized in their expected environments. The realization of 'v' as /v/ rather than the Indian variant was consistently high (close 100%) in all speakers, but 'w' was much more likely to be realized as the Indian /ʋ/. We think that 'w' is therefore a more interesting variable and in our results we concentrate on the percentage of standard /w/. There may be lexical differences here: the /ʋ/ variant tends to occur very frequently in **which**, but less so in *was* and *would* but we have not explored this aspect here.

Results

The full dataset showing token sizes for both variables is given in Appendix 1.

Use of American Postvocalic /r/

Figure 1 shows the percentage of American postvocalic /r/ for each agent in the Mock Call (MC) and the Free Speech (FS). As explained above, use of this feature through convergence, or even just through 'scripting', would mean that it appears in the MC rather than the FS. The MC score is indeed higher in eight of ten agents, but the difference is not a statistically significant one overall, probably because there are only two or three agents where this difference counts.

Turning to the MC data, agents performed as follows on the MC, in descending order: Sanju (43%), Akshata (42%), Gargi (28%), Vijay (26%), Sharan (23%), Ravindran (10%), Jasmine (8%), Ashwin (3%), Kartikeyan (2%) and Kiran (0%). Sanju and Akshata are the obvious candidates for possible convergence, and we will therefore examine these agents closely, but we will also consider Gargi, Vijay and Sharan.

Akshata

Akshata is the most clear-cut case for convergence, as, together with Sanju, she shows the most /r/ in the MC (47 out of a possible 112 environments), but unlike Sanju she has a negligible amount of /r/ in the FS (only four instances). Table 1 shows that with words which appear more than once in the MC transcript, Akshata's pronunciation of them is variable, with the possible exception of **computer**. In other words, her use of postvocalic /r/ is not restricted to a small number of lexemes, and that it occurs in both common

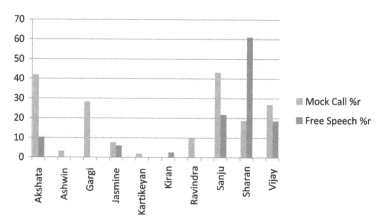

FIGURE 1 American postvocalic /r/ across all 10 speakers in MC and FS

Table 1 Realizations of lexemes: Akshata MC

Type	Tokens with /r/	Tokens without /r/
For	3	8
Your	5	15
Four	3	
Information		2
Computer	1	6
Papers	3	
Restart	1	2
Letters	1	2
Support	2	
Sure	1	1

There is only one token of the following words which is realized with /r/: **service, purpose, keyboard, serve, pleasure, first, here**

The following lexical items are never realized with /r/: **hardware, reconfirm, confirm, uniform, understand, regarding, survey, form, future, our, where, number**

function words like **for** and **your**, and content words such as **computer** and **keyboard**.

Despite the variability she shows for *your* in the mock call, Akshata does not produce any of the 8 tokens of **your** in the FS with /r/. There is some evidence that Akshata produces more /r/ in scripted sections of the MC – in the utterance below she has an /r/ in **support, here, your** and **service**.

A: thank you for\<r\> calling XYZ har\<0\>dwar\<0\>e suppor\<r\>t this is Akshata her\<r\>e may I have your\<r\> ser\<r\>vice tag number\<0\> please

However, Akshata's use of American /r/ is certainly not confined to these kinds of opening and closing lines. Her production of an /r/ in **letters,** for example, comes in the middle of her 'resolution' section:

A: but I guess the best thing you can do now is retype your letter\<r>s and then save it immediately okay

Sanju

Sanju's performance is very similar to that of Akshata. In fact, we should not make too much of her score on the FS, which is based on relatively few tokens. The five cases of realized /r/ (out of a possible 23) are: three tokens of **later** and the phrase **perfect homemaker.** Table 2 shows that Sanju too has variable realizations of **your** and **for** on the one hand, and **computer** and **information** on the other.

Sanju's use of /r/ is however slightly more script-dependent than Akshata, judging by the level of /r/ in the following two openers and one closer:

S: Thank you for\<0> calling XYZ har\<0>dwar\<r>e suppor\<0>t, this is Sanju her\<r>e. May I have your\<r> ser\<r>vice tag number\<r> please?

S: OK, thank you for\<0> the infor\<0>mation. May I hav\<v>e your\<r> fir\<r>st and last name please?

Table 2   Realizations of lexemes: Sanju MC

Type	Tokens with /r/	Tokens without /r/
Your	4	40
For	13	9
Number	3	1
First	3	
Confirm		2
Confirmation	1	
Information	1	2
There	4	1
Or	1	2
Properties	1	1
Over	1	1
Computer	1	1
Survey		3

There is only one token of the following words which is realized with /r/: **service, oscar, slower, easier, server (both syllables), yesterday, faster, our, serve, hardware, here**
The following lexical items are never realized with /r/: **support, more, understand, regular, were, internet, normal, stored, works, regarding, further, pleasure, form**

S: ok it is er w w w dot, suppor<0>t dot XYZ dot com. OK? This is a XYZ suppor<0>t site it's just infor<0>mation about XYZ, your<r> computer<r> and frequently asked questions.

Yet Sanju's use of /r/ in the MC is also not restricted to opening and closing lines and she uses /r/ in the troubleshooting section of the call:

S:Yah, you need to delete the files so that your<0> browsing would be a lot easier<0> for<r> you

Gargi

Even though Gargi and Vijay show similar amounts of /r/ in the MC, Gargi has no /r/ at all in her FS, making her a better candidate for convergence, although note that there are only 11 possible environments for /r/ in the FS:

You can gain a lot you can look into the wor<0>ld and maybe . . . er . . . go forward to things maybe you can achieve your<0> goal and with knowledge em so many things have come out people er . . . er . . . ya I em ya of cour<0>se I do not say that er you gotta know each and everything but a little bit of it I guess so that at least em maybe you can speak about it and if you do not know you can ask a per<0>son and gain knowledge. . . .

Table 3 below shows Gargi's variable realization of words like *your* and *number*, which pattern similarly to Akshata and Sanju, yet the table does also flag the way

Table 3   Realizations of lexemes: Gargi

Type	Tokens with /r/	Tokens without /r/
Your	10	10
First	1	1
Quimberg	2	4
Information	2	
Computer	8	6
Monitor	1	3
There	1	10
Number	1	3
For	1	5

There is only one token of the following words which is realized with /r/: **cord, or, order** (1st **syllable**), **card, form, uniform, Oscar.**

The following lexical items are never realized with /r/: **hardware, support, service, four, confirm, purpose, survey, customer, better, understand, working, circuit, wire, keyboard, tower, under, regarding, further, where.**

that alpha-numerics like Oscar and Uniform tend to be produced (in opening scripts) with /r/:

> G : thank you . . . just to confir<0>m L as in Lima I as in India L as in Lima O as in Oscar<r> Y as in Yankee
>
> C : its two Ls and there's no O
>
> G : ok sorry about that . . . and your<r> last name goes Q as in Quebec, U as in unifor<r>m I as in India M as in Mike B as in bravo E as in echo R as in . . . Romeo G as in Golf am I right
>
> C : mhmm
>
> G : for<0> verification pur<0>pose may I have a telephone number<r><link> and your<r><link> address the zip-code fir<r>st please

Gargi's production of the phrase 'your computer', which appears frequently in her MC is interesting. The first three uses have /r/, such as:

> G : ther<0>e's a w<w>ir<0>e that goes to the CPU – that's the tow<w>er<0> beside your<r> computer<r>

But the following three are all without /r/. The shift occurs at a problematic segment in the conversation in which Gargi is struggling to resolve the problem. This stress is then compounded by some misunderstandings:

> G : . . . no no . . . its not that you got to go to your<0> wor<0>k station
>
> L : I have to go to my work station
>
> G : mhmm
>
> L : what dya mean . . . I got to go to my job
>
> G : no at the place you have bought your<0> computer<0> from

Even though we would argue that Gargi's /r/ is not entirely lexicalized, she probably finds it easier to use /r/ in phrases such as 'your computer', but this goes when she is under stress.

Vijay and Sharan

Briefly, Vijay's performance on the mock call is similar to Akshata, Sanju and Gargi, but Sharan's is not. Vijay variably produces /r/ in both function words (**for, your**) and content words (**computer, port, pointer**). Sharan, on the other hand, produces /r/ variably in **number, support** and **computer** and he even uses /r/ consistently in **printer**, but **your** and **for** never appear with /r/ in his

MC. Sharan thus illustrates a more lexicalized use of /r/ which we would not associate with convergence. This is probably also true of Ravindra who has relatively few lexemes with /r/ in his MC **(cord x2, confirmation, there, start, information x2).**

While Ravindra uses postvocalic /r/ to a lesser extent than some of the others, the points at which he does use it are not situations where he is confident, as you would expect, but situations where he is stressed by the customer:

R: er<0>, hav<v>e you hear<0>d of the XYZ suppor<0>t site?

C: erm, what is that? (hostile tone)

R: it is er<0><unstr>, infor<0>, er<0><unstr>, XYZ suppor<0>t site has infor<r>mation about XYZ, your<0> computer<0><int> and frequently asked qu<w>estions.

C: ok,

R: er<0><unstr>, ther<0>e times probably w<V>hen you could also log on into it and er<0> solv<v>e your<r><int> issue. Er<0><unstr>, because frequently . . .

C: ok, (discouraging tone)

R: resol-issues ar<0>e resolv<v>ed ther<0>e and answer<0>ed ther<r>e

Peculiarly, Sharan shows a relatively higher use of /r/ in his FS. Again, tokens are small (8 out of 11), yet enough to illustrate that the range of lexemes produced with /r/ is greater: **or x 2, course, their, forty, work, under, years**. The content of Sharan's FS is markedly different to his peers. He presents himself, perhaps ironically, as enjoying the American dream:

Trust me people, I'm one among the top ten richest business-business tycoons in the next twenty five year<r>s. Thank you.

This kind of posing could explain Sharan's use of /r/ in the FS. But we should be cautious. Vijay's FS contains five tokens of /r/ **(first x 2, there, cover, water)** out of a possible 27 environments, but the content is comical:

I'm selling a product out her<0>e . . . okay I'm presenting this product which is called freeze dry water<0>

In conclusion, we have evidence in four cases that use of American /r/ goes beyond scripting and confinement to certain lexemes. In Akshata and Sanju /r/ in the MC is over 40%, surely an indicator that at least some agents are accommodating to the accent of their interlocutor.

Finally, let us take a look at some of the typical non-convergers. The transcript of Ashwin's MC shows that even the phrases most likely to contain /r/ for the agents analysed above, occur without /r/:

A: okay . . . thank you . . . thank you for<0> the infor<0>mation how may I help you

C: um actually I forgot why I called now okay . . . ya . . . um I wanna set up a screensaver

A: as I under<0>stand you want to set up a screensaver<0> I can help you with that

C: okay

A: okay please right click on the screen of your<0> computer<0>

Agents such as Ashwin and Kiran do not even reflect a symbolic use of American features. We discuss them further below.

Standardness of Indian English as Reflected by /w/

Figure 2 shows that overall there is no significant difference between the production of the standard variant /w/ on the Mock Call and on the Free Speech. Although this *is* the case for six out of the ten agents, the overall difference is not sufficient to be significant. Either agents are not treating the two tests as sufficiently distinct in terms of formality, or, it is not important (or possible) for them to manipulate this feature across the two contexts. Wiltshire and Harnsberger cite Saghal and Agnihotri (1988) as reporting that their speakers who only use /w/ between 20 and 33% of the time do not adjust this

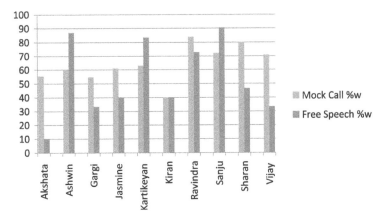

FIGURE 2   Percentage of /w/ for all 10 speakers in MC and FS

for more formal speech 'indicating that this feature is perhaps not associated with prestige or the lack of it in IE' (2006: 100). This is surprising given what we know about the presence of /w/ in the most prestigious varieties of Indian English, but it does suggest that there is much more sociolinguistic groundwork to be done for this variable.

Akshata's transcripts are the only ones which show a marked contrast for /w/. Her FS has almost no /w/. The Indian variant is shown in the coding here as <V>.

> . . . but right now if you think in our fast going social life pace it is just not happening . . . the first thing w<V>hich comes to your mind w<V>hen you buy phones like now you consider it as the mobile phones the first thing comes to your mind I bet it's your parents picture . . . you never do you never do things w<V>hich you w<w>anna do w<V>ithout telling your parents

Her MC demonstrates considerable variability as illustrated by these two sections:

> A: ok w<w>hat I can do for you is right now as you haven't saved your um two letters now I am sure that w<V>e w<V>on't be able to do it because your computer is hung so w<V>e have to shut down your computer and re-start your computer and then you 'll have to . . . again type your letters and then save it w<V>ill that be ok

> A: ok that's great so w<w>hat you can do is just press on the three keys I mean just press on the Shut Down option and . . . that w<w>ill shut your computer immediately

Akshata is not in fact as standard as some of the other agents in that she does not have the same level of /w/, yet she was the most promising 'converger' candidate. Ashwin and Ravindra on the other hand, who didn't use /r/ at all, are clearly /w/ users. The usefulness of looking at this feature is that it signals that may not be a relationship between the Indianness/standardness of an agent's accent and his or her propensity to accommodate to the accent of the customer. Since the 'standardness' feature, /w/ does not differ systematically for the MC and FS, in Figure 3 we compare %/r/ and %/w/ in the MC only:

It is clear that to the extent that standardness is reflected by /w/, these are a relatively standard group of speakers. They vary considerably however, in their production of /r/, and while there is a positive relationship between the two variables the correlation is not a significant one. While we can say that not all standard speakers are convergers, we cannot make observations about whether relatively non-standard speakers can and do accommodate, as we don't really have any non-standard speakers. The least standard, Kiran, is not a converger.

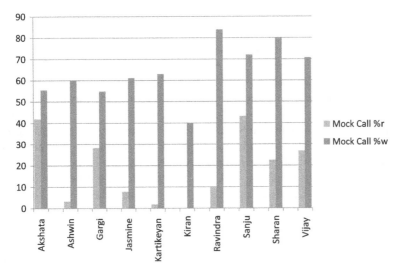

FIGURE 3   %/r/ in the MC and %/w/ in the MC

Explaining Difference and Future Research

In conclusion, we have found evidence that some agents can do more with American accent features than produce them in single words and phrases. We have also found that it is not necessarily the most elite or acrolectal speakers of Indian English who do this, and that acrolectal speakers of Indian English are not necessarily more likely to accommodate to an American accent. Our aim in this chapter was to demonstrate methods for identifying different patterns of accent shifting among agents. Ideally, we would also want to provide explanations for each agent's behaviour. In this study however, our sample is too small and our information on each agent insufficiently detailed to reliably relate performance to external factors. Yet this small-scale investigation can to some extent provide a heuristic for developing such explanations in future research. We think the following factors may have a role to play:

(i)   Call centre experience with American customers: Akshata, Sanju, Vijay and Jasmine all had experience of working in call centre speaking to American customers. Ashwin and Ravindra had worked in call centres but not with an American customer base. It is striking that the two most obvious convergers have this experience and may in fact have been engaging in this practice for some time. It is hard to know whether these agents have simply had more exposure to an American accent, or been more enculturated into identity practices encouraged by some call centres. The fact that this work experience has not made a difference in the case of

Jasmine cautions us that not all agents might respond to it in the same way.

(ii) Indian identity and attitude to American posing: Poster (2007) conducted 50 detailed interviews with agents at three Indian call centres and rated them on their attitudes towards 'American posing', the assumption of an American identity or some aspects of an American identity on calls with US customers. 13% of her respondents 'assimilate', 33% actively resist and the rest reluctantly 'accommodate', meaning that they may not agree with the principle of identity management but comply for 'various pragmatic reasons involving getting the job done' (2007:289). According to Poster some agents have noticed the 'benefits of acting American in their personal lives' (2007: 293). This is partly through the raised profile of American English in India, thanks in part to the temporary and permanent return of Indian migrants to the USA (Non-resident Indians or 'NRIs'). Murty (2007) has described changes in attitude towards American English among younger age groups. Without detailed interviews we cannot assign a score to our agents' position on American identity but we think it is highly likely that this is behind differences in performance. American posturing imposes a cost on ethnic or Indian identity (Poster 2007: 273) and agents with a stronger sense of local identity will be less comfortable with it. Furthermore, we know that the realization of an ethnic identity is going to be experienced differently for men and for women, and we don't think it is a coincidence that our three best candidates for convergence (Sanju, Akshata and Gargi) are women. Poster does not comment on gender differences in her respondents but it would be interesting to explore whether they are more likely to belong to the assimilator, accommodator or active resister group.

(iii) Motivations for convergence in call centre interactions: In our review of accommodation theory we noted that a convergence strategy needs to be considered in relation to microscopic conversational episodes as well as the overall profiles of the agent and caller. In section 2 we drew attention to the way that some of Orr's agents converged even with an angry customer, and this is something we have found examples of in our data as well. Thus a convergence strategy is not simply a question of positively identifying with the customer or wanting to elicit positive identification from the customer. It may also be about projecting competence and maintaining a professional image which is associated with a particular accent. We should also bear in mind that 'communication efficiency' and 'social approval' are both relevant criteria for an agent's success (Coupland 1984: 54–55) and convergence may for the agent be a **perceived** way of increasing intelligibility where a misunderstanding has arisen.

Appendix 1

Name	MC r	N	MC r%	FS r	N	FS r%	MC v	N	MC v%	FS v	N	Fs v%	MC w	N	MC %	FS w	N	FS w%
Akshata	47	112	42	4	39	10.3	29	32	90.6	16	17	94.1	15	27	55.6	1	10	10
Gargi	32	113	28.3	0	11	0	18	18	100	9	9	100	17	31	54.8	3	9	33.3
Sanju	51	118	43.2	5	23	21.7	18	23	78.3	19	19	100	31	43	72.1	19	21	90.5
Vijay	22	82	26.8	5	27	18.5	27	32	84.4	9	14	64.3	29	41	70.7	15	9	33.3
Sharan	9	40	22.5	8	12	66.7	17	19	89.5	6	7	85.7	16	20	80	21	15	46.7
Jasmine	6	77	7.8	2	33	6.1	34	37	91.9	27	30	90	33	54	61.1	7	20	40
Kartik	1	53	1.9	0	28	0	18	22	81.8	40	46	87	17	27	63	9	18	83.3
Ashwin	2	62	3.2	0	16	0	22	27	81.5	3	3	100	15	25	60	20	23	87
Ravindra	8	82	9.8	0	28	0	15	16	93.8	13	15	86.7	26	31	83.9	8	11	72.7
Kiran	0	77	0	1	40	2.5	32	35	91.4	7	10	70	8	20	40	8	20	40

References

Adamson, D. and Regan, V. (1991), The acquisition of community norms by Asian immigrants learning English as a second language: A preliminary study. *Studies in Second Language Acquisition* 13, 1–22.

Bansal, R. K. (1990), The pronunciation of English in India in *Studies in the Pronunciation of English: A Commemorative Volume in Honour of A.C. Gimson* (ed.) Susan Ramsaran. Routledge: London and New York.

Coupland, N. (1984), Accommodation at work: Some phonological data and their implications. *International Journal for the Sociology of Language* 46, 49–70.

Cowie, C. (2007), The accents of outsourcing: The meanings of 'neutral' in the Indian call centre industry. *World Englishes* 26(3), 316–330.

Cowie, C. (forthcoming), The demand and supply of accents in the Indian call centre industry: 'Anyone doing something phonetic can attract business these days'. *Language and the Market* (eds.) Helen Kelly-Holmes and Gerlinde Mautner. Basingstoke: Palgrave-Macmillan.

Forey, G. and Lockwood, J. (2007), 'I'd love to put someone in jail for this': An initial investigation of English in the business processing outsourcing industry. *English for Specific Purposes* 26/3, 308–326.

Gargesh, R. (2004), Indian English: Phonology in *A Handbook of Varieties of English Volume 1: Phonology*. (eds.) Edgar W. Schneider, Kate Burridge, Bernd Kortmann, Rajend Mesthrie and Clive Upton. Berlin: Mouton de Gruyter.

Giles, H. (2001), Speech Accommodation in *Concise Encyclopaedia of Sociolinguistics* (ed.) Rajend Mesthrie. Amsterdam: Elsevier.

Jenkins, J. (2007), *English as a Lingua Franca: Attitude and Identity.* Oxford: Oxford University Press.

Kachru, B. B. (1994), English in South Asia in *The Cambridge History of the English Language Volume V: English in Britain and Overseas: Origins and Development.* (ed.) Robert Burchfield. Cambridge: Cambridge University Press.

Krafft, C. (2008), *Standard American English and South African English in a Call Centre Environment.* Linguistics MA dissertation, University of Cape Town.

Murty, L. (2007), Accents and BPO industry: Issues of attitude. Paper presented at *Talking Across the World* conference, Manila 2007.

Orr, S. (2003), *Hanging on the Telephone: A Sociophonetic Study of Speech in a Glaswegian Call Centre.* MA dissertation, University of Glasgow.

Poster, W. R. (2007), Who's on the line? Indian call center agents pose as Americans for U.S.-outsourced firms. *Industrial Relations* 46(2), 271–304.

Regan, V. (2004), The relationship between the group and the individual and the acquisition of native speaker variation patterns: A preliminary study. *International Review of Applied Linguistics* 42(4), 335–348.

Saghal, A. and Agnihotri, R. K. (1988), Indian English Phonology: A sociolinguistic perspective. *English World-Wide* 9, 51–64.

Sharma, D. (2005), Dialect stabilization and speaker awareness in non-native varieties of English. *Journal of Sociolinguistics* 9 (2).

Shockey, L. (1984), All in a flap: Long-term accommodation in phonology. *International Journal of the Sociology of Language* 46, 87–95.

Wiltshire, C. R. and Harnsberger, J. D. (2006), The influence of Gujarati and Tamil L1s on Indian English: A preliminary study. *World Englishes* 25/1, 91–104.

Part III

Language, Culture and Training in the Globalized Workplace

Chapter 9

Talking about Talking: Comparing the Approaches of Intercultural Trainers and Language Teachers

Jane Hayman
International Consultants Centre, Melbourne, Australia

This chapter compares the ways in which language educators and intercultural trainers approach the teaching of language and culture and notes that in some ways the practitioners are mirror images of each other. I look at the constraints and expectations of intercultural training and suggest methodologies which can assist trainers to meet their objectives. The chapter also looks at attitudes towards stereotypes in language learning and cultural training.

Introduction

This chapter draws on my own recent experience and observations, informed by my transition from being a TESOL professional to working as an intercultural trainer for expatriates in the corporate sector. I am employed by a human resources firm which provides consultancy services for all areas of expatriation. In this role I design and deliver pre-departure intercultural training for Australians moving offshore and for international professionals arriving into Australia.

I will look at some of the similarities and differences between the approaches of intercultural trainers and language teachers and areas in which they could draw on each other's approach. Language professionals may be interested to learn more about the assumptions made in intercultural training and the ways that scenarios, tools and frameworks are used to bridge anticipated gaps in communication styles. I will suggest that language teachers could benefit from some of the direct insights and strategies offered to their clients by intercultural trainers and that intercultural trainers could benefit from a deeper understanding of the relationship between language and culture. Both professions offer a kind of mirror to each other; an exploration may assist practitioners to develop their own awareness of the particular assumptions and components embedded in their practice. I will additionally discuss how the use of an online tool has increased the capacity of myself and my colleagues to provide corporate training with a reflective component.

Culture through the Eyes of Language Professionals

It is widely accepted among language teaching professionals and researchers that language and culture are inevitably entwined and that language reflects and in turn shapes its wider cultural context. (Halliday 1979; Hymes 1972). Linguistic competence is inseparable from communicative competence and intercultural competence (Kramsch 1993) is an intrinsic aspect of linguistic proficiency.

Language professionals acknowledge to various degrees the importance of intercultural understanding, but do not always succeed in seamlessly weaving cultural awareness, let alone analysis into their practice (Baker 2003). English language teachers often struggle with the imperialism which is perceived to be historically embedded into the very act of teaching the language. Pulverness, suggesting a more direct engagement with culture as part of language learning, observes

> At a time when Britain no longer occupies a dominant political position in the world, it is perhaps reassuring for teachers to feel that they are permitted to treat English purely in forms of a language system uncomplicated by any cultural sub-text. (1995:3)

Sensitivity to past or present inequities between native speakers and aspirational speakers can lead teachers to back away from explicit teaching of cultural attitudes or behaviours. The rapid changes in society, economics, employment patterns and access to information which come under the umbrella term of globalization have muddied the cultural waters further for language teachers. As Kumaravadivelu observes 'Cultural Globalisation is a huge elephant that has stealthily intruded into the arena of language education' (2008:27).

Where Tomalin and Stempleski offer a range of tasks to assist learners with explicit recognition of culture in the language classroom (1993), Guest (2002) calls on language teachers to 'provide an indirect and covert introduction of culture' to their learners, in order to avoid the dangers of simplistic, fixed and 'otherised' representations of cultures.

Language through the Eyes of Intercultural Trainers

In contrast to the ambivalence demonstrated towards overt teaching of culture by language teachers, intercultural trainers are explicit about imparting contrastive cultural information and thus are in danger of a number of pitfalls. One of the most important of these is that intercultural trainers are not always able to acknowledge the extent to which a culture is embedded and reflected in its language(s). Corporate trainers are often in a position where they are teaching cultural awareness without the time, expertise or resources to look at any but the broadest linguistic aspects of the new culture.

Intercultural trainers work from a defined view of culture informed by the classic 'software of the mind' (Hofstede 2004) and the Trompenaars' (1995) description of culture as: 'the way in which a group of people solves problems'. Trompenaars further describes culture as 'the organization of meaning' and describes the ways in which different cultures attribute different meanings to the same events or interactions.

The issue of multiple perspectives is obvious yet so central to intercultural understanding that the construct deserves some explicit consideration. A personal experience of mine illustrates it. When I lived in Vietnam in the mid-nineties, I had a conversation with a Vietnamese taxi driver about the Swedish backpackers he observed roaming about Ho Chi Minh City. He expressed his concern that they had no home to stay in and had to look for accommodation. Where were their families? Some of them did not even have enough clothes! This is a somewhat endearing example of multiple cultural perspectives at work. Where the Swedes were experiencing independence and adventure, this Vietnamese man saw homelessness and absence of family protection. Where the Swedes presented themselves in casual shorts and sleeveless tops as appropriate hot weather holiday wear, the Vietnamese saw a lack of dignity and loss of face.

This cross-cultural misunderstanding is specific to time as well as place; in the early to mid-nineties, Vietnam was just becoming a fashionable tourist destination and many Vietnamese were patently unfamiliar with the whole dynamic of the tourist transaction. Globalization in the form of increased contact and observation of Northern European tourists will have given this driver more familiarity with backpackers. It is possible that he has now internalized the dual perspectives himself and can organize the meaning as it is intended.

Intercultural researchers are enamoured with concrete images to demonstrate the nature of culture. Notable among these are Trompenaars' 'onion' (1995), a useful tool to convey the many layers of explicit and implicit culture and the ubiquitous iceberg with its air of menace and the threat that the 90% that is not observable under the surface is what will sink you. Foster suggests an update of this image:

Cultures are no longer discreet 'icebergs,' reflecting unique, perceivable behaviours above the surface with invisible values below. Instead, cultures are part of a much larger sea of many icebergs, all of which are impacted by overpowering forces of globalization that are simultaneously re-shaping, melting, and melding the icebergs, and, in some cases, emphasizing differences. (2007:3)

The Task of the Intercultural Trainer

The impact of different cross-cultural perspectives on international business is increasingly well-documented. Its relevance to the success of an increasingly global work force is self-evident. Cross-cultural misunderstandings can delay, or indeed sink, the most meticulously planned and risk-audited project. However, cross-cultural issues are still often insufficiently identified as risk factors in international project design. The literature abounds with case studies of project disasters brought about by cultural misunderstanding. A classic example is the experience of the beer producers Fosters in China. Chung (2008) describes how the venture suffered from the Australian management's belief that attending banquets with local officials was a waste of time and money. This failure to nurture local relationships, critical and fundamental to any venture in China, resulted in various levels of disaster. Similarly there is considerable analysis available of the Chrysler Daimler merger and the cultural differences which emerged between the German and US partners, both at the level of national culture and at the level of the specific corporate cultures (Weber and Camerer 2003).

These are famous large-scale disasters but the opportunity for small-scale misunderstanding or failure is a feature of any international assignment or any project involving global or indeed diverse team members.

It is this awareness of potential cultural misunderstanding and the dollar value of failed international postings or joint ventures that leads corporations to invest in intercultural training.

A typical training assignment for an intercultural trainer consists of preparing an expatriate for a management, technical or influencing role in any one of a huge range of countries. The trainer is attempting to alert the client to the more predictable pitfalls and to equip them with skills and awareness to enable them to perform to the highest level of their professional ability in a new culture. The format is often a one or half day pre-departure programme for the assignee and spouse, paid for by the employer. The training objectives of this kind of session tend to be multipronged; informational, so that the expatriate knows some key 'facts' about her/his destination; awareness raising so that the expatriate begins to develop a sense of their own existing culturally determined values and how her/his personal style will impact on those of a different culture: and strategic, equipping the assignee with the skills to identify and manage any areas of tension arising from cultural difference.

These are notably ambitious objectives to be realized in a few hours of pre-departure training. Ideally the assignee and their family would be given several months of pre-departure language and cultural training. This kind of time frame and investment is of course extremely rare. Intercultural trainers are compelled to make their training as effective as possible in a very short space of time and with clients who have only a few weeks or even days to prepare themselves for every aspect of their departure. Two recent examples from my own experience illustrate the kinds of pressure that clients and trainers are under.

– We were asked to provide intercultural training to a couple in their home, while they were packing and simultaneously negotiating with removalists. (This did not take place.)

– We prepared a pre-departure intercultural briefing for an assignee going to Singapore. Two days before the training he phoned and informed us the assignment had now been changed to the Philippines and he was leaving in less than a week.

The very short time available even outside these more extreme situations, and the requirement of many corporate clients for instant fixes tends to compel the trainer to adopt a very direct style. Managers funding the training often request that the training not waste time with discussions but provide very concrete 'take-aways'. Trainers are in danger of finding themselves in the role of the 'top-down' imparter of information rather than allowing the participant to learn through a more typical adult learning experience of reflection, exploration and testing of new concepts. The assignee often presents with little pre-training reflection about the new culture due to the intrusion of issues such as shifting departure dates (and destinations), domestic disruption, current workload and mixed family responses to a relocation. Feeling under pressure the participant can express impatience with a more exploratory approach and request just to be told what they need to know, rather than undergoing a process of eliciting and exploring the ideas. It is one of the challenges for the intercultural trainer to meet the client's requirement for the training to be specific, targeted and time effective while ensuring that there is a reflective and awareness component which will enable some deeper learning to take place.

One of my clients articulated this attitude perfectly when she said to me; At company X we are focused on solutions. We don't want you telling us about cross-cultural problems without handing out the solutions.

The task for the conscientious trainer then is to balance on the one hand the client's desire for hard facts with on the other hand the responsibility to convey the ambiguity and complexity at the heart of intercultural analysis. In terms of training methodology there is an ongoing tension between top-down imparting of information and a more developmental approach.

Just as the language teacher may feel the need to be covert about culture, the intercultural trainer can feel pressure to be covert about learner-centred training.

The Methodology of the Intercultural Trainer

The intercultural trainer is required to make cultural difference navigable without resorting to cheap tricks and dodgy stereotypes. Simultaneously and like all trainers, the intercultural trainer is dealing with limited time and unrealistic client expectations. While it is tempting to hang training sessions on to lists of neat do's and don'ts, or broad, static generalizations, an important step for cultural trainers is to be open to testing out and challenging the received wisdom of cultural stereotypes and to allow the client to do so too. Effective intercultural training looks at the typical values and behaviours of a particular culture through the prism of all the variables such as corporate culture, regional and local culture, individual personality differences, age specific culture and educational backgrounds and ideally enables the participant to distill all these variables into some useful information and strategies which will be relevant to their own specific contexts.

One of the most important aspects in intercultural training is the participants' level of self-awareness. Any cultural interaction has more than one participant and more than one set of reactions. One of the tasks of intercultural trainers is to raise the assignee's awareness of his or her own style and how it is perceived by others. Once the assignee recognizes their own impact – that they are not culturally neutral – they are able to take responsibility for their contribution to any culturally based tension. The role of the intercultural trainer is to assist the participant to recognize their own preferences and prejudices and to understand that there is no such thing as normal, only a series of culturally determined norms. This self-awareness helps defuse the tendency to 'otherisation' criticized by Guest (2002) and the tendency to judge, blame and criticize which can be the hallmark of the culture shocked expatriate (Marx 1999).

The awareness raising dimension of cultural training can take a number of forms. One of the best known is the simulation game and its descendants, as outlined by Barnga (Thiagarajan, Sivasailam and Steinwachs 1990). This is an experiential activity where participants are put into teams each following slightly different rules. Language teachers will recognize this as a role play and information gap format. Delivered in a focused and abbreviated version this kind of activity is usually highly successful with corporate clients as long as it is not seen to take away time which could be used in giving facts and instilling information. A further successful technique is the discussion of the cultural dilemma or critical incident. Guest is scathing about this approach and asserts:

> Many of the anecdotes seem to be nothing more than formulaic manifestations of highly prejudiced deterministic paradigms. (2002:159)

However my own experience of using short scenarios and critical incidents in training sessions is that they are effective in a number of ways. First, a well-designed intercultural dilemma has ambiguity built into it and can function to shatter formulaic expectations. Secondly, participants find a narrative stimulus very memorable, and will recall an anecdote or a situation they have imagined themselves into more readily than a PowerPoint slide full of facts. Thirdly the discussion of a dilemma appeals to the problem-solving nature of the adult learner. Thus the judicious use and selection of critical incidents can support effective training in a range of ways.

Interculturalists have developed a number of different proprietary tools and systems to measure cultural awareness, or suitability for an overseas assignment. These include Culture Compass ™, The Cultural Detective ™, The Cultural Navigator™ and The Intercultural Competence Scale ™.

In my own workplace we utilize an online contrastive tool, Argonaut ™, to underpin the training by developing the client's awareness of their own cultural biases and potential impact on others. Argonaut, (copyright Power of Learning Pty Ltd and Coghill and Beery International), is a tool which enables individuals to assess their own cultural preferences through answering a series of multiple choice questions on line. The questions detect preferences in twelve different cultural dimensions. The results of this assessment are presented in the form of a wheel, showing potential gaps between the individuals' responses and the responses typical of the new culture. Each potential gap is supported by a suggested strategy and further information. Each dimension is represented along a continuum.

Used as the basis of individual coaching Argonaut is a powerful tool for developing multiple perspectives while demonstrating that there is no right or superior answer.

How Intercultural Trainers Describe Communication

To provide a more specific basis for comparison between the two disciplines of language teaching and intercultural training, I will highlight the cultural dimension of communication and how interculturalists account for and manage for differences in communication style.

The intercultural trainer's focus on communication style typically analyses the purpose, content and organization of the information and interpersonal exchanges that the expatriate is likely to participate in at work, often using the cultural dimension of directness as a comparative measure. Almost invariably these exchanges are expected to take place in English. There is little or infrequent focus on the linguistic differences between the interlocutors and the fact that the expatriate is typically speaking her/his native language while the other is speaking a second (or third or fourth) language.

There is likewise little opportunity for focus on the lexico-grammatical structure of the host language, except in terms of how it impacts on the aims of the expatriate. Expatriates might be told, for example, there are 10 different meanings for an Indonesian of the word 'Yes' and only one of them means the project is coming in on time! This information is typically linked with an exploration of group harmony versus individual aspirations and of attitudes to power and management hierarchies. The assignees thus will be taught that for an Indonesian team member the desire to save the manager's 'face' may override the need to impart unpalatable information. This approach will be contrasted with the typical Western business values of transparency and individual responsibility and the assignee will be warned that this may present an area of cultural tension. What is missing from this is further analysis of the features of the Indonesian's first language (which may not be Bahasa) or an acknowledgement that the Indonesian may have learned some Western workplace cultural habits as s/he learned the English language. The assumption is that the English spoken by local colleagues will represent a direct translation of what they would have said in their first language with no cultural shifts accompanying the language shift.

Although it is always recommended by intercultural trainers, it is very rare that there is a requirement or expectation for the typical corporate expatriate to learn and use the language of the host country in the workplace. In the majority of cases the expatriate will be communicating with colleagues who are using English as a foreign language. Where the expatriate is coming in to a senior position s/he may be dependent on more junior local colleagues to translate and interpret. Corporations and individuals rarely invest in a level of foreign language training which would assist the expatriate to use the host country language at their professional level in the workplace. (A notable exception is Toyota, where Australian engineers and foremen sent to Nagoya, Japan are required to use Japanese to communicate with colleagues on the shop floor.) There are various ways to justify this approach: expatriates are often by definition working for multinational corporations for which English is the language of the organization no matter where each branch is located. Expatriate assignments are often organized at very short notice, giving the assignee only a few weeks to prepare for their relocation. Likewise 'career' expatriates are often moved between different host countries after a one or two-year assignment and can not be realistically expected to master a new language in each destination.

Differing communication styles form one of the key areas of difference between cultures and this has been explicitly highlighted by interculturalists. From the important distinction of Hall (1976) between high and low context cultures through to the current work on cultural intelligence (Peterson 2004), communication is a dimension where cultural differences play out. Where applied linguists look at the creation of meaning through lexico-grammatical choices, discourse patterns and genres, shaped by the context of communication and the context of culture, interculturalists look at aspects such as whether information is presented directly or indirectly, the influence of hierarchy on communications and whether conflict is addressed or circumvented.

Stereotypes and Generalizations

One of the major areas of difference between intercultural trainers and language teachers revolves around the use of generalizations. Language teachers demonstrate significant tension around the usage of stereotypes and generalizations. Guest urges teachers not to fall into the trap of contrastive analysis.

> The reduction of an entire culture to a few convenient essences which then serve as interpretive pegs is predestined to misrepresent a culture by conflating it into monolithic static categories. (2002:155)

Wright voices a common view.

> First, we must work to move beyond viewing students as Russian students, Taiwanese students, etc. and approach each person as a unique individual. (2004:3)

Kumaravadivelu (2008) on the other hand is more pragmatic.
'Stereotypes reduce an unmanageable reality to a manageable label.' Having said this, however he goes on to demonstrate the limitations of stereotypes by surveying the recent literature on student stereotypes and their classroom behaviour. He concludes

> There is no empirical evidence to confirm any causal connection between the cultural beliefs and practices of students from Asia and their classroom behaviour. (2008:63)

Language teachers deal with this anxiety about stereotyping by studious attempts to broaden the diversity of the protagonists in textbooks. To the extent that TESOL professionals have developed a strong awareness of the simplicity and limitations of cultural stereotypes enshrined in unenlightened text books and the cultural imperialism embedded in some traditional approaches to language teaching. Thornbury (1999) bemoans the heterosexual stereotypes found throughout EFL textbooks. Otlowski (2003) observes that EFL textbooks still contain outmoded images of women in domestic roles while men go out to work.

ELT professionals are encouraged to focus on the immediate context of language use and language choices, and an analysis of how the relationship between the participants can determine the specific discourse between them guides learners in making their own choices. In language teaching materials development, the concept of authenticity is highly valued. Language educators believe that by analysing the features of an authentic piece of spoken or written text learners are being exposed to a real rather than an idealized or aspirational version of the target language. Parallel with the quest for authenticity there is increasing acknowledgement of global English as an international language which is not always tethered to a particular place or demographic. If two non-native speakers are using English as a mutually convenient way to communicate, who owns the discourse? Where is the authenticity?

Armed with certified authentic texts, language educators have been taught to analyse and identify the common features of particular text types and use them as signposts to make generalizations about particular genres or discourse patterns. So language teachers are in fact comfortable with linguistic stereotypes in terms of genres where they are not comfortable with cultural stereotypes.

Interculturalists are braver (or less enlightened or less politically correct) in this area. Some seek to make a positive distinction between stereotypes (bad) and generalizations (potentially useful). Stereotypes are seen as a negative uninformed response to cultural difference while generalizations can be used as signposts and a guide to accepted norms. Peterson describes it thus:

> Generalizations that come from research and from the insights of informed cultural experts and professionals allow us to paint a fairly accurate picture of how people in a given country are likely (but never guaranteed) to operate. (2004:27)
>
> Adler goes further and reminds us of the importance of the effective stereotype.
>
> We have failed to use stereotyping as a natural process and have failed to use it to our advantage. (1997:27)

The great pillars of Hofstede's and Trompenaars' research and writings still form the support structure of the interculturalists' belief system. There is a natural danger, particularly in short training courses, of a dilution of the complexity of their research into bald and static 'take-away' statements. No-one who has lived or worked with another culture can fail to recognize the inadequacy of statements such as 'Australians are more direct than Chinese people.' And yet, there is a truth in there despite the enormous overgeneralization that is so unpalatable. If you were sending an Australian employee to work in China – next week – you would prefer that s/he had this information, woefully inadequate though it is, than not.

Like any attempt at capturing explicit cultural information, the structure of Argonaut and other contrastive cultural tools could be accused of perpetuating stereotypes. However, when these tools are used in training, clients invariably understand that we are providing them with a fixed point of cultural norms as a navigational tool. The dimensions measured in cultural research are never intended to be the last word on that culture; rather they form the opening lines in a perpetual dialogue.

To be effective in an ever-changing global economy, intercultural trainers need to offer their clients a deeper view of culture; by grounding cultural theory with linguistic knowledge and by allowing their clients opportunities to process, reflect and engage in the learning. Most of all they need to engage with ambiguity; this will enable their clients also to engage with ambiguity which they will encounter in every day of an international assignment. Conversely language trainers could add value for their learners by engaging a little more directly and explicitly with culture and acknowledging cultural patterns and norms just as they illuminate and commentate on discourse patterns and lexi-co-grammatical choices for their learners.

References

Adler, N. (1997), *International Dimensions of Organizational Behavior*. Cincinnati, Ohio: South Western College Publishing.

Baker, W. (2003), Should culture be an overt component of EFL instruction outside of English speaking countries? The Thai context. *Asian EFL Journal.* http://www.asian-efl-journal.com/dec_03_sub.wb.php. (accessed 18 February 2009).

Foster, D. The Future of Cross-cultural Training: Making a Good Idea Better. www.global-excellence.com/getfile.php?g=48 (retrieved on 19 February 2009).

Guest, M. (2002), A critical 'checkbook' for culture teaching and learning. *ELTJ* 56/(2), 154–161.

Hall, E. T. (1976), *Beyond Culture*. New York: Doubleday.

Halliday, M. A. K. (1979), *Language as Social Semiotic*. Victoria. Edward Arnold.

Hofstede, G. and Hofstede, G. J. (2004), *Cultures and Organizations: Software of the Mind.* New York: McGraw-Hill U.S.A.

Hymes, D. (1972), On communicative competence in Pride, J. and Holmes, J. (eds.) *Sociolinguistics*. Harmondsworth: Penguin.

Kramsch, C. (1993), *Context and Culture in Language Teaching*. Oxford: Oxford University Press.

Kumaravadivelu, B. (2008), *Cultural Globalization and Language Education*. New Haven: Yale University Press.

Marx, Elizabeth. (1999), *Breaking Through Culture Shock*. London: Nicholas Brearley Publishing Limited.

Otlowski, M. (2003), Ethnic diversity and gender bias in EFL textbooks. *Asian EFL Journal.* www.asian-efl-journal.com/june03.otlowski.pdf. (retrieved on 20 February 2009).

Peterson, B. (2004), *Cultural Intelligence*. Yarmouth, Maine: Intercultural Press.

Pulverness, A. (1995), Cultural Studies, British Studies and EFL. *Modern English Teacher* 4 (2) April 1995, reprinted at http://www.elt.britcoun.org.pl/elt/forum/bsandefl.htm, (retrieved on 4[h] February 2009).

Thiagarajan, S. and Steinwachs, B. (1990), *Barnga: A Simulation Game on Cultural Clashes*. Yarmouth, ME: Intercultural Press.

Thornbury, S. (1999), Window-dressing vs. cross-dressing in the EFL sub-culture. *Folio* 5/2, 15–17.

Tomalin, B. and Stempleski, S. (1993), *Cultural Awareness*. Oxford: Oxford University Press.

Trompenaars, F. (1993), *Riding the Waves of Culture*. Great Britain: The Economist Books.

Weber, R. and Camerer, C. (2003), Cultural conflict and merger failure: An experimental approach. *Management Science* 49(4), 400–415.

Wright, S. (2004), Perceptions and stereotypes of ESL students. *The Internet TESL Journal,* 10(2), http://iteslj.org/ http://iteslj.org/Articles/Wright-Stereotyping.html (retrieved on 10 February 2009).

Intercultural Training Tools

http://www.argonautonline.com
http://www.countrynavigator.com/login.cfm
http://www.culturaldetective.com/
http:// http://www.imo-international.de/index_englisch.htm culture compass
The Intercultural Competency Scale http://icsprofile.org/ics/about.jsp

Chapter 10

Reconceptualizing Culture for Workplace Communication

Neil Elias

Logica (Philippines) Inc., Philippines

This chapter describes the process of the development of intercultural awareness training in a Philippines call centre. The centre was set up as a wholly owned subsidiary of an American insurance company, and provided customer service to policyholders based in the USA. These customers had previously dealt with US on-shore call centre agents, and the company was concerned that the Filipino agents would not be able to provide a call experience that was 'familiar in feel to the customer'. It was decided that training in American culture would be applied to help achieve this.

Initially, it was expected that an existing programme would be suitable for implementation, perhaps with some customization, since the US market was the major customer of commercial call centres in the Philippines. Discussions with local call centre managers and a vendor search provided several course and course outlines described as 'American Culture'. In general they were unsuitable for one of three reasons, in that they provided:

- Information about America with little relevance to the context
- Analysis of American culture with little relevance to the context
- Assumptions about American behaviour and preferences with no basis

Frameworks for Looking at Intercultural Training

In critiquing much of what is done in the name of 'intercultural training' in American call centres, I draw on a body of literature that situates culture in a sociolinguistic framework that sees language, behaviour and culture as essentially intertwined (Bakhtin 1984; Halliday 1984 and Martin 1997; Norton and Toohey 2002; Vygotsky 1986) and is constantly being negotiated in a dialogic process. In the BPO context and in call centres in particular, the ideational meaning (the field or content of what is being transacted and discussed); the tenor, i.e. interpersonal meaning (the complex relationship between the customer services representative and the customer) and the mode (the textual unfolding of the call on the phone) interact with each other to produce very specific intercultural register. These are constantly negotiated and interpreted and form the basis of success or otherwise in intercultural communication. Other intercultural communication theorists (Byram 2000 and Earley and Ang 2003) have investigated the multidimensional and communicative competency skills (also grounded in sociolinguistic theory) required for successful intercultural interaction and training. All are concerned with the 'situatedness' of speech meaning the functional use of language in specific sociocultural contexts as a way into understanding how language and culture, in their symbiotic relationship develops. In understanding and accepting these frameworks, we then need to view intercultural training in the call centre environment as something that is much more that sets of facts and assumptions about the target language and its speakers.

> Language learning engages the identities of learners because language itself is not only a linguistic system of signs and symbols; it is also a complex social practice in which the value and meaning ascribed to an utterance are determined in part by the value and meaning ascribed to the person who speaks it. . . . Thus, language learners are not only learning a linguistic system; they are learning a set of sociocultural practices, often best understood in the context of wider relations of power. (Norton and Toohey 2002:115)

How then do current examples of intercultural training in call centres reflect this complexity?

The Range of Existing Courses

The intercultural courses under scrutiny in this article relied solely upon information. They seemed to assume that if enough facts were crammed into a course they would adequately equip an agent to use them effectively on a call. Typical is a course from a Philippines call centre servicing several customers in different industry segments in the USA. The course consisted of an introduction followed by sections on Dress, Sports and Recreation, and Celebration Holidays. It was delivered using Powerpoint slides with a paper handout, and there was no assessment of knowledge acquisition. Figure 1 shows the introduction section.

It is difficult to imagine what use any of this would be to a call centre agent. Points 4 and 5 seem to contradict each other, while point 6b may be true but it is doubtful whether anyone alive now would either know or care. There is no context in which it can be applied.

CULTURAL UNDERSTANDING – AN INTRODUCTION

1. The American people express their culture through traditions:

   a. In food, clothing, recreation, ceremonies
   b. Through the education system and institutions of learning, including museums and libraries
   c. Through the arts, encompassing the visual, literary, and performing arts.

2. American culture is rich, complex, and unique. It is made up of contributions from European, African, Asian, and North American cultures.
3. Americans are strongly committed to Democracy. They believe that majority should prevail and there should be equality in law and institutions.
4. Its popular and democratically inclusive features, such as blockbuster movies, TV comedies, sports stars, and fast food, more often define American culture than by its more cultivated aspects performed in theaters, published in books, or viewed in museums and galleries.
5. Americans are avid readers of books and magazines, attending museums, operas, and ballets. They listen to country, classical, jazz, folk, classic rock-and-roll, and new wave music.

FORCES THAT SHAPED THE AMERICAN CULTURE

6. Imported Traditions
   a. In early history, the U.S. was considered culturally provincial and its art second-rate, especially in painting and literature. Britain served as the touchstone of culture and quality because of its role in America's history and the links of language and political institutions.
   b. Throughout the 19th century, Americans read and imitated British poetry and novels such as those written by Sir Walter Scott and Charles Dickens.

FIGURE 1   Call Centre Course 'American Culture'

The United States became the world's first modern democracy after its break with Great Britain in 1776 and adoption of a constitution (1798). During the 19th century, many new states were added to the original 13 as the nation expanded across the North America continent and acquainted a number of overseas possessions. The two most traumatic experiences in the nation's history were the Civil War (1861–65) and the Great Depression of the 1930s. Buoyed by victories in the World War I and II and the end of the Cold War in 1991, the US remains the world's most powerful nation-state. The economy is marked by steady growth, low unemployment and inflation and rapid advances in technology.

FIGURE 2   Call Centre Course: 'American Culture'

Figure 2 shows an extract from another international call centre course. This course was developed in India and used in Philippines when the company set up operations.

Again, the relevance to the call situation is unclear. Like the previous example, this course was delivered using Powerpoint and Word document hand-outs.

Apart from lacking a pedagogical framework for selecting the content, neither of these in-house developed courses had a curriculum or purpose document, and neither provided for assessment, a problem common to language communications programmes also (see Lockwood this volume).

While these courses may reflect the inexperience of trainer developers, of more concern was the course developed for the Philippines tertiary vocational training agency TESDA (Technical Education and Skills Development Agency, Philippines Department of Education). This course was developed in conjunction with the Business Processing Association of the Philippines (BPAP), the Philippines industry body, as a way to raise the skill levels of potential call centre agents. It was approved for use in colleges. The curriculum covered 356 hours with 12 hours on American Culture. The Culture segment curriculum contained the following:

- Contents cover

    o Cultural variables and how it affects communication. E.g. time zones, holidays and cities
    o Basic geography – map reading and state abbreviations
    o Accent improvement

- Assessment includes
    o Geographic variables identified and acted upon
        ▪ Identify cultural variables and values of targeted customer
        ▪ Geographic variables identified and acted upon

                                                              TESDA (2005:74)

Describing time zones and cities as cultural variables is a strange use of the term, and map reading and accent improvement are equally questionable in cultural awareness modules. The assessment tasks of identifying cultural variables and values consisted of a questionnaire based upon Hofstede's (1980) cultural values study. This framework is evaluated later in this article.

These courses and course approaches all share a lack of rigour or rationale for what they do. A particularly striking example of this is the outline from an American intercultural training company, Tucker International. Tucker International, in what they call *English Language and American Culture Program for Indian Call Centers*, describe their programme as follows:

Bangalore, India. Call Center agents in India are generally highly motivated and energetic in servicing their American customers. However, because English is a second language for them and they know little about America or Americans, they often leave their customers frustrated and unsatisfied. Unable to connect and relate, agents come across as aloof and unconcerned.

There have been a variety of language and culture training programs offered in India, both general programs for people looking to become call center agents and programs offered by American companies for new hire agents. However, these programs have not proven to be effective in training Indians to communicate clearly and effectively with their American customers.

This situation is about to change dramatically. **Tucker International** has launched a new program that has a remarkable effect on Indians. By using a 'surgical' approach to correcting the unique Indian difficulties in English pronunciation, speed, tone and style, graduates of Tucker's program sound quite different than when they started. Also, they are better able to relate to their American callers because Tucker's program teaches Indian Call Center Agents how to build rapport 'American Style.'

The Program includes video segments, songs, games and a great deal of practice to build individual skills. It is certain to increase satisfaction of American customers while also helping to reduce the high turnover rate at Indian Call Centers (40% to 60% per year). Companies that offer Tucker's training will attract the best Indian employees who are likely to 'succeed and stay.' (Tucker: 2006)

The situation where culture training is a random selection of facts and assumptions was humorously summed up by India's Consul General in San Francisco

In these schools, [training schools for those who wanted jobs in call centers] they teach you more about America than most Americans know about themselves. They teach you about baseball scores, beach ball escapades in the latest shows on American television and the critical differences between McDonalds and Burger King. Why? Don't ask me.

Not satisfied with all this they also run courses on how to take abuse and not to get into trauma while taking a 800 call. The assumption is that the average American caller whose call is being processed in India is one of the following: a chatty chap who wishes to discuss the weather, baseball scores, or politics before inquiring about flight schedules, or is a masochistic pervert who will taunt or abuse the person at the other end of the telephone line or an intellectual hell-bent on establishing your ethnic identity. (Prakash: 2005)

So, the problems with this information-driven type of cultural course are, in summary:

- Lack of any rigour in defining what culture training is, how it is assessable and what is its purpose;
- Lack of focus on communication and the relevance of the information, and little apparent needs analysis; and
- The assumption that culture is a fixed set of learnings which, when mastered, give cultural understanding

The second type of course which our review encountered attempted to describe the values of Americans in order to show how to understand them. The courses found: one in India and one in Philippines, were developed independently by American trainers with a master's degree in cross-cultural studies, and both were based on Hofstede's (1980) framework of work-related cultural values. Briefly, Hofstede's values were derived from an analysis of more than 100,000 IBM global staff in 40 countries in the late 1960s and early 1970s. Hofstede described the culture of each country along four continuums: power distance: the degree to which the less powerful members of society support and expect differences in the levels of power; individualism to collectivism: the extent to which people are expected to put themselves first or alternatively act mainly as a member of the group; masculinity to femininity: masculine values are those which favour competitiveness, assertiveness, ambition and the accumulation of wealth while feminine values are those of relationships and quality of life; and uncertainty avoidance: the extent to which a society attempts to avoid anxiety by minimizing uncertainty. He then scored each of these continuums for 40 countries as a measure of national work-related values.

Hofstede says that 'culture is learned, not inherited' (1991:4), and is shared with people 'within the same social environment, which is where it was learned' (1991:5). He proposed that societies have a set of social norms which allow culture patterns to be maintained across generations (1991:22). Culture, then, is a longlasting and stable system of values.

The courses examined took Hofstede's findings to show that Americans were individualistic, masculine and tend towards equality in power, while Asian countries are at the opposite end of the continuum. Again, there is the tacit assumption that this information is accurate today, and it will impact the behaviour of the call centre agent. Both of these are debatable.

Hofstede's four dimensions of cultural work values now constitute 'a virtually uncontested paradigm' (Holden 2002:34), in which 'the questions and the dimensions are used as taken-for-granted assumptions' (Sondergaard 1994:448). While it is beyond the scope of this chapter to analyse Hofstede's work, it is worth addressing three issues which raise questions about the existence and relevance of the national culture paradigm.

First, the assumption that culture is stable and relatively unaffected by events must be questionable. As Holden (2002) says:

> It seems hard to imagine that the work values of 1980 – or rather the late 1970s when the data were gathered – have not undergone significant shifts owing both to new pressures on individuals 'to deliver' and new possibilities for self development. (Holden 2002:35)

This is obviously a critical question. Hofstede does not discuss how cultures may be impacted by events or social changes, although he does note that culture is supported by, among other things, institutions. If institutions change, as, say, the decline of the state sector and 'iron rice bowl' in China, then presumably the cultural values will change. Since Hofstede first published there have been many changes in society with major global effects. The impact of the internet, in both communication and information dissemination, has changed the pace of life for hundreds of millions of people. The rise of China as an economic power and its development of its own form of capitalism has surely impacted work values there. The impact of feminism and increase in gender equality – there would have been relatively few female respondents in Hofstede's survey of IBM sales staff 40 years ago, and, perhaps most crucially, the rise of globalized business and off-shoring of work, all must impact the ways in which people respond to the world.

Secondly, Hofstede notes that any person has many layers of culture including national, regional or ethnic, gender, generational, social, organizational, and says 'additions to this list are easy to make' (1991: 10). While he states that national cultures are characterized by values and organizational by 'shared perceptions of daily practices' (1991: 183) it is unclear, at least to this author, why that should be the case and why, even if it is, it places a national culture as the major influence on values and lessens the impact of the differing levels. Furthermore, if additions are easy to make, then potentially each individual has a unique cultural mix, and potentially the impact of purely national culture on behaviour may be very small. A Japanese computer game designer may well have more in common with an American computer game designer than with a Japanese salaryman, and the use of cultural mapping at a national level must be unreliable.

Finally, the use of this in a call centre context is surely inappropriate. As Hofstede himself wrote, to apply national values to the level of the individual is an 'ecological fallacy' (1980:29), shifting from one level – culture – to another – individual. Since all call centre interactions are individual interactions, the use of a statistical cultural norm in planning effective interaction is misapplied.

The third category of courses found were based upon assumptions about how Americans expect to be treated. These tended to be prescriptive, and measured by compliance to a scorecard. Scorecards are the way in which many customers attempt to measure the quality of calls, and are especially used by customers with outsourced call centres. A service level score based upon the elements of a scorecard is often used to determine whether financial penalties or bonuses should be applied to a call centre providing service. There is little published research on the effectiveness of scorecards in offshore locations (Lockwood: 2008; Lockwood, Forey and Elias 2009), but they typically are prescriptive, with marks being added or subtracted for compliance with scorecard items. These scorecards are sometimes constructed by customers with no appreciation of how non-native speakers apply them, and sometimes by local Quality staff with assumed ideas of how Americans expect to be treated. Typical items found included:

- Never use the word 'sorry'
- Always use the caller's first name at least three times
- Always end the call by asking 'is there anything else I can help you with?'

Given the potential financial loss for non-compliance, centres drilled agents with these rules. They have no relevance to effective communication, and often impede it, such as when a caller called 'John' replied testily, 'My name is Mr Jones', and the agent responded, 'Right. John Jones', so that he could meet the score of three uses of the first name.

This scorecard-led training ignores the context of the interplay between customer and agent, and in a customer service context in which the customer can ask a range of questions and cover a number of concerns, provided no real benefit.

Further, if the interplay of cultures is complex, and the incidences of convergence and divergence are contingent upon the situation, the importance of cultural sensitivity and openness to new situations rather than rules, tips and techniques, becomes the key to success. The focus moves from analysing what the cultures *are* to working with them as they occur. As Holden (2002) notes

> The essentialist concept of culture . . . does not seem to resonate with firms' and managers' experience of cultural complexity in the business environment which is becoming globalized: globalized not only through the emergence of a consumer culture with converging tastes and demands, but through worldwide collaboration and competition supported by the borderless communication technologies. (Holden 2002:27)

In short: an ability to interact with culture in action rather than culture as a set of knowledge is the requirement for business communication.

Developing the Intercultural Awareness Course for a Philippine Call Centre

The initial survey of available courses described above was carried out by a team with representatives from management, training and quality assessment, and the whole team agreed that the main problem was that nothing succeeded in applying the learning to the call centre situation. The team therefore decided to develop the training in-house, and to start by looking at the aims of a cross-cultural course; something generally lacking in the examples found. A workshop decided that a course needs to cover three areas:

- Knowledge – information about how cultures operate generally and specific information about the country that is relevant to managing a call with someone from that country
- Skills – ability to manage an interaction with that country using authentic transactions and calls
- Exposure – to different accents and dialects to ensure that callers can be understood

This is similar to what Earley and Ang (2003) term 'cultural intelligence': a concept with three elements: cognitive training, which means having the relevant information, having knowledge about a culture and how to process it; motivation, meaning interest and capability to deal with new cultures; and capability, the skills to use the first two. The team also found Byram's (2000) 'intercultural competence' a useful expansion of this concept. Byram defined five elements of competence:

- Attitudes: curiosity and openness, readiness to suspend disbelief about other cultures and belief about one's own.
- Knowledge: of social groups and their products and practices in one's own and in one's interlocutor's country, and of the general processes of societal and individual interaction.
- Skills of interpreting and relating: ability to interpret a document or event from another culture, to explain it and relate it to documents from one's own.
- Skills of discovery and interaction: ability to acquire new knowledge of a culture and cultural practices and the ability to operate knowledge, attitudes and skills under the constraints of real-time communication and interaction.
- Critical cultural awareness/political education: an ability to evaluate critically and on the basis of explicit criteria perspectives, practices and products in one's own and other cultures and countries. (Byram 2000:2)

Both of these stress the need for openness and willingness to engage as well as knowledge and skill in working within another culture: in other words, the attitude towards intercultural transactions is as important as the skill or knowledge.

This seemed to provide a more open framework to teach and assess intercultural ability in the call centre, and also identified the importance of the need for capability rather than knowledge in a real-time interaction. Cultural understanding exists in the interaction and is negotiated in that interaction.

1. **Appropriate asking and responding to questions, and avoidance of 'dead air'** This refers to appropriate use of the language, including good vocabulary knowledge and accuracy, and overall fluency of the call

2. **Familiarity in feel for the customer** This involves language used appropriately depending on contextual factors such as the status and accent of callers, idiomatic language used, to build customer rapport

3. **Responding to the type of call** The ability of the CSS to understand the call context and structure and to provide coherent, well-focused replies for claims, surrenders, etc.

4. **Keeping the call pleasant for the customer** The ability of the CSS to keep the call on track and repair misunderstandings when they occur

5. **Knowledge to provide first time completion** This involves the subject domain knowledge including insurance in general as well as specific policy and product detail. It also requires system knowledge.

FIGURE 3   Elaborated characteristics of a successful call

Cultural training must therefore be focused on the actual transactions targeted in the training.

From this, the group, in conjunction with the US-based customer service managers, developed a chart of what customers want in a successful service call. This is shown in Figure 3.

They also produced a 'context sheet' which was used to work with employee focus groups to identify gaps in being able to achieve them. The 'context' sheet was as follows:

How do we interact with American customers?
Objective is calls which are:

- Pleasant for the customer
- Efficient
- Familiar in feel for the customer

The gaps the US-based Customer Service managers see in Filipino agents are:

- Inability to fill 'dead air'
- Inability to ask/respond to questions quickly
- Inability to deal effectively with angry or demanding customers.

This was used as a thought starter for focus groups of agents and trainers to look at how to make Filipino agents more effective dealing with Americans. The focus groups addressed why Filipinos may have problems identified by the Americans either because of inexperience or lack of skills. On the experience front, the findings included:

- Call Centres in Philippines are different from USA. Generally people in Philippines are more accepting of things not being done, and people do not confront problems. Expectations of the customer are low. When dealing with US callers, often the perception is that they are angry, that they 'know their rights'.

- Anger is very much avoided in Philippines. If someone gets angry, the normal response is to ignore them – it is more polite than to confront. Filipinos may not be comfortable dealing with perceived 'angry' callers – they may be silent or uncommunicative.

On the issue of skills, and using authentic calls analysis, the top four specific skills gaps identified were:

- Handling irate callers (response is to put them on hold or mute the phone, or feeling unable to respond)
- Inability to get to the purpose of the call
- Inability to effectively close the call – 'I tend to over-explain.'
- Difficulty in organizing information in the way the customer wanted

As noted, these gaps were identified using real call experience. An example of the first skill gap, lack of response, is in the following call segment:

Customer (very frustrated and towards the end of the call): 'I'm waiting for an underwriter to call me back and it's going to be almost a month because nobody has called me. I've been corresponding with Andrea Carlton and I've said to her . . . this is absolutely . . . you're going to be the 12th person that I've talked to, two from Milwaukee, I cannot tell you how many from Texas, I cannot tell you how many from Illinois and this is absolutely pathetic. I expect a call back within a week's period of time and all this mess cleared up. And I don't care who you tell but I appreciate that this will be done within a week because I've been waiting since November 12th and nobody is doing their homework'.

Agent: 'Yes ma'am'. (Silence)

An example of difficulty in organizing information effectively is in this segment:

Customer: 'How does XYZ policy work . . . you know my husband did all this kind of thing'.

Agent: 'Even if you've been a member for some time, it depends on how much you're sending in. It depends if you've been making payments. If you've missed out on payments . . . uh . . . a a portion of that will be deducted from your cash value . . . do you know exactly how much your cash value is Maam'?

Customer: 'Sorry, can you go through that again . . . how does it work? I mean tell me why my husband would buy this kind of policy in the first place . . .'

Agent: (Silence)

Using these authentic calls enabled the team to see culture within the transaction in a very relevant situation.

These analyses were used to build a training programme structured on the purpose, content and audience and type of transaction, for the range of call types serviced, and give the agent exposure to recognize different categories within these call types. For instance, the purpose may vary from purely informational ('how much is a premium?') to more relational, as in responding to a death claim notification. The transactions included death claims, premium receipt enquiries, policy cancellations and other insurance matters. This analysis enabled the team to focus on the potential cultural differences which could impact the specific interactions, such as:

- What does it mean for an American to be bereaved? Is it different from Filipino?
- What is the attitude to money – specifically to delayed payments, IRS returns, etc.
- What are 'normal' customer reactions or expectations in a service call?

The course was piloted with a cohort of agents, and their quality scores (an internal measure) and customer satisfaction scores (an external measure) were compared with a control group over a 3-month period. The scores showed little difference in quality measures but a 10% improvement in customer scores for the pilot cohort. The course was then rolled out in the centre.

Conclusion

The intercultural course development identified four key needs for course effectiveness:

- The need to identify what is the purpose of the training in specific and assessable terms. 'Culture' must be related to the specific situation (Halliday 1985), in call centres and this typically is the voice interaction.
- need to find out where the gaps are and train into those rather than provide general information
- need to constantly review and refine as more authentic data is available
- need for cultural training to be measured against the specific outcomes

It also identified a need to reconceptualize 'culture' from 'an all purpose concept which has as many meanings as the number of people who use it' (Holzmuller 1997) towards a 'cultural intelligence'-based concept. A move away from the anthropological and essentialist approach to culture is needed to make effective intercultural communication training.

References

Bakhtin, M. M. (1981), *The Dialogic Imagination: Four Essays* (C. Emerson and M. Holquist, trans). Austin, TX: University of Texas Press.

Byram, M. (2000), 'Assessing intercultural competence in language teaching', *Sprogforum* 18 (6), 8–13.

Earley, P. C. and Ang, S. (2003), *Cultural Intelligence: Individual Interactions across Borders*. Stanford: Stanford University Press.

Halliday, M. A. K (1984), 'Language as code and language as behaviour: A systemic – functional interpretation of the nature and ontogenesis of dialogue'. In Fawcett, R., Halliday, M. A. K., Lamb, S. M. and Makkai, A. (eds.) *The Semiotics of Language and Culture*. Vol 1: *Language as Social Semiotic*. London: Pinter, 3–35.

Hofstede, G. (1980), *Culture's Consequences: International Differences in Work-related Values*. Newbury Park, CA: Sage.

Hofstede, G. (1991), *Cultures and Organizations: Software of the Mind*. London: McGraw-Hill.

Holden, N. J. (2002), *Cross-cultural Management: A Knowledge Management Approach*. Great Britain: Prentice Hall.

Holzmuller, H. (1997), 'Kulturestandards', translated in Holden (2002).

Martin, J. (1992), *English Text: System and Structure*. Amsterdam: Benjamins.

Lockwood, J. (2008), What does the Business Processing Outsourcing (BPO) industry want from English language assessment? *Prospect* 23(2).

Lockwood, J., Forey, G. and Elias, N. (2009). In Belcher, D. (ed.) *English for Specific Purposes in Theory and Practice*. Ann Arbor: University of Michigan Press.

Norton, B. and Toohey, K. (2002), Identity and Language Learning. In Kaplan, R. (ed.) *The Oxford Handbook of Applied Linguistics*. Oxford: Oxford University Press, 115–123.

Prakash, B. S. (2005), *Reversing the Call Culture*, downloaded 16 May 2009: 19:50 http://www.rediff.com/news/2005/jul/13guest.htm

Sondergaard, M. (1994), Research note: Hofstede's consequences: A study of reviews, citations and replications, *Organisation Studies* 15(3), 447–456.

Sorge, A. (1983), A review of culture's consequences: International differences in workplace values', *Administrative Science Quarterly*, December, 625–629.

TESDA (2006), *Course Design of Contact Center Services National Curriculum* 11. TESDA issue to colleges 2006.

Tucker International (2009), *English Language and American Culture Program for Indian Call Centers*, downloaded 16 May 2009: 19:42 http://www.tuckerintl.com/callcntr_prog/indian_callcntr.html

Vygotsky, L. S. (1986), *Thought and Language*. Cambridge, MA: MIT Press.

Chapter 11

India Rising: The Need for Two Way Training

Barry Tomalin
International House, London, UK

Based on my work auditing language usage, culture and empathy in Indian call centres and interviews with call centre personnel and with the Business Process Outsourcing Industry in the UK, this chapter explains some of the key problems Indian call centre agents face in working with British customers and clients and how to overcome them. It also suggests how British clients and customers need to adapt their perspective on how best to work with Indian suppliers and makes recommendations for improving training.

> When old words die out on the tongue,
> New melodies break forth from the heart;
> And where old tracks are lost,
> A new country is revealed with its wonders.
> (Rabindranath Tagore)

For some years now more and more of us have been living in a brave new country and the new melodies that go with it are globalization and outsourcing. According to Thomas Friedman (2005) in his book *The World is Flat* , globalization effectively means that if anything can be produced or carried out more cheaply anywhere else in the world, it will be and the means of achieving this process is outsourcing via telecommunications and the Internet and, for the time being at least, the English language.

Apart from cost-cutting, part of the rationale for outsourcing is commonality of language. The aim of British, US and Australian firms outsourcing both back office and voice work to countries like India is that they have a well-educated graduate workforce which speaks English. The first two are certainly true. It is the third one, the use of the English language, that poses problems.

According to David Crystal (2006) in 'The English Language', India's 1.2 billion population contains an estimated three hundred million English speakers but the variety of English that has developed on the Indian subcontinent is significantly different from the English used by the majority of speakers in the British Isles.

In his work on varieties of English, the Indian linguist Braj Kachru (1992) has identified circles of English usage. Originally identifying three concentric circles of a native speaker core, an English as a second language-speaking inner circle and an English as a foreign language-speaking outer circle, he later rationalized it as two circles, the inner native speaker core and the outer second and foreign language-speaking circle.

In looking at the use of English by Indians we find that there are perhaps three levels of usage. The first, used by Indians who are highly educated and who have lived and worked internationally, is native speaker level.

The second, used by Indians who are part of the diaspora, living and working abroad, can vary between native speaker level and fluent user. These are sometimes referred to as NRIs (Non-resident Indians).

The third level, used by Indians using English uniquely in the subcontinent, is highly influenced by India's national languages. It is call centre representatives at this third level who form the majority of call centre personnel and who experience the greatest difficulty in communicating with the UK general public.

In summary, the majority of Indian call centre representatives speak a variety of English that is still localized to the Indian subcontinent, although a number of words and expressions have increasingly filtered into other varieties of English both as a result of the Raj (The British Empire) and the non-resident Indian diaspora. Some of India's English-Hindi words have been captured in Baljinder Mahal's entertaining book, *The Queen's Hinglish*.

In working with major call centres in India between 2004 and 2008 I discovered that over 80% of call centre employees had done all their studies within India and had never travelled abroad. This is not particularly surprising and would be the same for the population of any large land mass, such as the USA, Russia or China. **What has changed, however, is that for the first time since Britain left its former Indian colony, ordinary Indians are talking to ordinary British people and they are doing so not face-to-face but by telephone and email and they have only just realised they don't understand each other, linguistically or culturally.**

The problem is that UK customers expect no difference between the way they talk and the way they would expect an Indian in their community to talk. Therefore, they experience a degree of shock when they fail to understand a call centre representative and tend to fall back on condescending assumptions about the call centre representative's level of education and competence.

Indian call centre representatives, on the other hand, tend to assume that their use of English is more or less the same as that of their UK customers, barring their accent and that their accent neutralization course during their induction training as new hires will overcome any discrepancies.

The communication gap is complicated by the inherent challenges of telephone communication. The call centre representative has to deal with a wide variety of customers of differing backgrounds, cultural experience and language and has to do so without the aids of body language, lip movement or background environment. Teachers of languages agree that no task is more challenging than talking to a stranger on the telephone in a foreign language. Devoid of the face-to-face aids to meaning, such as lip movements, facial expressions and gesture, understanding can be much more difficult. In addition, the call centre telephone process itself adds complications, such as the quality of the telephone line, the time the customer has been held in a queue and the often sensitive topics that are being handled. From our observations the key tensions come from a variety of misunderstandings, some of which are linguistic and some of which are to do with socio-cultural and psychological factors.

Linguistic Factors

Accent

Indian call centre representatives complain that the most difficult British accents to understand on the phone are Northern Irish, Glaswegian, Scouse (Liverpool), Geordie (Newcastle) and Brummie (Birmingham). Obviously, no-one is going to teach people from these areas to neutralize their accents, although it happens naturally through school, work or travel. However, a lot of work is done in call centre induction training on accent neutralization. It is common to sit in a training room listening to twenty inductees pronouncing names by rote. It seems that the problem of accent itself is not so big as the confusion caused by different pronunciation of particular sounds, such a 'v' or 'b'. Amusing examples, such as 'Jolly pine' (fine) or 'Bestern society' (Western) are nevertheless confusing for British customers. No Indian representative can be expected to pronounce every UK place or personal name correctly. The fact that on the whole they do so is a testimony both to their intelligence and to their training. British customers have no idea how to pronounce, 'Vizag', 'Hyderabad' or 'Chennai' or even 'Mumbai', let alone personal names, such as Gopilal.

The trick is, therefore, to focus less on individual names and more on strategies for recognizing unfamiliar names and for finding out correct pronunciation. The right strategy in training is to focus on teaching expressions such as 'Sorry, how do you spell that?' and 'what would you like me to call you?'. Gradually, through practice, representatives become familiar with the most common names they need to know and it is no longer a problem but representatives could be forgiven for not recognizing the Yorkshire town of Hawick when they hear over the phone, its pronunciation 'Hoik'!

Stress

On the phone, word and sentence stress is a major threat to successful understanding, even more than accent. In monitoring phone conversations, it is probably the leading factor causing customer incomprehension. Putting the stress on an unfamiliar syllable is confusing to the customer and destabilizes the positive relationship the call centre representative is trying to create on the phone. The fact that both the customer and representative think they are speaking correctly only makes the situation worse. Our examples suggest that typical problems that arise are these.

Customer: How much is the ticket?
Representative: FOURteen pounds.
Customer: FORTy pounds! That's too expensive.

The representative needed to stress the second syllable in fourteen to make a clear distinction between the two amounts.

Customer: I've received no reply to my insurance claim.
Representative: I'm sorry, I have no reCORD of your claim.

The representative needed to stress the first syllable, not the second. Although the meaning wasn't impaired in this case, the message was lost as the customer was distracted by the wrong stress. In the following exchange, the representative fell into both the stress trap and the formality trap.

Customer: I need to report my phone isn't working.
Representative: Do you have an alterNATive instrument?

The representative needed to stress alTERnative but it would have been better to simply say, 'have you got another phone?'

Even more than the 'accent neutralization' programmes beloved of call centre induction courses, understanding the stress patterns of international English is even more important. However, sitting in on training programmes you hear words and sentences being practised that have nothing to do with what is actually said on the phone. There is a need for a database of wrong utterances used in phone conversations, which can form the basis of training.

Part of the problem faced by British customers is that English is a stressed timed language whereas many of India's languages mainly put equal stress on each syllable. The result is that stress is often misplaced and the hearer often feels put under pressure by the apparent speed of delivery.

The conclusion is therefore that the teaching of correct international English stress patterns is crucial to successful communication between call centre representatives and British customers.

Vocabulary –Too Many Words

Another factor which creates pressure on the phone is Indian use of vocabulary and grammar. Since the job of a language and cultural trainer is to raise performance levels of Indian call centres to the level of the UK equivalents, it is instructive to compare the way in which a typical UK and Indian representative deals with the same problem. The situation is banking and the customer needs to check his credit balance. Notice how the UK and Indian representatives approach the ID check.

UK	INDIA
CALLER:	CALLER:
I need to check my credit balance, please.	I need to check my credit balance, please.
REPRESENTATIVE:	REPRESENTATIVE:
Sure. Just a couple of quick questions. Could you give me your mother's maiden name?	Thank you, Mr Smith. I will be absolutely happy to help you with that. Could I first of all ask you a couple of quick questions just to verify your account?
CALLER:	CALLER:
Jones.	OK.
REPRESENTATIVE:	REPRESENTATIVE:
Fine. And the name of your first pet?	Thank you. First of all would you be kind enough just to tell me your mother's maiden name?
CALLER:	
Woody.	CALLER:
REPRESENTATIVE:	Jones.
Fine. I'll just check your balance. Your current balance is £X and the credit available is £Y. Anything else I can help you with?	REPRESENTATIVE:
	Thank you, Mr Smith. That is absolutely correct. And could I also ask you the name of your first pet?
CALLER:	CALLER:
No. Thanks very much.	Woody.
REPRESENTATIVE:	REPRESENTATIVE:
Pleasure. Bye.	That is absolutely correct, Mr Smith. Thank you for your patience. Now I will just go into your account and check the amount of credit that is available to you. Please be online while I do so.
CALLER HANGS UP.	

On the face of it the Indian representative is doing everything right, checking ID, being polite and courteous, keeping the customer aware of what he/she is happening. The problem is that it seems to be taking so long.

Comparing the Indian and the UK representative's delivery three differences jump out:

1. The UK representative uses 'half sentences' for the routine exchanges to check ID. This both emphasizes that the exchange is routine and gets it out of the way quickly and efficiently. The Indian representative uses long indirect questions, which prolong the exchange. Done out of politeness, it can actually be counterproductive as it draws out the exchange beyond what is necessary.
2. The UK representative doesn't need to encourage or comment on the quality of the caller's responses. The Indian representative does.
3. The UK representative explains what will happen in one sentence, 'Fine. I'll just check your balance.' The Indian representative needs three.

The effect of this is less efficient and slower call handling and can lead to impatience and irritation on the part of the customer. What is happening here is that partly as a result of the representative's wish to be polite and the introduction of elements of Indian English grammatical forms into the conversation, the transaction is extended with no increase in the quality of information exchanged. If you then lengthen the conversation and introduce other elements of Indian English, such as the use of extraneous adverbs and adjectives, as in 'May I even know your good name?' you have a situation where communication is impeded rather than enhanced. Once again the effect on the UK customer is often to question the professionalism of the Indian representative, maybe an understandable reaction by the British customer but usually wrong.

Indianisms

Apart from the 'wordiness' of Indian English, we need to recognize that Indian English and British English are quite separate in some respects. 'Indianisms', such as 'prepone' (bring forward), 'No issues' (No problems) and 'I will do the needful' (I'll do what is needed) cause amusement rather than bafflement on the part of British customers, whereas the British use of slang, idioms and jokes over the phone causes genuine confusion among call centre representatives.

Another feature that can cause problems is the use of call centre jargon in conversations with customers. I noticed a number of examples of 'call centre English' creeping into conversations, such as 'I will enter a dispute on your file' (enter a query) or 'I will do a warm transfer' (I will transfer you direct). These are specialist uses of English only used within the call centre environment and should not seep into usage with the customer, who may not understand them.

Pitch and Intonation

Pitch describes the height or depth of the voice. According to the person the voice can be pleasantly modulated or it can be high pitched and grating or low pitched, deep and hard to understand. Many UK customers find high pitched delivery grating on the ear. They often find very low voices difficult to understand. Teaching call centre representatives to modulate the pitch of their speech is an important part of induction training. The other factor that can cause irritation is the 'sing song' intonation perceived by many British customers, particularly on the part of female representatives. One of the key features in training therefore is to teach a more relaxed speed and pacing and also to help the more 'emotionally sounding' representatives to adopt a slightly flatter intonation, without losing the lively and welcoming quality of their voices.

It is a fact that some of the most successful representatives I listened to have a flat, matter-of-fact, almost laconic style of delivery which could be seen as betraying lack of interest. In fact, it comes across as professionalism, which is an attractive quality to British customers. We were also advised that such speakers often achieved the highest sales results in the team.

Speed and Pacing

Pacing determines where the speaker pauses in the sense group and between sense groups and therefore the perceived speed of delivery. Our observations of calls, especially where sales calls were concerned, affected both comprehension and willingness to listen. Where a call centre representative was delivering a sales pitch, for example offering the financial benefits to the customer of a new credit card, the speed of delivery appeared to come at the listener like an express train, making it almost impossible to take in the relevant information and make a judgment about the value of what was on offer. The result is that British customers sometimes complained of 'machine gun' delivery.

In discussing the speed of delivery in English with Indian linguists, this is due to interference from Indian national languages which are often spoken faster than British English and also to the fact that Indian national languages carry equal stress on words. Therefore the British listener is looking for stress that is not there and experiences difficulty in identifying the most important information in the communication.

Culture and Empathy Factors

For two countries with a long history together, young Indians know relatively little about modern Britain and young Britons know even less about modern India. Our surveys showed that Indian call centre representatives felt they knew more about the USA, largely because of TV soaps, such as 'Friends'. 'East Enders', sometimes cited as the British accent and cultural training vehicle of choice, according to British media, was either unknown or locked in a cupboard out of sight. Unsurprisingly, the best-known British TV series was the spoof on British and Indian life, 'Goodness Gracious Me' and 'the Kumars at Number 42' , featuring the Indian comedian Sanjeev Bhaskar and his wife Meera Syal. Equally unsurprisingly, the popularists have turned their attention to the call centre industry with a comedy series, entitled, 'Mumbai Calling'.

Surprisingly, our data showed fewer cultural errors than I had expected. This may be partly due to the nature of the calls themselves (routine financial and data enquiries) and partly to the knowledge and expertise of the call centres representatives. However, there are some real howlers and call centre representatives themselves recall these with glee. One is the customer who rang a call centre in Delhi to cancel her registration for an event because her partner had 'passed away unexpectedly'. 'Oh' replied the representative brightly. 'Would you like to nominate somebody else?' Another concerns the British customer who allegedly rang a white goods call centre in Mumbai to complain, 'My dishwasher isn't working', only to receive the reply, 'Well, why don't you fire him?' Apart from the fact that in Indian English 'fire' is often used to mean 'reprimand' rather than 'sack' the cultural assumption that the caller is referring to a man rather than a machine is indicative of the cultural misunderstandings that can occur.

I have heard call centre representatives visibly floundering as they struggle to identify the cultural reference and provide the right solution. One example was this exchange.

CALLER: I'm in St Helier and I'm travelling to the mainland next week and I want to know if I can use my card.'
REPRESENTATIVE: And where will you be travelling to?
CALLER: The mainland.
REPRESENTATIVE: And where will you be travelling from?

The representative clearly did not understand that St Helier is the capital of Jersey in the Channel Islands, which is an offshore dependency of Britain and that therefore the mainland in question was England.

However, a simple question resolved the conundrum. 'Where will you be landing?, asked the representative. 'Heathrow', was the answer. So the mainland referred to was England. Problem solved through intelligent strategic questioning by the representative.

Another example concerned the now beached cruise liner, the Queen Elizabeth 11 (QE2) that used to carry passengers between Southampton in the UK and New York in the USA. Here is the conversation.

CALLER: I'll be travelling on the QE2 and I want to know if I can use my card.

REPRESENTATIVE: Yes, Madam and where will you be travelling from?
CALLER: Southampton.
REPRESENTATIVE: Yes, you can use your card in England.
CALLER: Yes, I know that but I'm travelling on the QE2.
REPRESENTATIVE: Er, and where are you travelling to?
CALLER: Well, we're flying back from New York.
REPRESENTATIVE (with relief) Ah yes, Madam, I'll make a note on your file
that you will be using your card in England and in the USA.

In this case, the representative clearly missed the fact that the caller wanted to
know if she could use her card to pay for services while on board ship. A few
more exchanges clarified the situation and all was resolved successfully but it
took time.

The point is that it is impossible in a short training period (typically
24 hours) to prepare representatives for every cultural reference they are
likely to come across. What they need to develop, therefore, is the skills of
how to recognize a cultural reference and then how to ask clarification questions. Indian call centre representatives often don't ask questions because they
are afraid of losing face. They think they ought to know. But imagine if the boot
was on the other foot. Would you expect a British call centre representative to
know the distance from Pune to Mumbai by car or how to get from Vizag to
Darjeeling?

What is needed is less cultural knowledge training, although it is obviously
useful and re-assuring, and more cultural strategy training, which helps representatives learn the skills of recognizing cultural references and asking the right
questions to clarify them. Knowing the right questions to ask and how to ask
them is probably more valuable than knowing the right answers, which will
anyway come with experience.

Formality and Informality

One of the major cultural assumptions that Indian call centre agents have about
Britain is that it is still a formal society, whereas, in fact, it is very informal.
Therefore, when British English-speaking customers hear rather formal and
archaic expressions, such as, 'May I even know your good name?' or 'I would be
assisting you today,' they tend to feel amused and then embarrassed. The British
style is typically relaxed. People use first names very quickly and enjoy a relaxed
easy communication style with humour and charm.

Therefore, when an Indian call centre representative addresses a British
customer with the formality demanded by respect, the British take it completely
the wrong way and think the representative is being obsequious and even
'colonial'. They don't see it for what it is, politeness.

It is therefore useful to encourage call centre representatives to adopt a more informal style of communication and teach them the phrases to do so. It is also important to teach British executives dealing with India the importance of courtesy and respect and to recognize that formality of expression is out of ignorance of current British style rather than any feelings of inferiority.

The Big C and the Little c

Keeping representatives up to date with cultural developments will make them feel more confident in interacting with British customers. Culture covers the big C – cultural icons, events and monuments and the little c – daily life, items that people like to talk about and discuss, such as weekends, holidays and gossip about celebrities. Some call centres can and do enhance their representative's experience and knowledge by introducing ways of keeping up to date with British culture. Here are some of the most positive things I have seen.

- Installing a TV screen in the downtime area or canteen with a subscription to BBC World Television.
- Putting regular cultural information, quizzes and news on the call centre Intranet to keep representatives motivated and informed about developments in UK life.
- Decorating the walls or panels dividing the work areas with travel posters of scenes in the UK and even flags.
- Making online editions of newspapers available – particularly the tabloid press.

Other strategies include, keeping a print log of culturally inappropriate calls (names and voices concealed), keeping a similar log of culturally appropriate calls, getting a log of UK equivalent calls for education and comparison. Strategies like this will encourage representatives to feel more in tune with the UK and more motivated as a result. The practical results will be greater productivity, more harmonious working conditions and lower attrition rates.

Other more cost intensive investments are equally valuable, such as employing UK nationals as floorwalkers, available to give language and cultural advice and even creating a programme of secondments to UK call centres. I have seen that in as little as 2 weeks, Indian representatives completely change their view of Britain and consequently their style on the phone when they get back to work in India. This also has a trickle-down effect on other representatives in the team. A programme of secondments between UK and Indian call centres also creates a more cohesive working team, increases British awareness of India and Indian life and work and helps create, through building personal relationships, the family atmosphere that is so important in Indian business.

Empathy

Call centre experts and employers believe that the key skill that a successful representative needs to cultivate is empathy. Empathy means developing the ability to put oneself in the customer's position and to see things from their point of view. Since India is one of the most empathic nations on earth, this is not difficult but call centre representatives need training in how to use their natural instincts to optimise performance. Lots of techniques such as 'Smile when you dial' are used to manufacture empathy but the truth is that it can be difficult to create empathy on demand, especially when you are under pressure. However, there are a number of empathy 'evaporators' that representatives need to be trained to deal with and one is timing.

On the whole you do not call people in the UK unless they are family or close friends after 9pm at night or before 8.30am in the morning. You are also sensitive about calling people during football matches on TV and on Sunday mornings. Call centre shift schedulers are sensitive to this but sometimes mistakes are made. Call centres need to learn that empathy demands that you don't launch straight into your script but apologise for intruding on your customer's privacy. Respecting privacy is very important to the British and if you suspect you are intruding on it, always apologise. A phrase like, 'I'm really sorry to bother you at this time but . . .' goes a long way to establishing empathy with the customer.

Active listening is another important skill. This involves really listening to the customer, to the stress level in their voice and the noise in the background as well as to the words they use. One representative asked a customer 'What's the weather like today?' and got the reply, 'Look, I've just had a bereavement and I can't really handle this.' 'Oh, the weather is very nice here. About twenty-five degrees.' Apart from the cultural error (twenty-five degrees is pretty hot for the UK), empathy demanded she say, 'I'm so sorry. Please accept my condolences.' Another representative, trying to do a customer survey, encountered a woman with a baby crying in the background. The customer was clearly stressed but didn't want to be impolite and end the call. The representative responded brilliantly. She left her prepared script, asked the baby's name and asked the customer if she would prefer she called back later, which the customer gratefully agreed to. In this case the reputation of the company was enhanced and the representative was assured of a positive response when she called back.

As a general rule it is useful to teach representatives the FIVE STAR CODE for improving empathy. When you sense stress or resistance in a call, do the following:

- Slow down – don't go so fast. Something is going on, What is it?
- Listen – listen actively to the voice, to the words, to the mood of the speaker and to any background noise you can hear.
- Feel – feel what's going on. Is the customer tense? Do you feel they wish they were somewhere else?
- Don't assume – Don't assume the customer doesn't want to know. They may be tense, offhand or even abrupt for completely different reasons from your call.
- Ask – Be prepared to ask if it is OK to proceed or whether the customer would prefer you to call back another time.

Doing these things will really help improve the atmosphere of calls and make the representative a more relaxed and effective operator on the phone.

Email and Conference Etiquette

Within companies back office work is often outsourced to India. The representatives asked to do this work are often people who are judged not to have the degree of proficiency required for voice work. However, they are often required to be in email and sometimes in voice communication with their UK counterparts. Although perfectly knowledgeable and expert in their work, written and spoken communication problems get in the way of efficient processing, especially in programming and systems testing. As a result there is a need for email queries and voice queries and periodic roundups by teleconference and videoconference calls. Emails are often confounded by what is sometimes called in the UK, the 'never say no' culture.

A positive feature of Indian life is its 'can do' optimistic attitude. A negative feature is the tendency, out of politeness, to write what people think the reader wants to read rather than what is actually the case. As a result the style of emails is often roundabout and indirect or flowery and over-explanatory. It also means that the information given is unclear or incomplete. It is also not timely. Indian executives need to cultivate greater directness of style in emails and greater frankness in acknowledgement of problems and proposing solutions, while preserving the politeness and courtesy common to both cultures. The British colleagues, on the other hand, also need to cultivate greater directness in saying what they need. In our experience, an email which says, 'Could you possibly do this by next week?' is an invitation to the Indian counterpart to put the request on the backburner as it is obviously not priority. An email request which says clearly 'I need this by Friday at 5PM, UK time' is far more likely to get an acknowledgement and a result.

The problem with conference calls, either video or telephone is silence. It is not uncommon for the Indian side to listen without responding, largely out of respect for authority (the leader of the Indian group) or for the foreigners. This 'dead air' unnerves the British who then start to lecture. As a result, both sides end up unsatisfied. The Indian team needs to be more direct and tighter in communication and also to be prepared to speak up in response. The UK team needs to be prepared to listen more and to give time to the Indian team to formulate responses. They also need to motivate the Indian team to feel confident in voicing their reservations and objections as well as to propose their solutions, which may be very different but far more effective in the Indian context than the British ones.

As well as the linguistic features impeding communication we have also to consider the impact of cultural references. On the whole, the teaching of cultural issues is given much less time than is spent on accent neutralization and is primarily devoted to what we used to call British and American life and institutions rather than to the development of cultural skills. The contention in this chapter is that it is much less important to teach the major supermarkets in Britain, for example (they can find it on Google in 1 minute) than to teach the skills of probing cultural references politely to find out what is meant.

Implications for Language and Culture Training

Given the problems identified above, it is clear that in the first case, call centre representatives need to understand the differences between Indian English and International English usage and to adapt their usage to the British customer. In the second case, representatives need to learn techniques for probing cultural references and for building empathy with the British customer. In business environments where meetings are often held by video and teleconference, Indian executives need to understand the customs of international remote communication and, even in 'back-office' email communication, representatives need to understand how to structure messages to achieve successful communication.

The training in cultural awareness and empathy should be part, not only of the induction accent neutralization training, but also of the process training, 'nesting' period on the floor and of on-the job training during operations. It harnesses the natural instincts of call centre representatives in India, while providing focus and context for the development of cultural and empathy skills.

Differences in British and Indian Business Culture

During the British Council 2nd policy dialogue in Kolkata in 2008 I asked the group to identify the key qualities British customers needed to recognize in Indian colleagues and counterparts. The answer was:

- Understand the Indian psyche.
- Exercise patience.

One of the interesting developments of recent years and a phenomenon of India's economic growth is that companies who used to provide services to British companies have now become their owners and partners through joint ventures and mergers and acquisitions. The most famous examples are the Tata group who bought British car manufacturers and the Mittal group who bought British Steel. However, there are also cases where Indian call centres are using their experience and expertise to set up their own companies in the UK and USA. This process has put a premium on making sure that British and US business understands and can deal with Indian expectations of the business relationship. The differences in communication styles and cultural expectations put increasing strains on people from different English-speaking cultures working together, using different varieties of English. We have highlighted key differences in English usage but we also have to take into account the fact that different communities have:

- Different cultural expectations of the client supplier relationship
- Different working procedures

If both sides are not aware of these differences and take them into account in their strategic and operational planning and implementation then the losses are likely to be considerable, both financially and in public reputation.

What then are the key issues which highlight different cultural expectations between Indian call centres and British corporate clients?

First, is the issue of relationships. As mentioned by the British entrepreneur Paul Davies in his 'What's This India Business?', India sees relationships as the basis of a business transaction and contract as one step in building a long-term relationship, which can be amended and modified according to need. The UK is primarily a 'job done' culture in which the contract is the basis of work to be done and which may in due course lead to a personal relationship, if things go well.

Secondly is the style of communication. One of the key issues at the operational level is that UK managers prefer a 'hands-off' relationship conducted through email while many Indian operational personnel are used to a hands-on approach with close monitoring and personal interest. The danger that many British executives remark on is that the above-the-line cost savings achieved by outsourcing to India are built back in below-the-line by increased time involved in operational management.

Thirdly, is the issue of respect. This has both organizational and communication repercussions. India is a high respect culture which still tends to believe in that her British colleagues and clients preserve the formality they left with in 1947! Indian management itself is like, many other countries, very 'top down', with operational as well as strategic decisions being taken at or referred to the top management. This is seen by British clients as both inefficient and frustrating.

Even worse at operational level is the politeness and formality of language used by Indian call centre representatives dealing with British clients. This is seen by many to be at best amusing and slightly irritating and at worst as time-wasting and embarrassing. Much of this stems from interference from Indian English, referred to above.

A fourth and more contentious issue in British Indian relationships is that, unlike British executives, Indians are less likely to voice their opinions and risk speaking out of turn. This means that they will do exactly what is suggested, right or wrong, and will not challenge opinions or statements they think are wrong. It is not that they can not do so (in the Indian environment, people often challenge decisions). In the international environment they do not seem to think it is their place to do so, causing delays which prompt many British executives to say: 'Frankly, I could have done things quicker myself!'

Fifthly, is the issue of timeliness. Although in my experience Indian Business Process Outsourcing units are fierce in their monitoring of Service Level Agreements and Key Requirement Areas, they are much less prompt in responding to emails and completing tasks by due date. Worse still, they are not always good at advising on slippage and suggesting new deadlines for delivery.

These are the main complaints that British executives involved in outsourcing programmes at the operational level make about their Indian colleagues.

The saving grace in the relationship is often the quality of the young graduate representatives themselves, who, are intelligent, well qualified, eager to do a good job, tolerant and resilient in the face of sometimes angry (call centres in India tend to use the word 'irate') customers and willing to learn. However, the main problem that British and Indian colleagues share with each other is communication.

Implications for Two Way Training

Our audits of language use in Indian call centres suggest the following conclusions regarding accent neutralization and accent refresher training in Indian call centres.

- The training in understanding and saying correctly particular English words and place and personal names is less important than the teaching of strategies to find out from the customer how to pronounce them without causing offence.
- The training in sounds is less important than the focus on sound differences that cause confusion, such as the difference between b/ and /v/ or voiced and unvoiced sounds, such as /s/ and /th/
- There needs to be more emphasis on the understanding of stress patterns in British English words and sentences.
- There needs to be more emphasis on levelling out intonation and adopting a more relaxed pacing and speed of delivery.
- There needs to be a clear understanding of which words and phrases are common in Indian English or call centre jargon but are likely to be unfamiliar to UK customers.
- On the UK side there is a case to be made for training teams in regular contact with India in the following areas and skills.
- Respect for Indian English as an independent and very widely spoken variety of English, equivalent in the number of speakers to the UK and US varieties. This is happening naturally through interaction with India and through increasing familiarity with Indian accents through movies and pop music. As an example, in 2009 the movie *Slumdog Millionaire* won eight Oscars in the Hollywood awards ceremony.
- Understanding of the key words and phrases most commonly used in Indian English.
- Understanding how to use English in a way that eases comprehension on the part of those using a different language or dialect. This includes strategies for making English clearer and more comprehensible through pacing, clearer explanation of acronyms and initials, avoidance of idioms and especially jokes and the better structuring of communication.

Implications for Training

Cultural knowledge is important but even more important is teaching strategies for recognizing cultural references and how to ask questions to elicit relevant cultural information. This would include real-life scenarios which illustrate the cultural problems that arise and the teaching of language designed to probe cultural reference and elicit information. Telephone role-play is also involved in this process.

It cannot be stressed how important it is to teach cultural information that is relevant to the customer call centre interaction. I have reviewed training manuals which contain the complete list of British monarchs. Honestly, if I was learning to support Indian customers, would it really help to know about Ashoka, Aurangzeb and Mohamed? In the same way, most British customers only know the names of three or four British monarchs (William the Conqueror, Henry VIII, Elizabeth I and Victoria plus, of course, our own dear Queen Elizabeth II!) and forgot the rest by the time they left school, if indeed they ever learned them.

The development of empathy training and how to harness Indian natural empathy to the demands of call centre customer service is very important. Indians are extremely good at maintaining courtesy under pressure but need practice in active listening – recognizing mood and stress and background interference – and responding appropriately.

Trainers on both the British and the Indian sides need to recognize that not just voice process representatives but also back office representatives, and support executives, need communication training in how each side normally communicates both in emails and in voice communication through telephone and video conferences. In the Indian case, the email and conference training may be a supplement to the general accent neutralization and cultural training programme and be offered as a half-day or one-day programme, with possibly a coaching follow-up element introduced to provide support for handling email exchanges.

Last of all, British executives working with Indian executives on site and in the UK need training in understanding Indian expectations of the working relationship and how people communicate, organize their work, take and communicate decisions and how they expect to interrelate with each other on the phone, through emails, video and teleconferencing and face-to-face contact. This can be done in half-day or one-day courses and more and more British client companies working with Indian companies recognize the need for this kind of orientation.

Conclusion

Business Process Outsourcing may wax and wane as some processes are pulled back inshore and others are exported but it won't go away. A key factor in its development will be the increase in process as call centre representatives demand better remuneration and the danger of the 'gene pool' of English-speaking graduates drying up. Already we are seeing signs of old call centre cities being used up and new ones coming on stream. Above all, for young Indian graduates, call centres represent their initiation into the world of international relations and the opportunity to learn language, cultural and empathy skills that will stand them in good stead in their future careers.

In his research for the British Council, entitled 'English Next' the researcher, David Graddol has predicted that in 2050 India will be the world's third largest economy after China and the USA (according to Goldman Sachs) and British business must disabuse itself of its prejudices and learn about modern India if she is to reap the benefit of trade with one of her oldest natural allies. This is a long-term reason why investing in language and cultural training ON BOTH SIDES is a must for future prosperity.

Acknowledgements

Thanks to the British Council and the English Speaking Union for the opportunity to visit India in 2007 and 2008 and to the companies with whom I have had the privilege to work. Thanks also to International House, London, CultureSmart Consulting and Intuition Languages, London for their support. Above all, thanks to the magnificent teams of call centre representatives and training managers who have shared their experiences and work hard and well to meet the challenges of international customer service.

References

Crystal, D. (2006), *The English Language*. London: Penguin.
Davies, P. (2004), *What's this India Business?* London: NB Books.
Friedman, T. (2005), *The World is Flat*. London: Allen Lane, the Penguin Press.
Graddol, D. (2007), *English Next*. London: The British Council.
Graddol, D. (2010), *English Next- India*. London: The British Council.
Kachru, B. (1992), *The Other Tongue*. Illinois: University of Illinois Press.
Mahal, B. (2006), *The Queen's Hinglish*. London: Collins.
Tagore Rabindranath (1913) Closed Path: Gitanjali.
Tomalin, B. and Nicks, M. (2007), *The World's Business Cultures and How to Unlock Them*. London: Thorogood Publishing.
Tomalin, B. and Stempleski, S. (1995), *Cultural Awareness*. Oxford: Oxford University Press.
Tomalin, B. and Thomas, S. (2009), *International English for Call Centres*. New Delhi: Macmillan India Ltd.

Chapter 12

Call Centre Training and Language in the Philippines

Eric Friginal

Georgia State University, USA

This chapter overviews language training, personnel recruitment and performance monitoring practices commonly observed in outsourced call centres that are located in the Philippines. Implications for language policies specifically addressing the use of English in this context of cross-cultural interaction between Filipino call centre agents and American callers are discussed in relation to performance issues and language-based threats that are potentially impacting the quality of outsourced service transactions. This study briefly summarizes the present state of outsourcing in the Philippines and describes the Philippine advantage and its various opportunities to develop its human resources. It is argued that the use of English by Filipino agents, together with the prevailing American perceptions of outsourcing and the dynamics of cross-cultural interactions, directly influence the success or failure of many service encounters. The chapter suggests that more detailed analysis of communication in this setting is needed, which will help improve training practices in Philippine call centres and better define the language-based needs of Filipino professionals in serving their American callers.

Introduction

Customer call centre services in the United States (USA) have been gradually outsourced overseas due to the increased business demand to lower costs incurred in maintaining these call centres on the US mainland. To improve their overall financial structure, companies ranging from Fortune 500 businesses to smaller internet-based firms have relocated their customer service operations to countries with available English-speaking human resources and relatively low labour expenses compared to the USA (Friginal 2004; Friedman 2005; Magellan Alliance 2005). Because of its tradition of bilingual education (in English and Tagalog-based Filipino) and cheap labour market, the Philippines has become one of the major centres for US-based outsourcing, second only to India (Teves 2003; 'Service Alert' 2004; 'Philippines Sees Jump in Outsourcing Business by 2010' 2007). The Philippines produces over 400,000 English-speaking college graduates every year. Of these, 80,000 are in the fields of information technology, computers and engineering. Another 110,000 come from business-related fields, such as commerce, finance and accounting (BPAP 2007). The international perception of the Filipinos' English language competency and overall trainability is positive because of the high number of college graduates in the workforce compared to other countries (Cabreza 2007). Also, the growing Philippine population estimated at over 90 million in 2007 appears to complement the requirements of US outsourcers for increased manpower and staffing. The country's demographic structure ensures the sustainable flow of skilled and relatively young workers in the labour force. Only 4% of Filipinos are above 65 years old in 2002 (Rodolfo 2005).

Over the last 10 years, the Philippines has established its capabilities and reputation for delivering high-quality, productive call centre services (Tschang 2005). This high-profile sector, which has also been referred to as the 'sunshine industry' of the Philippines (Uy 2004), continues to influence the economic and educational policies in the country. It is also evident that many US and other foreign investors recognize the Philippine advantage in maintaining call centres outside of India (or the mainland U.S.). During the initial boom of the industry in 2002, a survey conducted by Garner, of corporations engaged in call centre services in the Philippines shows that these corporations are relatively satisfied with business operations and staffing as well as the level of government assistance for outsourcing in the country. A related survey by Tschang (2005) also supports these prevailing impressions. The most commonly cited positive or 'advantageous factors' for outsourced call centres in the Philippines from this survey include: the Philippines' long history of cultural affinity with the USA; the Filipinos' 'strong interpersonal skills'; Manila's livability and reasonable quality of life for expatriates; and the strong telecommunications infrastructure and the availability of real estate, government incentives such as the Philippine Economic Zone Authority (low taxation) zones and low employee turnover rates.

By Philippine standards, the average entry-level salary of customer service agents (heretofore 'agents') in outsourced call centres is competitive. A newly hired agent's basic salary of approximately PhP12, 841 (U.S. $264 at the current exchange rate in November 2008) per month is higher than that of many technical and white collar workers in government and private corporations. For example, a geologist working for the Department of Environment and Natural Resources earns a monthly salary ranging from only PhP8,000 to 10,000 (salary range data taken from the Department of Labor and Employment

[Philippines] website: http://www.dole.gov.ph). Financial benefits, additional incentives and opportunities for immediate promotions are major reasons why there has been a continuing increase in the number of applicants for positions in the call centre industry in the Philippines since the late-1990s. Additional remuneration such as overtime pay, productivity bonuses, transportation allowance and medical insurance make the financial package attractive, especially for recent university graduates. Because outsourced call centres employ mostly young, English-speaking professionals, the industry has cultivated a dynamic, fast-paced and competitive atmosphere which appears to capture the interest of a greater number of fresh college graduates. Many call centres in the Philippines are also tapping college graduates from provinces outside the capital, Manila, and are branching out to other cities in order to find qualified potential agents who are able to speak English proficiently. Most job fairs conducted in universities and various malls across city centres regularly showcase call centre companies competing for trainable English speakers (Ochoa 2006; Olchondra 2006). Experienced agents and management staff are easy targets for promotion to supervisory and managerial positions in other call centres. There is considerable demand for, and aggressive recruitment of, experienced/trained agents in the Philippines because of the constant growth of the industry and the continuing flow of new start-up call centres seeking qualified Filipino professionals (Magellan Alliance 2005; BPAP 2007).

This chapter reports language training in English and performance monitoring practices in outsourced call centres in the Philippines and discusses some implications for language policies addressing the use of English in this context of cross-cultural interaction between Filipino call centre agents and American callers.

Training Practices in Philippine Call Centres

American customers who need assistance for products and services usually call a toll-free number that directs them to available agents in the Philippines. Calls are entertained during regular business hours in the USA, which requires that the agents in the Philippines work on nightshift (usually from 10pm to 6m) to accommodate the differing time zones. Some agents serve businesses that operate for 24 hours, 7 days a week. There are generally two groups of call centre agents: those who work directly for a particular offshore international corporation (e.g. agents in India employed by Dell computers with offshore operations in India) or those who are employed by a third-party (outsourced) call centre. In a third-party call centre, the agents are employed by the call centre company and not by the particular firm they serve. In other words, agents may be handling customer calls about the iPhone and have received technical training about the product; however, they are not considered to be

Apple employees. The agents receive salaries and benefits from the call centre outsourcer, which, in turn, collect revenues from their clients for manpower services and use of technology and equipment. The call centre, in coordination with representatives from these clients, provides English and phone-handling training and coaching to the agents and regularly evaluates agents' performance and customer satisfaction scores in the transactions.

The combination of cheap labour and the available supply of skilled applicants in the Philippines makes it possible for US-owned call centre companies to use managerial practices very different from those generally found in the USA or other developed countries. In 2004, Hagel finds that these offshore/outsourced call centres invest heavily to recruit staff, since 'they can afford to be more selective'. Table 1 below summarizes results of a case study by Hagel of the recruitment and screening process for prospective call centre agents by a major US-owned company which is one of the biggest outsourced call centres in the Philippines.

Table 1   Summary of agent recruitment and screening processes from Hagel (2004)

Factors	Descriptions
Recruitment	[XX Company] employs a recruiting team of over 30 human resources staff that puts applicants through a rigorous seven-stage screening process (an equivalent U.S. call center operation might have around four people on a similar team. A two-stage process—a resume and a short interview—is typical in U.S. call centers). Because of this process, [XX Company] is able to offer positions to only two percent of its applicants while enjoying a 90 percent acceptance rate, compared with an average acceptance rate of 50 percent in U.S. call centers.
Managers to staff ratio	In terms of managers-to-staff ratio, high wages in the U.S. are a major reason for the understandable tendency of high-performing companies to strip out layers of middle management and to increase the operating span of the remaining managers, forcing them into administrative and supervisory roles. In the Philippines, by contrast, the ratio of managers to staff is much higher because companies can afford to sustain managers' salaries. This allows the managers to spend more time building the skills of employees. The higher ratio of managers to workers also allows companies to pay greater attention to identifying and implementing process improvements that enhance their operational performance; at [XX Company], no less than 10 percent of a team leader's (frontline managers) time is spent in this way. [XX Company] maintains a ratio of one team leader to eight customer service agents, compared with a ratio of 1:20 or more for similar U.S. operations.

(Continued)

Table 1 (Cont'd)

Training programs	The company invests heavily in formal training programs, which are reinforced by apprenticeship, coaching, and mentorship. Agents who handle complex mutual-fund advisory calls, for instance, take a 16-week training course leading to the NASD Series 7 examination for broker certification. By organizing employees into smaller teams that have more exposure to managers, the company can follow up with ad hoc coaching and detailed reviews of every agent's perform-ance—at least an hour a week for seasoned reps and more for newer ones. Agents at [XX Company] enjoy an average pass rate of 81 percent on the NASD tests (recently, in fact, the pass rate has been 100 percent), compared with an average U.S. pass rate of 59 percent.
Handling time	The benefits are evident as soon as the company takes over a client's call center. One client, in its own operations, was used to an average handling time of about eight minutes. Within six months, [XX Company] had reduced this to four and a half minutes by refining call-handling procedures; revising the order in which information was gathered and entered, with a view to minimizing the impact on performance; and altering computer screens to reduce the number of page changes required in most transactions.

Language Training and Quality Monitoring

All agents hired by third-party call centre companies in the Philippines typically attend a short, 2-week 'core-skills' training for new employees designed as an orientation programme that covers language use, US culture and phone-handling topics, as well as business and procedural account matters before they attend their 'product training'. This core-skills orientation programme for agents is conducted by the training departments of these call centres in collabo-ration with the human resources (HR) and quality assurance (QA) depart-ments. New-hires have passed a series of interviews, oral performance tests and written examinations based on their knowledge and understanding of the services and products offered by the specific clients and their ability to communicate effectively in English. Product training focuses on the concrete support processes that the agents will provide their callers once they start taking actual calls. This training may be conducted for a period from 2 weeks to 4 months depending on the particular skill requirements of the clients. For example, agents serving high-value clients such as investment or banking serv-ices are often required to train for examinations in order to obtain US-required certifications or licenses. Some agents are sent to the USA or other training centres outside of the Philippines for product training.

Once the agents start taking actual customer calls 'on the floor', quality monitoring of performance is conducted on a regular basis. An agent may be grouped with a particular team under a team leader who acts as a coach and also conducts client-specific evaluation of performance. Typically, internal, client-specific evaluations are matched by additional monitoring from the QA department. Results of weekly or monthly performance evaluations are of great interest to US clients. The QA department of the call centre also conducts customer satisfaction surveys by calling recent customers and asking a series of questions about their interactions with the agents. Data from internal team-leader evaluations, QA monitors and feedback from American customers are sent to the US clients, and reports of problems as well as customer satisfaction or dissatisfaction scores are regularly scrutinized. US clients make frequent and necessary checks of the performance of their outsourced division comparing data from their local operations in the mainland with the group of agents from the Philippines. Conference calls between US-based managers and supervisors from various companies are conducted regularly with the QA officers of call centres in the Philippines. Clients hold the call centre responsible for improvements in agents' performance and can recommend the termination of low-performing agents. Customer complaints – especially those related to language and task performance (e.g. intelligibility, accuracy of support, average time spent in transactions) – are internally addressed in the Philippines by providing the agents additional training and coaching.

Different language and quality scorecards are used by many call centre companies to match the specific needs of clients. Some of these clients have very strict compliance requirements regarding agents' support processes which are all reflected in the assessment instruments used to evaluate agents' performance. For example, there are clients that require agents to meet a certain average length of time in completing transactions ('AHT' or Average Handling Time). In these AHT-specific transactions, agents attempt to solve issues in the shortest amount of time possible. Agents are trained to initiate closing spiels (e.g. 'Is there something else I can help you with?') to signal and encourage the conclusion of the transaction. In addition, some clients also require their agents to sell products or offer callers-related services. In these instances, successful sales lead to incentives and bonuses.

In general, agents have monthly scorecards that show quality monitoring scores, language proficiency ratings, number of customer complaints or positive feedback and average length of completion of support. These indicators yield a monthly performance rating for each agent. These data are considered during the provisionary status of the agents' employment with the call centre (usually during the first 6 months) and are used as the basis for financial incentives or possible promotion, or – in the case of poor performance – additional training, extension of the provisionary status, or termination of employment. Although it may seem that these rigorous quality monitoring processes might create too much pressure to allow agents to perform well, it is apparent that most agents are able to adjust to the demands of their clients and maintain very good, collegial relationships with other agents, their team leaders and managers. The benefits and the internal employee development programmes of call centres seem to outweigh the constant on-the-job anxiety resulting from the 'performance surveillance', even for those agents working with problematic accounts. Filipino agents also seem motivated by available opportunities for upward mobility in call centres and the prospects of overseas training and employment.

Performance Issues and Language-based Threats

Proficiency in English

As call centres continue to hire qualified agents, especially recent college graduates, at a relatively rapid pace, some sectors raise concerns about the overall skill level of the remaining pool of potential hires (Domingo 2006). In the first few years of the industry in the Philippines, many call centres were able to be selective in hiring agents and staff as reported by Hagel (2004). However, with call centres competing for agents with high-level language proficiency and effective sociolinguistic skills, some companies are currently not able to fulfil staffing requirements especially for high-end accounts such as banking and investment services. In March 2006, a report from a US-based think tank, John F. Kennedy Center Foundation-Philippines (JFKCF-P) said that the fast-growing outsourcing and call centre sector in the Philippines was in danger of losing steam because the supply of qualified workers was drying up (Domingo 2006). According to the JFKCF-P, less than 3 out of every 100 new college graduates were hired by the call centre industry from 2004 to 2006. The JFKCF-P study showed that the declining supply of qualified workers in this sector could arrest the projected growth of the industry and keep it from matching the level of call centre employment in India. Among the solutions offered by the JFKCF-P was to 'adequately prepare fresh graduates in the Philippines for a job in a call center firm by providing them quality training, especially in the declining proficiency of graduates in the English language' (Domingo 2006: B11). This general perception of the 'declining proficiency of graduates in the English language' (Monsod 2003) has been constantly talked about by industry insiders, educators, media practitioners and lawmakers in the Philippine Congress.

Language and Cross-cultural Understanding

It appears that there are cross-cultural discontinuities impacting the ability of Filipino agents to deliver high-quality customer service responses to American callers. These deficiencies can likely be addressed, or at least mitigated, through additional training and experience in transaction handling. It is not easy to project and act sufficiently like 'an American' as prescribed by many internal call centre trainers so as to satisfy American customers (Pal 2004), given the types of available training currently offered by many call centres in the Philippines while, at the same time, make a quick transition from skills and product training to actual phone support. The language and communication factors threatening the sustainability of the call centre industry in the Philippines clearly show the importance of effectively addressing English proficiency and interactional strategies to serve US callers successfully. As it is, productivity and service quality are inextricably bound to each other in outsourced call centres, whether measured empirically or experientially (Granered 2004). Considering factors related to cultural sensitivity and language proficiency, the non-native English speaker engaged in service trans-actions needs to have effective cultural understanding of customer needs, pro-ficiency in English and successful communicative strategies in transferring information to the callers. The interplay of these factors is expected in every single call to ensure customer satisfaction and loyalty. Moreover, a sincere, patient and service-oriented call centre agent is highly desirable in order to relate to the customer and show adequate, personalized service (D'Ausilio 1998; Granered 2004). Providing 'total quality service' is important in main-taining customer loyalty (Albrecht and Zemke 2001; Pal 2004), and the use of effective language in transactions is a major factor in facilitating a kind of service that will guarantee customer patronage (Anton and Setting 2004). For the Filipino agents, it is ideal to display high-level English as a Second Language (ESL) abilities and awareness of cross-cultural pragmatics and strate-gies in service encounters in order to efficiently address customer needs and avoid misunderstanding.

In addition to proficiency in the target language, cross-cultural competence is very important in service interactions involving speakers from different lan-guage backgrounds (Korhonen 2003). Training programmes that integrate instructions and tasks intended for the acquisition of cross-cultural compe-tence is necessary in outsourcing (Granered 2004). Korhonen states that training in international communication which is facilitated without a direct link to the cultural norms of the target language has proven to fail. The fail-ure to utilize cross-cultural communicative or linguistic (e.g. repetitions, use of numbers, references or response forms) strategies potentially leads to miscommunication with fatal consequences, as in the studies conducted by Cushing (1994) and Jones (2003) about the cross-cultural communication problems experienced by air-traffic controllers and pilots who do not share the same first language background. In call centres, miscommunication, as in most business-oriented settings, is harmful in transactions and must be avoided to assure the completion of support and save valuable contact times. To be successful in this context, therefore, Filipinos need to continue to develop a customer service culture congruent with American expectations and not largely following Filipino norms and communicative conventions in service encounters.

As Filipinos gain experience serving American callers, they learn about the value of control and 'leveling' with the common culture of the callers. Americans have been characterized as having a 'distance/individualistic' culture (Hofstede 1997) which opposes the Filipinos' family/collectivist norms. In Hofstede's collectivist/individualist scale, the USA. is ranked as the most individualistic culture directly opposite of the Philippines on the other end of the scale. According to Hofstede, freedom and equality of individual opportunity shape the social structure in the USA while family and harmony in social structures appear to be defining norms for Filipinos. The drive for status and achievement means that Americans work a lot, are mobile and expect immediate returns from their time and effort invested. Americans are known to be results-oriented with the main goal being profit and achievement as they want to see – and get to – the bottom line right away. In communicating with Americans in outsourced call centres, Granered (2004) suggests that offshore agents have to make their points obvious and direct immediately instead of trying to appeal to emotions or build trust. These agents need to stress points clearly and repeat them a few times for clarity and then get to the 'fix' or solution to the callers' problem as quickly as possible. Relationships and 'harmony' should be a secondary by-product, rather than a primary objective for Filipino agents trying to successfully meet American customer needs. In sum, Filipino agents need well-designed language and culture training, as well as sufficient experience serving American callers, to slowly gain cultural awareness that is vital in successful outsourced call centre interactions.

Clearly, culture learning cannot be accomplished overnight and even Americans coming from different regions in the USA will encounter cultural problems among themselves in service interactions. The lesson here is knowing how to solve these culture-based conflicts successfully, as most native speakers would be able to do in service interactions. Filipinos have to learn to properly and efficiently ask for additional contexts and explanations whenever they experience difficulty in understanding the callers culturally. Some might argue that as customers, Americans ideally should also learn to be more accepting and accommodating of the language and culture-based limitations of the Filipino agents. Unfortunately, and realistically, because of the inherent dynamics of customer service and the political and economic implications involved in the outsourcing of US jobs, the burden is left to Filipino agents to support customers efficiently and avoid constant miscommunication in order to sustain the flow of the service transaction.

Training Materials

Because of limited training materials specifically designed for Filipinos, many language and culture training programmes in Philippine call centres use materials from the USA. These references and activity manuals on call handling practices and mock transactions are primarily written for native speakers of English or those with high-level language proficiency. Training topics in telephone support which address service competence include appropriate speech techniques; establishing rapport and personalization of support; and clarity, effectiveness and accuracy of information. The foci of these topics already assume fluency in the English language. These common topics are universal in the context of outsourcing but, as pointed out by Korhonen (2003), the need is for more grounding of these skills in cross-cultural competence, and consequently effective language usage. However, even with the obvious concerns about these issues in training curriculum and materials, the prevailing training environment in many call centres appears to address the basic requirements that support the preparation of agents in customer service. More provisions for practice are given and constant monitoring and coaching are provided by language trainers employed by the companies. Call centres employ American expatriates and Filipinos with advanced ESL teaching experience to work with agents in various areas of language production and task performance. Once the agents start taking actual calls from American customers, they gain valuable experience in the real-world use of the English language in addition to exposure on the range of issues and concerns coming from the customers.

Language Policy Implications

With the boom of employment in outsourced call centres, the goals of fluency, accent reduction and the acquisition of high-level English skills have influenced the direction of recent macro and micro language policies and shaping of popular opinion about English language use in the Philippines. As a key growth industry currently providing jobs and revenues to the country, the government and the education sectors are ready to respond to the language needs of foreign call centres. This direction influences future guidelines for organized, top-down language planning implemented by the Department of Education and private language training institutions. The question is, 'Does the country need to advocate for "fluency" as the definitive goal of English teaching – and is this realistic?' Or, to what extent should national education policy support 'fluency' in English? (and with what costs?). Highlighting the importance of fluency following the American variety could define the nature of language policies in the Philippines as evidenced by recent developments such as the proposed Gullas Bill which is attempting to (re)legislate English as the sole medium of instruction in schools (Luz 2007). As the country may pursue this focus in the coming years, it would be fair to ask if 'educated bilingualism' and designs to teach fluency following an exo-normative model (i.e. 'standard' American English) could lead to the acquisition of native-like mastery in the target language taking into account the language realities in the Philippines.

Given that 'schooled bilingualism has achieved only minimal proficiency, within very limited registers or domains of usage' (Kaplan and Baldauf 1997:134), the outcome of these potential policy changes could still be a disappointment for sectors demanding the immediate acquisition of native-like fluency in English from the Filipino workforce in outsourced call centres.

It is important not to 'rush' the formulation of language policies intending to address language-based threats to call centre operations. A strong set of industry-supported macro and micro language policies that combine essential variables such as cross-cultural competence and effective phone-handling strategies with language proficiency should be carefully planned and evaluated. In the light of these policy issues, collaborations between US call centre companies and public and private universities in the training of future call centre employees and the language assessment and monitoring of existing call centre agents have been established. In June 2007, a local university in northern Philippines, the University of the Cordilleras, started piloting a preparatory course in English proficiency, technical competency and customer relations designed by a US-owned corporation, Sitel Philippines. Rod Spiers, Sitel northern Philippines (Baguio) site director, reported that the firm has partnered with the university for a 5-year testing project (2007–2012) to flesh out a curriculum designed for call centre firms. The Sitel director added that the preparatory course was designed to give college students 'a concrete idea of what it is like to work in a call center, [where] the final stretch of training will be an onsite, hands-on lesson at Sitel Baguio' (Cabreza 2007:B13). Many call centres are also very supportive in providing monetary assistance to their employees who want to pursue higher education. Attendance at external language-based training and various performance certifications offered by private agencies is highly encouraged. Companies continue to send their employees overseas for corporate meetings and additional training, and these exposures to trends and recent business practices contribute to the holistic development of Filipino professionals in international business settings.

Friginal (2007) finds that the level of professional English spoken by university graduates in the Philippines does not readily match the English proficiency expectations of American call centers and customers. However, the Filipino agents' education in English, overall ESL proficiency and trainability allow these agents to work in outsourced call centres successfully and attain adequate achievement in the industry when provided appropriate training and experience on a micro level. Schooled bilingualism in the Philippines has provided opportunities for Filipino professionals to work in international business satisfying the standards of many multinationals and international organizations (Ramirez 2001). Nevertheless, for particular industries requiring native-like fluency in English, the English-in-education policies in the Philippines still leave gaps in training its professionals in the acquisition of fluent speech. Specific pragmatic features of English, contextual domains of usage and cultural sensitivity are, as expected, not thoroughly learned in schools.

Conclusion

The first 10 years of outsourced call centres in the Philippines brought much-needed investment money and provided jobs for many Filipino professionals. It is clear that the country is doing its best to continue to lure US corporations to operate business processes in the Philippines by addressing the training needs of its human resources, especially in the use of the English language. Cheap and sustainable customer service is an important consideration for many US companies and the Philippines has quite a lot to offer when it comes to human resources, available technology and governmental support provided to these multinational investors. There is sufficient incentive and support even with the present global economic turmoil in 2008–2009 to ensure that outsourcing will continue to flourish. It is also possible that American customers will continue to adjust and accommodate the limitations of foreign agents in language and cultural awareness during service transactions. In consideration of and response to this possible – or likely – scenario, language training in most call centres needs to continue to improve and include relevant, real-world materials that contribute to effective learning and the acquisition of high-level communication skills in English by Filipino professionals.

English proficiency and cross-cultural communication training and the call centre companies' English-based policies are important in addressing the gaps brought about by language limitations in outsourcing. In addition, actual experience in transactions with Americans increases the confidence of the agents and provides them the best venue to practice their language skills and task performance. These language and communication experiences lead to higher scores in English tests and service quality monitoring (Cowie 2007; Friginal 2007). It would be interesting to investigate in a longitudinal study if such improvements eventually lead to the acquisition of native-like proficiency in English after a period of time. High-level ESL in customer service is required but this alone does not determine success in transaction handling and accuracy. Other factors that will ensure effective delivery of service such as establishing rapport, personalization of support, comprehension and correctness of information in transactions are equally important. A successful interplay of product knowledge, cross-cultural communication skills, service personality and language skills is needed by Filipino agents in this context of customer service to effectively provide assistance to American customers. Outsourced call centres in the Philippines would benefit from devoting additional training time and resources to these other areas to achieve improvement in agents' overall task performance.

References

Albrecht, K. and Zemke, R. (2001), *Service America in the New Economy*. New York: McGraw-Hill.

Anton, J. and Setting, T. (2004), *The American Consumer Reacts to the Call Center Experience and the Offshoring of Service Calls.* Retrieved 15 March 2006 from http://www.kellyconnect.com/eprise/main/web/us/kcnt/en/kc.pdf

[BPAP] Business Processing Association Philippines (2007), [Homepage on the Internet] Back office outsourcing in the Philippines. Retrieved 12 January 2007 from http://www.bpap.org

Cabreza, V. (2007, 6 July), College-level workforce attracts outsourcing investors to RP. *Philippine Daily Inquirer,* B13.

Cowie, C. (2007), The accents of outsourcing: The meanings of 'neutral' in the Indian call center industry. *Word Englishes* 26(3), 316–330.

Cushing, S. (1994), *Fatal Words: Communication Clashes and Aircraft Crashes.* Chicago: The University of Chicago Press.

D'Ausilio, R. (1998), *Wake up Your Call Center: How to be a Better Call Center Agent.* Indiana: Purdue University Press.

Domingo, R. (2006, 18 January), Siemens' RP unit opens 450-seat contact center. *Philippine Daily Inquirer Online.* Retrieved 10 February 2007 from http://inquirer.net/

Friedman, T. L. (2005), *The World is Flat.* New York: Picador.

Friginal, E. (2007), Outsourced call centers and English in the Philippines. *World Englishes* 26(3), 331–345.

Friginal, R. V. (2004, 18 March), *Call Center Industry to Supply 50% of World Demand.* Retrieved 5 October 2004 from http://www.malaya.com.ph

[Garner] Garner Strategic Analysis Report (2002), An in-depth assessment of the Philippines for offshore IT-enabled services. Garner Strategic Analysis Report. Retrieved 28 January 2005 from http://www.neoit.com/pdfs/Philippines-Competitiveness.pdf

Granered, E. (2004), *Global Call Centers: Achieving Outstanding Customer Service across Cultures and Time Zones.* Boston, MA: Nicholas Brealey International.

Hagel, J. (2004), Offshoring goes on the offensive. *The McKinsey Quarterly* 2, 45–46.

Hofstede, G. (1997), *Cultures and Organizations: Software of the Mind.* New York: McGraw-Hill.

Jones, R. K. (2003), Miscommunication between pilots and air traffic control. *Language Problems and Language Planning* 27(3), 233–248.

Kaplan, R. and Baldauf, R. (1997), *Language Planning from Practice to Theory.* Clevedon, UK: Multilingual Matters Ltd.

Korhonen, K. (2003), Developing intercultural competence as part of professional qualifications: A training experiment. Paper presented at the 10th NIC Symposium on Intercultural Communication. Retrieved 20 October 2004, from www.immi.se/intercultural/nr7/korhonen-nr7.htm

Luz, J. M. (2007, 22 January), 'English first' policy will hurt learning. *Philippine Daily Inquirer Online.* Retrieved 2 September 2008 from http://archive.inquirer.net/view.php?db=1&story_id=44752

Magellan Alliance (2005), *The Philippines as an Offshore Service Delivery Location.* Manila: John Clements Consultants, Inc.

Monsod, S. (2003, 12 December), How's our English? *Philippine Daily Inquirer Online.* Retrieved 25 September 2004 from http://www.inq7.net/opi/2003/dec/13/text/opi_scmonsod-1-p.htm

Ochoa, R. (2006, 3 October), As India gets too costly, BPOs turn to Philippines. *Philippine Daily Inquirer*, B12.

Olchondra, R. (2006, 23 August), Call centers seen creating 90,000 new jobs in 2 years. *Philippine Daily Inquirer*, B10.

Pal, Amitabh (2004, August), Indian by day, American by night. *Progressive*, 68(8), 29–33.

Philippines Sees Jump in Outsourcing Business by 2010 (2007, 24 January), *Balik-bayan Property*. Retrieved 3 March 2007 from http://www.balikbayanproperty.com/blogs/bernard_bajada/archive

Ramirez, V. (2001), Philippine maritime and nursing education: Benchmarking with APEC best practices. Retrieved 5 October 2004, from http://dirp4.pids.gov.ph/ris/pdf/pidspn020

Rodolfo, C. (2005), Sustaining Philippine advantage in business process outsourcing. Retrieved 10 November 2007, from http://www3.pids.gov.ph/dprm3/services%20papers/BPO%20Study%20- %20final.pdf

Service Alert (2004, 8 April), *Malaya* B7.

Teves, R. (2003), 14 December), The business of call centers. *Manila Standard*, 23.

Tschang, T. (2005), The Philippines' IT-enabled services industry. Retrieved 22 April 2006 from http://siteresources.worldbank.org/INTPHILIPPINES Resources/ Tschang-word.pdf

Uy, V. (2004, 8 October), Call centers join job fair in Manila; 20,000 workers wanted. *Philippine Daily Inquirer*, A12.

Chapter 13

What Causes Communication Breakdown in the Call Centres? The Discrepancies in the Communications Training and Research

Jane Lockwood
The Hong Kong Institute of Education, Hong Kong

This chapter explores causes of communication breakdown in the call centres in the Philippines and how these are reflected in the training programmes offered in the Business Processing Outsourcing (BPO) workplace. The training programmes capture common perceptions about the causes of communication breakdown when the second language speaker (L2S) customer service representative (CSR) tries to resolve the problems of the first language speaker (L1S) customer on the phones. In this chapter, the content of some training programmes are first described and then evaluated against the current linguistic research which discusses where communication has been seen to be problematic in the call centres. Interestingly, there appears to be a gap between what the workplaces are doing in their communications training programmes and what the applied linguistic research suggests they should be doing. The main discrepancies seem to relate to the priority given by the call centre trainers to teaching discrete grammatical and phonological items in an attempt to eradicate first language interference, rather than to train for improved discourse and interactive ability, which, current research is increasingly showing to be the key source of communication breakdown. These discrepancies will be described and exemplified in the present chapter. Finally, there will be suggestions for improving current call centre communications training programmes based on current research and improved understanding of applied linguistic frameworks for planning, delivering and evaluating training.

Introduction

The outsourcing and offshoring (O & O) of business processes from developed countries such as the UK, USA, Australia and New Zealand to cheaper destinations in developing countries such as India and the Philippines has been rapidly increasing over the last decade (McKinsey report-NASSCOM 2005). Furthermore, there is at least one school of thought that predicts with the latest global financial upheaval this industry is set to escalate as businesses become even more preoccupied with their bottom lines and search for cheaper ways of working (BPAP 2009).

This chapter looks specifically at how the call centres, in these new second language English-speaking call centre destinations are coping with the level of English language service they are expected to provide to first language English-speaking customers on the phones, and how training departments support this. I then look at what the applied linguistic research, including research into call centre interaction, can tell us about what frustrates smooth communication with customers and how this can be better integrated into the training. The final section of the chapter will look at suggestions for change and further areas of research and development that are needed to enhance communications training provision in the global business processing outsourcing (BPO) workplaces.

The Methodology

The data for this chapter has been collected over a number of consultancies carried out by FuturePerfect Business English Specialists* in the Philippines and India (2004 –2009) when working with call centres. The consultancies have included carrying out complete 'language audits' for the businesses and reporting on the quality and impact of existing communications training programmes and assessment processes on the business. Typically each 'language audit' encompasses multiple methods of collecting data including:

(i)   Focus group discussions with key stakeholders
(ii)   Observation of training programmes and assessment processes
(iii)   Collection and analyses of key documents such as assessment tasks, training materials and policy statements
(iv)   Collection, transcription and analysis of calls to highlight areas of communication breakdown on the phone.

For privacy reasons the identification of these call centres cannot be made, but they do represent a cross-section of captive offshored, as well as 3rd party outsourced, businesses and also a variety of industry types including IT, retail, telecommunications, banking and insurance.

---

*FuturePerfect Business English Specialists is a BPO communications consultancy firm based in Manila and Hong Kong.

What is the Business Expectation of the Language and Communication Ability of the CSR?

A colonial legacy left both India and the Philippines with English language competencies that have helped position them as favoured BPO destinations in Asia. While both countries are considered 'outer circle' (Krachu 1985) countries with their own unique varieties of English, businesses positively view these destinations for outsourcing and offshoring their work, precisely because of their belief that the English language skills are good. However, are these varieties of non-standard English sufficient to meet the English demands of speaking with native speaker customers on the phones when they contact the call centres? Up until the advent of this BPO industry, the standard of these varieties has been acceptable for those seeking work overseas evidenced by overseas employment success. This has been corroborated by the international benchmark levels (e.g. IELTS and TOEFL scores) being attained by nurses, teachers and engineers working overseas. Workers from the Philippines employed as professionals (and indeed domestic workers) around the globe have been welcomed world-wide as 'globally intelligible' in their ability to use good spoken English (Gonzalez 1997, 2004). As well, IT specialists and postgraduate students from India have flocked to the USA over the last 2 decades and have found success in their studies and employment in this new land of opportunity (NASSCOM 2009). However, with the growth of the BPO industry and the movement of call centres overseas in particular, the levels of spoken English have come under much closer scrutiny. There are undeniably convincing business reasons for this new concern. For example, Western businesses do not want to upset their customers with a lower quality communication service, nor do they want to upset their customers with the unpopular decisions of taking jobs out of countries such as the USA and UK to cheaper destinations in Asia (BPAP 2009). The demand therefore for 'native speaker-like' oral competency is now common in the call centre industry in Asian destinations. A corollary of this new concern has been the development of little tolerance for first language interference which many key business stakeholders in the BPO industry believe to be the main cause of communication breakdown. These businesses also have very high expectations for soft skills, intercultural and linguistic performance on the part of the CSR. But how realistic are these expectations? And how are these high order communications skills being sourced at recruitment, supported by training and evaluated for quality?

Unfortunately, the business expectation of strong communication skills operates one way in the call centre interaction, i.e. the business mantra is 'the customer is always right' dominates:

> As customers, the native English speakers ideally should also learn to accommodate the language and culture based limitations to the CSR.

Unfortunately, because of the inherent dynamics of customer service and the political and economic implications involved in the outsourcing of US jobs, the burden is left to the non-native English speaking CSRs to support customers efficiently and avoid constant miscommunication in order to sustain the status quo of outsourcing outside the US mainland. (Friginal 2007:335)

Many call centres are currently struggling to meet the native-speaker levels of English required for work and required for the stringent quality assessment benchmarks that form part of the service level agreements (SLAs) signed by the businesses. Subsequently businesses and governments are investing heavily in the assessing and training of both near and pre-hire call centre CSRs in the hope that these solutions will provide a reliable pipeline of CSRs onto the floor. But how successful are these call centre training departments in the communications assessment and training solutions they have created? Communications assessment in the call centres is highly problematic. The lack of language assessment expertise within the BPO, coupled with commercial language tests that are expensive and not tailored to the need of the industry, have resulted in poor recruitment processes and problematic quality assurance processes (Hamp-Lyons and Lockwood 2009; Lockwood 2008; Lockwood, Forey and Elias 2009). Such limitations negatively impact recruitment rates, which vary between the very low levels of 1–5% (BPAP 2009). In addition, these limitations also negatively affect success and threaten compliance with the SLAs, which in many cases require extremely high levels of language competency. Furthermore, there is an absence of valid and reliable assessment measures which are capable of having a positive washback effect on the training programmes. This chapter focuses particularly on content (e.g. language, culture and soft skills) decisions, made for inclusion as training materials in the programmes.

The Nature of the Call Centre Near- and Pre-hire Training Programmes

It has been observed in the BPO industry in the Philippines that although trainers are degree holders, very few of them have qualifications in the disciplines of education or applied linguistics/TESOL (Lockwood 2004). In addition, this business sector is currently poorly served by the English for Specific Purposes published communications materials. So who currently assumes responsibility for planning, implementing and evaluating the BPO communications curriculum? This burden most often falls on the shoulders of the underqualified trainers in the BPO workplace.

Apart from the trainers lacking the qualifications to develop such a specialized curriculum, a further issue that negatively affects the quality of the communications training programmes is that the solutions are often imported from call centres abroad (Friginal:2007). These 'transferred solutions' are problematic because they are either imported from native speaker call centres in the USA, UK, Australia or New Zealand or they are imported from other L2S call centre destinations such as India. Those coming from English-speaking countries are problematic because the communication needs of native, as opposed to non-native speakers of English are very different. Flying in native English speaker soft skills trainers from the USA to run English language communication courses for CSRs is common in the Philippines. In one training session however, it was observed that the USA soft skills trainer, who was on a 2-week secondment from the Head Office in Dallas, was instructing the pre-hire agents on the importance of 'apology and empathy'. The workshop provided a lot of input and was very USA ethno-centric. During one training session, the trainer showed a slide that simply said 'Never say – "Sorry"'. The Filipino participants were mystified as to what the implied message was, but as a native speaker I understood it to be that the CSR should perhaps be more effusive, and make careful word choices in their way of apologizing, by saying something like 'I really am terribly sorry about this, how about I. . .?'or 'I **do** apologise Ma'am'. This level of explicit deconstruction of language points, with simulated practice and feedback, is a standard approach when training for language and communication with second language speakers (L2S), but is uncommon in current soft skills training in the Philippines being conducted by non-language native English speaker specialists. Subsequent to this particular training session, a CSR was heard to say to a grieving insurance claimer whose husband had just died . . . 'I do apologise for your loss'. Soft skills programmes designed for L2Ss need to be substantially revised to incorporate the linguistic and inter-cultural needs of the L2S CSR. An equally problematic approach is where 'transferred solutions' from other L2S speaker call centre destinations (such as India) are simply picked up and dropped in another L2S O & O destinations (such as the Philippines). This is problematic for two reasons. First the cultural and linguistic needs vary. For example, the wholesale transfer of Indian call centre training programmes, where 'accent neutralization' programmes proliferate, has not been helpful in the Philippine context where current research shows that accent is not a major cause of communication breakdown (Lockwood, Forey and Price 2008). The second reason is that in the call centre industry there is a great deal of swapping and imitating bad 'best practice' models pedaled by large multinational training departments. Such practices relate to for example, the very long recruitment assessment procedures that rely on 'counting' phonemic and grammar mistakes of the recruitees and then providing behaviourist-based training programmes to rid the new hires of L2S interference errors.

Who is responsible for making these important training decisions and what is the basis for such decisions? As mentioned earlier in this chapter, this task appears to be left to the trainers and sometimes to senior management who insist on often quite unrealistic outcomes for the time and money invested.

This combination of high (and often unrealistic) expectations; little expertise in the training teams; the mimicking of bad 'best practice' from other call centres, and no time for preparation and upskilling, is resulting in poor curriculum and questionable training in the call centres (Lockwood 2008).

The typical call centre communications programme for pre-hires lasts for 2 weeks full-time. This amounts to approximately 80 hours of training. Each day the pre-hire trainee attends around 8 hours of training that is split into discrete and unconnected lessons on grammar, accent neutralization, soft skills, quizzes and intercultural training. The syllabus documents comprise little more than a collection of activities with most often no stated training aims and objectives. They generally do not provide any pedagogical frameworks nor guides for use to help other trainers. The example of a typical day's training as shown below reflects the good intentions of a training team trying to pack in activities to remediate problems that have been highlighted by quality assurance personnel and team leads on the floor. These programmes however, lack rigour and integration in educational planning and do not draw on applied linguistic theory and good practice in language teaching and learning. Just as seriously, there are no principled measures for success, so we have very little idea as to the impact of the significant investment that call centres are currently making into their training programmes. Interestingly, in the call centre programmes reviewed in this chapter, there was very little listening material and very few examples of real calls for the trainees to practice listening skills. Below is a typical day out of a 10-day training programme. Although the days vary, they are similarly organized.

Such a training programme would be targeted to a group of pre-hire trainees, perhaps 10–20 in a class and the sources of the materials are typically downloads from the internet and homegrown materials.

There are a number of issues that contribute to the poor quality of the communications syllabuses being developed in the call centres. First, there is very little understanding within call centre training departments in the Philippines about the **nature of language.** This is reflected negatively in the curriculum

---

Monday

9–10.30 Grammar lesson: e.g. prepositions; verb/Subject agreement/tenses

10.30–12 Soft skills: Dealing with an irate customer

12–1: Roleplay

Lunch break

2–3.30: Accent neutralization drills: tongue twisters

3.30–5: Culture training: e.g. facts and figures about the state of Denver

5–6: Quiz

Adapted from 2-week call centre training programme in large Manila-based call centre

FIGURE 1   A typical call centre daily training plan

documents such as the one described above. Non-linguists often believe that good language skills relate directly to a good 'knowledge' of the grammar items. This means that the programmes are often packed with discrete grammatical item practice that bears very little relation to CSR functional communication needs. There are two main problems with this view. First, 'grammar knowledge' does not automatically mean an ability to use grammar in real situations. Applied linguists, and particularly sociolinguists, explain the difference between language and parole (de Saussure 1916) and use and usage (Widdowson 1978). 'Langue' and 'use' here being the terms to describe a 'knowledge' of grammar; while 'parole' and 'usage' describe the ability to communicate (i.e. actively produce the language). This distinction is a critical one for trainers to understand as 'knowledge of' language does not translate into competent use of language in real situations. This lack of understanding was painfully obvious when consulting in a large BPO back office in Manila where one managing director who had just had all his middle management staff complete a exhaustive discrete grammar test developed internally, was at a loss to understand why supervisory staff who had scored 100% on the grammar test could not write or speak good English in the workplace. Structural grammatical items taught in isolation do not result in a functional communication unless the contextual information of content, purpose and audience is provided and explained. An ability to understand and use discrete grammatical items does not magically result in textual competency – that is the ability to make extended communication on the phones with customers successful. Good language use requires the speaker to use language as a 'system of choices' that relies on an understanding of the context. Without this understanding, effective choices cannot be made (Halliday 1985). A sociolinguistic description of the language of call centre customer service interaction is encapsulated in the authentic text of the call itself. Describing and analysing this 'grammar in action' provides the starting point for uncovering what needs to be taught as part of the language curriculum. Generally speaking, in the call centre pre-hire communication programmes investigated, discrete and decontextualized grammatical items are taught with no reference to the authentic texts. Descriptions and analysis by applied linguists of authentic texts will be invaluable for call centre communication programme development. Such analyses will inform materials developers as to the key lexico-grammatical features that cause communication breakdown and contribute to success on the calls. Furthermore, through the collection of data and the expansion of a corpus of call centre interaction, one is able to reliably source high frequency idioms for training. Examples of early research of the textual and linguistic qualities of authentic call centre exchanges are outlined later on in this chapter.

The second problem evidenced in the content of the BPO communication training programmes relates to an unquestioned belief in the call centres that first language interference is the source of many of the communication problems. There is a misconception that if we can only get rid of these L1 features, native speaker proficiency of the CSRs will magically happen. There is emerging research that challenges such assumptions. First, there is English as a Lingua Franca (ELF) research to show that many first language (L1) interference features do not cause communication breakdown. For example, the kinds of non-standard forms identified for Philippines English (Bautista 2004) are very often evident in call centre interactions. Some of the most prevalent of these include the lack of verb/subject agreement, pronoun switching, non-standard use of prepositions in phrasal verbs, altered use of tense and aspect (e.g. use of past perfect for recent rather than distant past, overuse of the future continuous **will+ ing** form,) and most notably the restricted use of modality and overuse of 'would'. In the current research (Lockwood, Forey and Price 2008) there was however, scant evidence of these features causing communication breakdown on the phones in the call centres with the occasional exception of personal pronoun switch, overuse of the modal 'would' and the mixing up of simple present and past tense. There is a growing body of research showing that L2 speakers of English are adept at negotiating meaning around L1 features (Bolton 2005; Kirkpatrick 2007).

When interviewing the trainers who were also the writers of the call centre training programmes, the main rationale for the inclusion of the grammatical items related to the mere fact that they were simply L1 mistakes, rather than if they caused communication breakdown. Relentless drills of decontextualized and discrete grammar items such as verb-subject agreement, tenses and prepositions are common in call centre teaching programmes.

What the Literature and Current Research is Saying

There is an extensive literature that deals with workplace and academic discourses (Bhatia 1993; Candlin, Maleyand Sutch 1995; Idema 1995 and forthcoming; Roberts, Davies and Jupp 1992; Swales 1990; Swales and Bhatia 1983). Perhaps one of the most powerful and relevant studies to emerge out of the applied linguistic literature in the UK, for the BPO is the framework informing the Industrial Language Training (Roberts, Davies and Jupp 1992). The value in this framework is that it links directly to practice. They say that theories of interaction have three major functions for trainer as a curriculum developer:

1. to describe: they provide descriptive accounts of what is involved in interaction and thus they can also help us to develop a critical awareness and analysis of the interaction;
2. to interpret: they provide analytical tools for understanding how people make sense when they talk to each other;
3. to explain: allied to interpretation, they can help us to relate the specific and local in interaction to the social institutions through which things get done and which determine our social and economic well-being

(Roberts, Davies and Jupp 1992:30)

Many theoretical linguists have picked up on these components of this framework. Candlin, C. N and Candlin, S. (2003) and McNamara (1990) have looked also at the medical profession; Idema (1995, 2003) has looked at, and is looking at, the discourse of the public service and administration in Australia; several studies have been carried out on the discourse of teachers in classrooms (McDowell 1995; Elder 2001; Gibbons 2006) as well as other professions such as accountants (Nunan and Forey 1996; Forey and Nunan 2002), the metals and engineering industry (Mawer 1993,1999), pilots and air traffic controllers (Alderson 2007) UN peacekeepers and business managers and leaders are also under investigation.

In recent years there have been a number of studies completed on the subject of English language communication breakdown in the Asian call centres (Clark, Roger and Murfett forthcoming; Cowie 2007; Forey and Lockwood 2007; Friginal 2007; Hood and Forey 2008; Lockwood 2008; Lockwood, Forey and Price 2008; Lockwood, Forey and Elias 2009). These studies have used a sociolinguistic framework to look at authentic call centres data, notably either conversational analysis (CA), corpus studies or systemic functional linguistics (SFL). Forey and Lockwood (2007) based their research into the textual flow of the call centre interaction and transaction based on listening to over 500 inbound call centres calls across a range of different industry types. After identifying what appeared to be the generic structure and identifying obligatory and optional stages, they focused on where, in the textual flow, the calls appeared to be breaking down. Specifically, it became evident that the major problems in communication lay in expressing and understanding the purpose of the call and in the servicing stages. Interestingly, the specific areas of breakdown appeared to have less to do with the phonological and lexico-grammatical choices made by the L2S CSR and more to do with the interpersonal, intercultural and discourse capabilities of the CSRs.

Lockwood, Forey and Price (2008) carried out a further study isolating the specific communication areas of breakdown in the calls and again this study was based on a range of calls collected in the Philippines. This study again used a communicative competency framework domains of phonology, lexico-grammar, discourse and interaction (Canale and Swain 1980, 1981) to investigate the nature of the communication breakdown. From an analysis of this data set it was found that there were examples of communication breakdown due to the Philippine English (PE) reduced consonant and vowel sounds, although these were extremely rare. Interestingly it was also found that customers complained about the CSR's accent being hard to understand when, in fact, the research showed it was other features (notably interactional and discoursal limitations) of the CSR's communication that was causing frustration as described below:

Example 1
CSR: I'm explaining it to you Ma'am, it's for privacy purposes, it doesn't show here in my system but you do have a beneficiary, it's just not showing

in my system , but I can request a letter indicating for you who your beneficiary is. . . .

Caller: Well, you know you're not very plain. You have an accent right? I'm having trouble understanding you. Are you saying it does not show a beneficiary? Are you saying that? Are you saying that? (Lockwood, Forey and Price 2008, p. 231)

In this study, it was also found that non-standard patterns of Philippine English (Bautista 2004) such as the lack of verb/subject agreement, pronoun switching, non-standard use of prepositions in phrasal verbs, and altered use of tense and aspect were prevalent, but rarely did they result in serious communication breakdown. Callers and CSRs appeared to be adept at negotiating meaning around these non-standard patterns if they threatened communication. More serious communication failure appeared to centre around the interactional and discoursal language choices and limitations displayed by the CSR in the calls. To a certain extent, caller frustration was more frequently found in the calls because the CSR appeared vague, robotic, rude, incompetent, confusing, long winded, etc.

This initial work has been further expanded by Forey and Hood (2008) who investigated the nature of the interpersonal interaction/transaction in the call centres and specifically the interactive rise and fall of emotion. The calls used for this research were based around problematic call in inbound telephone conversations collected from call centres in the Philippines. This study draws on Appraisal theory (Martin and White 2005) and shows that reliance on implicit (for example the use of phonological devices e.g. equal stress on words to carry the meaning of impatience), rather than explicit attitude (where the caller would say 'I am really fed up with you!') with both the caller and CSR is common, although this is manifested in different ways. While the caller frequently grades up FORCE in references to time taken, or number of contacts, the CSR employs such lexico-grammatical choices such as concessive contractors e.g. **just, already, once, yet** and **actually** to control the interpersonal aspect of problematic calls. Wan (forthcoming, and see current volume) and Cowie (2007, and current volume) have both researched the area of prosodic features in the call centre interaction. Wan (forthcoming and current volume) explores how voice quality creates meaning potential in conflict between the caller and the CSR. Cowie (2007) explores, through an ethnographic study, how 'accent training' in the Indian call centres impacts the employability of the CSR, particularly in American call centres. Friginal (2008) has researched call centre discourse in the Philippines involving US customers and local CSRs. His research design follows a quantitative multidimentional framework developed by Biber (1988) to extract and interpret linguistic co-occurrence in his corpus. The three linguistic dimensions analysed were first, 'addresse-focused, polite, and elaborated information vs. involved and simplified narrative; second, planned, procedural talk and third managed information flow' (Friginal 2008:715). Results showed variations in the linguistic composition of the discourse of agents and callers across the three dimensions. He plans to build on this research by extending it to Indian call centres which he thinks may differ. He is also interested in how social categories e.g. speaker roles, gender, the nature of the accounts may determine and predict the use of features across the three dimensions.

Another study (Clark, Rogers, Murfett and Ang 2008) was carried out with call centre data collected from a large insurance company based in Singapore. Response data from around 500 problematic calls were collected from call centres in Singapore. A 'grounded theory' qualitative together with a quantitative (cluster and regression) approach were used to analyse and interpret the data. Four categories emerged that appeared to relate to the notion of courtesy; namely 'shows solidarity', 'anticipates needs', 'shows attentiveness' and 'asks for direction'. The authors make the argument that 'solidarity expression challenged traditional views of politeness and is less about the presentation of self and more about enabling collaboration with the other' (Clark, Rogers, Murfett and Ang 2008:2). This is a significant finding and contributes to the field with implications for call centre communications training which currently appears preoccupied with the traditional emphasis on politeness markers such as empathy and apology.

Very little of this research however, is understood and currently used in the design and delivery of call centre communication training in the call centre destinations.

Discussion

The discrepancies between what the research is now suggesting and what is taught in the communications training programmes in the call centre training departments under investigation are huge. Significant communication breakdown in the call centres appears to relate to the domains of communication performance such as an ability to interact with ease with the customer and an ability to explain products and services, rather than discrete L1 interference mistakes in the grammar and the pronunciation. In order to teach such communication performance, one first has to describe and analyse it from a sociolinguistic standpoint. This means collecting and selecting calls, transcribing and analysing them for their communicative strengths and weaknesses and writing training material that reflect these findings. Counting and describing the number of discrete grammatical and phonological errors in the discourse does not account for communication breakdown. Regrettably this is exactly the approach that is taken by non-linguists working in this field. One trainer recounted the common practice in their call centre in the recruitment and post-course assessment stages, of simply counting the number of grammatical and phonological mistakes to determine suitability for work as a call centre agent. Another call centre recruiter explained that if a recruitee makes more than 3 phonological mistakes s/he is simply not hired (irrespective of whether the vowel sounds hindered communication). The unfortunate washback of such an approach means that recruitment officers and trainers simply concentrate on discrete grammatical and phonological items that research is showing are of minimal significance in communication success. Not only are potentially good CSRs not recruited for work as a result of such practice, but huge investments of time and money are wasted on such flawed assessment and training practices. More seriously, it would seem, good communicators are not getting access to jobs as CSRs.

Conclusions

Clearly on-going research will be invaluable to this important industry. Further research into the discourse and interpersonal functions of the calls will provide the potential for much better informed materials development and training and coaching within the workplaces in the future. Research into the precise curriculum planning, design and evaluation of call centre programmes may shed light on how best to train trainers in the call centres. It would also be of interest to research the impact of different kinds of communications training, not only in terms of content but also in terms of length, in the call centres; and to research the impact of the call centre communications training not only in terms of final assessment scores, but also in terms of performance on the floor. Much also needs to be done in the area of language assessment research in the call centres. There is a great deal of anecdotal evidence that communications assessment interviews are designed to keep recruitees out of employment rather than bring them in. There is also some evidence that new recruits improve their communications skills at an exponential level once they start work on the floor. A research project exploring recruitment assessment practices would highlight practices that may be hindering business development. In addition, a longitudinal study of a sample of new recruits moving onto the phones over a 6–12-month period would be of value insofar that such a study would help predict how fast CSRs become really competent in their jobs.

However, hand in hand with such research, there is a need for professional development of call centre workplace trainers as a way of ensuring that the research outcomes find their way into improved pedagogical approaches in the communications training programmes particularly in the areas of educational planning for adult learning, intercultural training, sociolinguistic theory and practice and language assessment approaches . As has been suggested in this chapter, the applied linguistic skills and approaches that help trainers to analyse their own calls, to integrate the culture, language and soft skills components into coherent programmes and to make accurate assessments for diagnostic and quality purposes is essential. Until then businesses may well question the wisdom of their investments in communications training and assessment.

References

Alderson, C. (2007), *ELPAC Final ValidationReport.* UK.

Bautista, M. L. (2004), The verb in Philippines English: A preliminary analysis of the modal 'would'. *World Englishes* 23(1), 113–128.

Bhatia, V. (1993), *Analysing Genre: Language Use in Professional Settings.* UK.

Biber, D. (1988), *Variation across Speech and Writing.* Cambridge: Cambridge University Press.

Bolton, K. (2005), Where WE stands: Approaches, issues and debate in world Englishes. *World Englishes* 24(1), 69–83.

BPAP, Business Processing Association of the Philippines www.bpab.com.ph (accessed February 2009).

Canale, M. and Swain, M. (1980), Theoretical bases of communicative approaches to second language teaching and testing. *Applied Linguistics* 1(1), 1–47.

Canale, M. and Swain. M. (1981), A theoretical framework for communicative competence. In Palmer, A., Groot, P. J. M. and Trosper, G. A. (eds.) *The Construct Validation of Tests of Communicative Competence.* Washington. D. C. TESOL.

Candlin, C. N. and Candlin, S. (2003), Healthcare communication: A problematic site for applied linguistic research. *Annual Review of Applied Linguistics* 23, 134–154.

Candlin, C. N., Maley, Y. and Sutch, H. (1995), Industrial instability and the discourse of enterprise bargaining. In Roberts, C. and Sarangi, S. (eds.) *Discourse at Work: Communication in Institutional, Professional and Workplace Settings.* The Hague: Mouton.

Clark, C., Rogers, P., Murfett, U. and Ang, S. (2008), Is Courtesy Not Enough? 'Solidarity' in Call Center Interactions. University of Michigan. Ross School of Business Working Paper.

Cowie, C. (2007), The accents of outsourcing: The meanings of 'neutral' in the Indian call centre industry. *World Englishes* 26(3), 316–330.

Elder, C. (2001), Assessing the language proficiency of teachers: Are there any border controls? *Language Testing* 18(1), 149–170.

Forey, G. and Lockwood, J. (2007), I'd love to put someone in jail for this. An initial investigation of English needs in the Business Processing Outsourcing (BPO) Industry. *English for Specific Purposes* 26(3), 308–326.

Forey, G. and Nunan , D. (2002), The role of language and culture in the workplace. In Barron, C., Bruce, N. and Nunan, D (eds.) *Knowledge and Discourse: Language Ecology in Theory and Practice.* Singapore: Longman, 204–220.

Friginal, E. (2007), Outsourced call centers and English in the Philippines. *World Englishes* 26(3), 331–345.

Friginal, E. (2008), Linguistic variation in the discourse of outsourced call centers. *Discourse Studies* 10(6), 715–736.

Gonzalez, A. FSC (1997), The history of English in the Philippines. In Bautista, M. L. S. (ed.) *English is an Asian Language: The Philippine Context.* Australia. The Macquarie Library Pyt. Ltd., 7–16.

Gonzalez, A. FSC (2004), The social dimensions of Philippines English. *World Englishes* 23(1), 7–16.

Halliday, M. A. K (1985), *An Introduction to Functional Grammar.* London. Edward Arnold.

Hamp-Lyons, L. and Lockwood, J. (2009), *The Workplace, the Society and the Wider World: The Offshoring and Outsourcing Industry.* In Language policy and language assessment, Bernard Spolsky (ed.) 2009 volume of the Annual Review of Applied Linguistics. Cambridge University Press.

Hood, S. and Forey, G. (2008), The interpersonal dynamics in call centre interactions: Co-constructing the rise and fall of emotion. *Discourse and Communication* 2(4), 389–409.

Iedema, R. A. M. (1995), *The Language of Administration: Write it Right Industry Research Report.* Sydney: NSW Dept of Education, Disadvantaged Schools program, Metropolitan East.

Iedema, R. (forthcoming), *The Language of Administration.* Sydney: NSW AMES.

Kirkpatrick, A. (2007), *World Englishes: Implications for International Communication and English Language Teaching.* Cambridge: Cambridge University Press.

Krachu, B. (1985), Standards, codification and sociolinguistic realism: The English language in the outer circle. In Quirk, R. and Widdowson, H. G. (eds.) *English in the World: Teaching and Learning the Language and the Literatures.* Cambridge: Cambridge University Press.

Lockwood, J. (2004), *Consultancy Report for Call Centre X. Philippines.* Submitted by Lexicon Consulting Group Ltd. July 2004, 1–29.

Lockwood, J. (2008), What does the Business Processing Outsourcing (BPO) industry want from English language assessment? *Prospect* 23(2), 60–75.

Lockwood, J., Forey, G. and Elias, N. (2009), Call centre communication: Measurement processes in non-English speaking contexts. In Belcher, D. (ed.) *English for Specific Purposes in Theory and Practice.* Michigan: University of Michigan Press.

Lockwood, J., Forey, G. and Price, H. (2008), *Englishes in the Philippine Business Processing Outsourcing Industry: Issues, Opportunities and Research.* In Bautistia, M. L. and Bolton, K. (eds.) *Philippines English: Linguistic and Literary Perspectives.* Hong Kong: Hong Kong University Press, 157–172.

Martin, J. and White, P. (2005), *The Language of Evaluation: Appraisal in English.* London: Palgrave Macmillan.

McDowell, C. (1995), Assessing the language proficiency of overseas-qualified Teachers – the English Language Assessment (ELSA). In Brindley, G. (ed.) *Language Assessment in Action.* Australia: NCELTR.

McNamara, T. (1990), Assessing the second language proficiency of health professionals. Unpublished thesis. Department of Linguistics and Language Studies. University of Melbourne.

Mawer, G. (1993), *Communication Syllabus Framework for the Metals and Engineering Industry.* Sydney: National Centre for English Language Teaching and Research.

Mawer, G. (1999), *Language and Literacy in Workplace Education: Learning at Work.* UK.

NASSCOM – McKinsey (2005), *The NASSCOM McKinsey Study 2005* (retrieved from www.nasscom.com.in 17 June 2007).

NASSCOM www.nasscom.com.in (accessed 15 February 2009).

Roberts, C., Davies, E. and Jupp, T. (1992), *Language and Discrimination Communication in Multi-ethnic Workplaces*. London: Longman.

Saussure, F. de (1983), *Course in General Linguistics*. Bally, C. and Sechehaye, A. (eds.) Trans. Roy harric. La sale, Illinois: Open Court.

Swales, J. M. (1990), *Genre Analysis – English in Academic and Research Settings*. Cambridge: Cambridge University Press.

Swales, J. M. and Bhatia, V. K. (1983), An approach to the linguistic study of legal documents, *Fachsprache* 3(3), 98–108.

Wan, J. (forthcoming), How voice quality features create meaning potentials and form alignments in telephone conflicts, *Proceedings of Semiotic Margins Conference*. Sydney 10–12 December 2008.

Widdowson, H. (1978), *Teaching Language as Communication*. London: Oxford University Press.

Part IV

Communication Skills: Assessment and its Uses

Chapter 14

Consulting Assessment for the Business Processing Outsourcing (BPO) Industry in the Philippines

Jane Lockwood

The Hong Kong Institute of Education, Hong Kong

This chapter reports on the development of a 'consulting assessment' (CA) approach to meet the specific needs of the BPO industry in call centres in the Philippines. Put simply, this CA approach aims to provide English language communications assessment processes and tools that key stakeholders can use to determine placement, diagnostic and achievement language levels of their employees. Specifically these tools and processes can be used at recruitment, training and on the floor in the call centres, thus providing an 'end-to-end' solution to the business requirement for constant communications measurement. As well, this chapter reports on the development of the Business Processing Language Assessment Scales (BUPLAS) that were created to provide speaking and writing scales and descriptors to be used for the CA approach within the BPO workplace. The data for this chapter is drawn from communications consulting work carried out in the Philippines in the period 2004–2007, with specific reference to two call centres. The first is a large well known 3rd party outsourced call centre with several sites in Manila and Cebu employing about 5,000 Customer Service Representatives (CSRs). The second site is a large USA-based insurance off-shored 'captive' company employing about 800 CSRs. This chapter does not provide a detailed impact study (beyond the anecdotal) on the BUPLAS tool and approach, as evaluative data is currently still being gathered.

Introduction

Traditional approaches to Business English language assessment are currently being challenged by the particular needs of new globalized workplaces such as call centres which are being set up in such non-native English speaker (NNES) destinations as the Philippines and India (Hamp-Lyons and Lockwood – 2009; Lockwood 2008). In these new BPO worksites NNES communicate with native English speakers from USA, UK, Australia and New Zealand and poor communication can threaten the smooth running of the business. It is therefore important to explore where these critical points of communication occur in the call centres, and how language assessments can safeguard and inform the business requirements resulting in good communication. The Offshoring and Outsourcing (O&O) industry is estimated to be worth in excess of US300 billion world-wide by 2010 (NASSCOM McKinsey Report 2005) and the current financial turmoil is tipped to add to these estimates where there is a business imperative for companies to find cheaper ways of doing business. The call centres, which form a sizable section of the O&O industry in these new NNES destinations, are currently experiencing problems in selecting, training and evaluating customer service representatives (CSRs) who mainly interact with USA or other English-speaking customers over the phones and who need to address concerns about a whole range of products and services. There is great anxiety currently within the call centre industry about poor English language skills, and the call centres are struggling to meet the demands of new client accounts being opened in the O&O destinations to serve the Western English-speaking world.

The business requirements for language assessment in the call centres are such that the traditional 'off-the-shelf' commercial business English tests do not fit the need for three reasons. First, the call centres attract very large volumes of potential employees with only 1–5% being hired. Clearly the companies are not willing to pay the high cost of language assessment in testing all interviewees with a commercial tool that charges on a per head basis. Related to this issue too, is the need for speed in assessment as the hiring process is often completed on the same day. Typically, commercial business English tests have a lead in and turnaround time of 2–4 weeks. The second reason relates to the specific placement information required for each client account. Each client account requires a language benchmark 'tag' to which an assessed newly recruited CSR is placed to work. For example, a simple directory enquiries account that provides routine information to callers will require a lower level of communicative competence than a high-end financial advisory call centre. No commercial test provides this kind of service. As well, the business wants the assessment process used in recruitment to provide information on which recruitees can be categorized as pre-hire, near-hire or far-hire, i.e. how trainable are they? Assessment 'granularity' and diagnostic information are expected of any language assessment process within the BPO business and such assessments need to be aligned to and support the communications training curriculum. Finally, even after hiring, the business requires on-going communications assessment information for training, for client account migration and for quality assurance. The interactive competency of the CSR is of important and critical concern to the call centre business that constantly measures its success in customer satisfaction statistics. To meet these different demands, the call centre companies themselves are developing their own solutions, often with problematic results (Friginal 2007; Lockwood 2008). The main objective of this chapter is to explore how one English communications training company based in Manila, has linked language assessment theory and best practice to the reality and requirements of the business in the BPO industry.

This chapter is divided into three main sections. The first section describes the business requirements for language assessment in the call centre industry, taking companies domiciled in the Philippines as examples. In the second section, I will consider the limitations of commercially available business English language tests for this industry context and review the limited literature; and in the final section I will describe and tentatively evaluate (albeit anecdotally), one solution developed by a training provider based in the Philippines. This final section will report on the efforts of a Philippines-based communications consultancy and training group (FuturePerfect Business English Specialists*) to develop a solution for this industry which we have termed consulting assessment (CA). CA is an industry approach to communications assessment which relies on analyses of the business requirements for assessment and responds with a systematic, tailored, valid and reliable set of tasks and assessment processes.

The business processing language assessment scales (BUPLAS) were developed by the author when consulting in Manila call centres (2004–2007) in order to provide a measurement tool and a process for carrying out speaking and writing assessments within the business context of the call centre worksite. First I document the decisions about selecting the domains for the speaking descriptors for BUPLAS and then how, as a result of the questions and problems being posed by the call centres, these scales and descriptors were embedded into the business systems at recruitment, training and quality assurance and then transferred to the key stakeholders to use themselves.

The Background and Methodology for This Study

This study was carried out as part of two consulting assignments in the two call centres in the Philippines. The first call centre was a 3rd party company with sites in Manila and Cebu which does work for different multinational companies across a number of industry 'verticals' including telecommunications, IT, finance and insurance, retail and tourism. It employs approximately 5,000 call centre representatives (CSRs). The second call centre was a large well-known American insurance company employing about 800 CSRs all locally employed by that company. This call centre processed insurance claims for American customers from all over the USA. Over a period of 6 months the key stakeholders in both the call centres were interviewed individually and/or as part of a series of focus group discussions. These were recorded and summarized.

---

* BUPLAS is the language assessment tool and set of processes tailored by FuturePerefct to the needs of the BPO industry.

As well, the consultant also surveyed a number of call centre supervisors about their needs and views on the language assessment and training requirements of their CSR teams. Language assessment tests and training documents were reviewed and observations were made by the consultant at recruitment, in training and on the floor where quality assurance processes take place. As well, the computerized assessment and monitoring for communications competence were studied on the floor in order to understand the principles behind the many metrics being generated as quality assurance standard procedure in the call centre. Call centres generate metrics related to all aspects of their operations including 'average handling time' (AHT) and success at 'first time resolution' (FTR) on the phones. These metrics form the basis of regular quality assurance (QA) reporting for each of the CSRs and feed into regular CSAT (customer satisfaction) ratings.

The qualitative and quantitative data were then analysed and written up in the form of a consultancy report together with a series of recommendations (Lockwood 2004).

The Call Centre Industry in the Philippines

The Business Processing Outsourcing (BPO) Industry or the Offshoring and Outsourcing (O&O) industry as it is becoming known as, in developing countries such as India and the Philippines, is currently reporting a serious shortage of proficient speakers of English to be employed in the call centres as customer services representatives (CSRs) (BPAP 2007; Forey and Lockwood 2007; Friginal 2007; Lockwood 2008; Lockwood, Forey and Price 2008; NASSCOM McKinsey report 2005). It is estimated that the $5 billion a year O&O industry in the Philippines is enjoying a yearly 75% increase in the coming 5 years (Tuchman 2004). Such call centres serve USA, UK and Australian multinational companies, answering customer queries and complaints related to a range of products and services. The O&O destination of the Philippines has been heavily promoted in Western English-speaking countries because of its perceived good language skills and its cultural affinity with all things American; it also boasts of being the 3rd largest English-speaking country in the world (Gonzalez 2008).

The Problems

The BPO industry in the Philippines is complaining that their recruitment success rates are very low (1–5%) and where the BPO industry aims to recruit 50,000+ new CSRs per year (BPAP 2008), this is a serious threat to the viability of the industry. The main cause of the low recruitment success is reported by human resource and training personnel to be the lack of acceptable English language-speaking skills to serve their native speaker customers (BPAP 2008; Dominguez 2006; Greenleaf and Ferrer 2006; Lockwood 2008; Magellan Alliance 2005). The Filipino government, the Chambers of Commerce and the O&O industry in the Philippines all bemoan the sliding English language competence of its school leavers and university graduates. At the same time, they have launched significant English language awareness campaigns e.g. 'English is Cool' to promote English language learning (BPAP 2003). While I do not wish to debate the validity of the government concerns in this article, it is certainly the case that the call centres require extremely high levels of spoken communication as many of the companies are insisting on a 'native speaker' variety to serve American customers. A Filipino variety of English, albeit internationally intelligible, appears to be rejected as inappropriate for this kind of work and mother tongue interference is commonly cited by recruiters, trainers and QA personnel as problematic when CSRs are serving Western English-speaking customers on the phones. Currently there are three tiers of recruitees that the industry looks for at recruitment, namely pre-hire (ready to go into employment with minimum induction training); near-hires (need 2–4 weeks of intensive communications training) and far-hires (need substantial training, sometimes up to 8 weeks of intensive training). Two questions are constantly being posed by BPO stakeholders as follows. How do we language assess for hireability and trainability at interview to ensure high-quality communicators on the floor? How do we measure and report on this at recruitment, at training and on the floor?

The Business Requirements for Language Assessment in the Call Centres

One of the biggest problems in call centre English language assessment relates to the complex and multidimensional nature of the language assessments required by the business. The nature of this complexity emerged during the consultancies carried out in the abovementioned call centres in the Philippines. The business requirements of 'captive' and third party call centres for valid, reliable and practical communications assessment at client account set up, at recruitment, at training and at quality assurance are described below.

An 'offshored' client account (sometimes called 'captives') is one where the parent company simply 'off shores' its back office functions to cheaper destinations overseas. It then recruits its own employees in the new destinations. An 'outsourced' client account is one where a company wants a third party to take the work offshore and do the work. In Manila, a big American insurance company from hereon named ERA has offshored much of its own insurance administration work and its own service centre now houses over 800 CSRs who deal with ERA customers all over America throughout the night. What we will refer to as PESAsia, on the other hand, is a large third party call centre that services the businesses of about 40 client across a range of 'verticals' or industry types such as IT support, retail, finance, insurance and telecommunications and employs around 500 CSRs. Each client account in PESAsia is different in that their products and services are different, the customer demographics and socio-economic backgrounds are different and organizational requirements of good service are different. For example, a large US investment bank headquartered in New York and whose customers are big corporate investors need CSRs who are able to communicate under pressure with a range of educated native speakers about complex financial products and provide good counsel. At the other end of the continuum, there are retail accounts that simply give customers directory information on their outlets. How can the call centres measure the level of language difficulty and challenge inherent in each account and place CSRs into them who are well matched for language level? How can this be achieved when the tools, processes and language assessment skills of the key stakeholders responsible for recruitment, training, management and quality assurances have no familiarity with English language assessments? The key stakeholders and processes are captured in the diagram below:

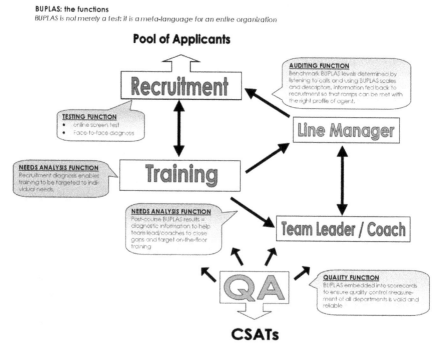

FIGURE 1   BUPLAS: The functions (Diagram taken from FuturePerfect publicity 2008)

The Business Requirements

The business requirements as outlined in Figure 1, relate to the following key areas. First, call centres need information about language levels **at set up**. When a new client account is set up in the Philippines, the call centre requires an assessment (or **audit**) of the language complexity and requirement of that account. As outlined above, some accounts are inherently more complex and demanding of communication skills than others. The company needs to know what the linguistic and intercultural challenges are of each of its accounts. The process of establishing this, is known as a language audit (Reeves and Wright 1996). Currently very few call centres carry out a language audit of their accounts, so how do they know what levels of English they need? Secondly, the call centres need information about how to measure language levels **at screening and recruitment.** As previously noted, the current successful recruitment rate is running between 1 and 5%. The most common complaint is that the recruitees lack good enough English language skills. However, the recruitment language assessment processes are highly problematic, sometimes resulting in the stronger candidates being unsuccessful and the weaker ones being recruited (Lockwood 2008). The O&O industry and the Philippine government have recently collaborated on a 'training voucher' system that provides English language support to a new pool of potential call centre recruitees called 'near hires'.

Thirdly, language assessment skills are required **for pre- and post-course training.** Most call centres in the Philippines invest heavily in pre- and near-hire communications training. Pre-hire training is short-term communications training, typically lasting 2 weeks, where candidates undertake language and communications training around the same time as their product training. The programmes generally concentrate on 'soft skills communication' and assume assured language proficiency levels that underpin choices of appropriate functional language. Near-hire and far-hire training, on the other hand, can last for anything between 2 and 8 weeks full time. Without having a capacity to measure language gain, it is difficult for training teams to target their programmes and measure outcomes. Furthermore based on observational data collected from such programmes, often their training needs analysis, training quality and reporting are frustrated by a lack of a principled framework for language assessment (Lockwood 2008).

Once the CSR has been deemed to be of a good enough level of English language competency and to be familiar enough with the product information for the client account in which they will work, they are normally put into 'incubation' or 'nesting' on the floors, similar to a trial period. This is where they receive **intensive mentoring or coaching support.** The coaching support is often carried out by team leaders in the call centres or 'veteran' CSRs (i.e. CSRs with a great deal of experience). Good diagnostic information about language and communication problems is required for the coaches to target their support, although this was not evident in the call centres visited. In many cases the team leaders work supporting and assessing the language performance of these new CSRs simply by intuition and 'gut' feeling.

The final business requirement for communications assessment is where **quality assurance is carried out on the floor.** Service level agreements (SLAs) revolve around successful communication with English-speaking customers. To this end, each account has its own quality assurance 'scorecard'. While these scorecards may work on native-speaker CSRs at home, no allowance has been made for CSRs whose first language is not English. For a full discussion of the scorecard as a language assessment tool see (Lockwood, Forey and Elias forth-coming). Many call centres report a lack of success with the scorecard as a judgmental tool for assessing the communication quality of the calls. As well, they report a lack of success in using it as a developmental and diagnostic tool for coaching on the floor.

All these points of contact within the business require language and commu-nications measurement skills for different purposes. The necessary task for language assessment research and development in the O&O industry is to build tools and approaches that meet these challenges.

Some Common Problems in Using Commercial Products

Tests of business English do exist. Large testing organizations such as Cambridgeesol (UK) and Educational Testing Service (USA) have produced a selection of business English tests (e.g. BULATS, BEC, TOEIC), claiming that they can be used within workplaces to meet their needs. But can they? These 'business English' skills tests appeal to a broad sector of the working population world-wide as they are offered by large well-known and respected examinations bodies and provide useful certification for entry into a variety of workplaces. For example, TOEIC and BEC are included in employment advertisements in business in Indian and Korean newspapers. However, such large-scale tests have been found to be ineffective in meeting the particular business require-ments for language measurement within the call centres. The approach is problematic insofar as the commercial tests give a one-point-in-time overall assessment score provided by an approved assessor for the test. How can such a testing model respond to the different dynamic and on-going needs outlined in the previous section? The business model is also problematic insofar as the per-head cost is deemed too high, when taking into account the call centres are screening hundred and thousands of possible candidates for 1–5% success. The turnaround time for results is also impractical for call centres wanting same-day recruits. However, more seriously, the call centres are wanting more informa-tion than most commercial business tests provide. They want diagnostic infor-mation for training purposes and they want extensive information about the 'interactive' domain of spoken English of each recruitee, as they see interactive capability as key to successful communication with their customers. Additionally business stakeholders in the call centres are also asking for measures of intercultural communication.

Government instrumentalities in the Philippines such as the Technical and Education Skills Development Agency (TESDA) in Manila are also frustrated about the lack of cost effective, valid and reliable assessment tools that can be used by the BPO industry to recruit, measure training and quality assurance (QA). TESDA is still seeking new assessment processes to be endorsed by them for the call centre industry after several years and a series of commercial language assessment test disappointments.

What the Literature Says

'Consulting assessment', as previously mentioned, relies on in-depth needs analysis of the workplace requirements for communications assessment and also relies on the capacity of the assessment tools and processes to be tailored to the specific business requirements. While the applied linguistic literature is rich on training needs analysis (Brindley 1984; Brown 1995; Dudley and St. John 1998; Nunan 1988; Willing 1988) the literature is scarce where language assessment needs analysis is concerned. Reeves and Wright (1996) address the specific issue of front-end language requirements of workplace posts through what they have coined 'a language audit'. They take a broad-angled ethnographic view of needs analysis in the workplace and encourage language providers to 'tailor' courses specifically to the needs of the workplace based on language benchmarking the 'work' within the organizations. Once these language needs and benchmarks are understood, planning for language improvement and measurement can take place.

> A language audit therefore should strive to help a company's management make the right strategic decision in recruitment, in modifying the organization and the behaviour of some departments, as well as allocating resources for training and quality assurance. (Reeves and Wright 1996:2)

The language testing literature is rich in the discussions about the relative merits of using different applied linguistic frameworks to achieve construct validity and reliability in the design and use of any test and much of the discussion has revolved around pushing criteria for assessment beyond the traditional preoccupations with pronunciation and grammatical accuracy to a consideration of broader communicative domains such as discourse and interactive capabilities (Bachman 1990; Bachman and Palmer 1982; Bachman and Savignon 1986; Canale and Swain 1980; Davies 1988; Hughes 1989; Weir 1990). Assessment practices that reflect communicative approaches to language training in Language for Specific Purposes (LSP) contexts is also well covered

(Lumley and Brown 1996; McNamara 1997; Douglas 2000; Elder 2001), and well-documented accounts of test development for different groups of occupations and professionals abound. McNamara (1990, 1996) and McDowell (1995) have both developed standardized and competency-based tests for a range of teachers and health professionals in Australia, Douglas (2000) looks at specific language use situations to develop test content and test methods for highly specific LSP, such as English for air traffic control. Such frameworks, however, have yet to be fully understood in an industry context and incorporated into business language assessment practices on-site to meet specific business requirements. Testing for professional performance in an individual test taker is not the same as embedded assessment in a worksite to meet a range of business requirements.

Revell (1994) talks specifically about language testing in the Hong Kong corporate context and makes an interesting and relevant link between language assessment and quality management practices in Hong Kong companies when he says:

> Internal and external customer requirements are first priority, but other sources of information may be needed and should be found to make sure training and assessment are aligned with the company's quality requirements. These may be found in training criteria, in job descriptions, or in external quality requirements. (Revell 1994:333)

While Revell (1994) has articulated the problem, he does not offer any solutions in the form of practical guidance or prevailing theoretical frameworks that may prove useful to the English language workplace assessment practitioner. Lockwood (2002), in a further analysis of workplace training and evaluation processes in Hong Kong workplaces, has argued for an interdisciplinary approach to curriculum and programme evaluation incorporating applied linguistic and business management models (Bramley and Pahl 1996; Goldstein 1993; Kirkpatrick 1994) to ensure business stakeholder involvement in these educational processes. This approach relies on educationalists taking a 'consultative role' in the workplace and gathering key stakeholder views to ensure that training and assessment make an impact on workplace performance. This research approach and frameworks have been key to understanding the business requirements for language assessment.

The History of the Business Processing Outsourcing Language Assessment Scales (BUPLAS)

In the early part of 2000 in the Philippines, the call centre industry started to experience great difficulty in getting a steady supply of CSRs with the right language levels and skills for work on the phones. When the O&O industry first started up in the Philippines, good English language speakers were sourced readily from the top universities in Manila. However, over the years that pipeline has dried up and there is now great reliance on lower tier universities and post-secondary colleges for recruiting CSRs. Not surprisingly, the level of English is not as good as their counterparts from the top schools. This has caused anxiety within the industry sector.

Call centres have responded to this recruitment crisis in a number of ways. Some have developed common sense, but layman solutions, to highly complex language assessment and training problems in order to meet the business requirements outlined earlier on in the chapter. Other companies have been importing 'ready-made' solutions from commercial business testing agencies with great expectations that one test would provide all the solutions to the call centre needs (and indeed they were marketed this way). A few call centres have been late to admit that there has been a problem at all. However, as recruitment has become more difficult over the years (BPAP 2007), call centres have been evaluating their business processes for communications training and assessment in order to develop improved recruitment processes, to target and shorten training and meet the requirements of the QA processes more effectively. In fact, call centres are now viewing improved and tailored assessment and training processes as a 'competitive edge' for their businesses (Lockwood 2008). It was in this context that BUPLAS was conceptualized and developed. The author was, at that time, consulting into the two call centres which are the subject of this article. The challenge was to find a workable solution to the business requirements and problems these call centres were posing for language assessment and communications training.

I first pose a series of business problems articulated by call centre senior managers at the time of the consultancies through the interviews and focus group discussions. Each of these problems articulated in the data pose different requirements for language assessment in the day-to-day call centre work. I then go on to discuss how the BUPLAS tool and consulting assessment (CA) process emerged to meet these business needs.

BUPLAS is a five-level scale (1 being the lowest and 5 being the highest with .5 being awarded where there are features of both levels), and comprises speaking descriptors across the domains of Pronunciation, Language accuracy and range, Discourse capability and Interactive capability. There is a separate rubric for writing that is not discussed in detail in this chapter.

The Case Study Questions

Each of the case study problems is derived from the two workplaces described above during the time of the consultancy. Each reflects different concerns around the issues of communications assessment in the BPO workplace. They are first described and then responded to.

Case study 1 – Company request (set up):
How do I know what level of English I need in my inbound call center? Our agents need to deal with some pretty complex calls? If I do all this testing, how do I interpret the results? How do I know the CSR is going to cut it on the floor? (Account Manager in ERA)

In the BPO industry, and call centers specifically, there are different language level needs depending on the account. Variables such as whether the account is inbound or outbound; what kind of industry the account is servicing; in which country the account is domiciled, are all factors affecting the language difficulty of the account. 'Tagging' different accounts with a BUPLAS level can be done by carrying out a language audit. This entails listening to a representative sample of calls, talking to the CSRs and their supervisors and reading about the product/service content. Typically the insurance and financial sectors inbound are tagged at a high BUPLAS level (4+), whereas outbound or routine inbound calls (e.g. directory enquiries) can be as low as BUPLAS 2.5. It takes approximately one day to audit an account.

Case study 2 – Company request (recruitment):
I need to ramp up to 250 call center agents within a six week period and I need to know who is ready for the account immediately and who needs training and for how long. We've got over 4,000 applicants for these jobs . . . where do I start? What do I do? (HRO manager of PESAsia-2003)

The volume of CSR applicants that need to be processed, especially at times of expansion, was particularly notable. Given that the industry only expects, at best, to recruit on average only 5 successful candidates out of every 100, communications assessment at recruitment needs to be as cost effective and time efficient as possible. Many large call centres employ casual teams of phone screeners who have the collective responsibility of screening out 50% of the applicants based on language requirements. The problems appeared to be threefold with the phone screeners. First, the level of English of the screeners was not good, indeed some of the screeners were high school students on vacation. Secondly, they had no scales and descriptors, nor assessment tasks to work from; and thirdly they had no training or calibration. Given these limitations, it was observed that the screeners made very haphazard and subjective decisions about who to bring in for the next round of assessment. Those who did make it through to the next round were generally given a test of grammar (these items related to first language interference mistakes e.g. verb/subject agreement), reading comprehension and a writing task. From there successful applicants would go onto the final speaking assessment carried out by an HRO or account manager. Not only was the process long, but it also was not based on sound language assessment principles and approaches (Hamp-Lyons and Lockwood 2009; Lockwood 2008).

To meet this need at recruitment, the author, who was then the consultant, decided to develop a set of scales and descriptors for call centre recruiters, account managers and trainers, and decided that these stakeholders would need to be screened themselves to ensure good proficiency levels. They would then need to be trained up to use the scales and descriptors and would require additional assistance in developing appropriate language assessment tasks.

Case study 3 – Company request (pre- and post-assessment for training):
We run both communications and product training before the agents go 'live' but we don't know if the communications training has any impact on our pre-hire group. What if I invest in putting longer communications training programmes on? Do these communications training programmes make any difference? How long does it take to get good enough to go on the phones? (Senior manager ERA)

The links between language proficiency development, end-of-course score reporting and short training programmes is a common concern in the call centres. Understandably there is a requirement for business to justify its expenditure on communications training but how this should be measured requires careful consideration. The author considered this issue in relation to the final domain areas selected and also in relation to the writing language achievement descriptors that related to the objectives of the communications training. While it was felt that a short training programme would not result in clear improvement in language accuracy and range and pronunciation (the proficiency domains); it was felt that improvements in the competency/skills domains of interactive and discourse capacity may show development. These latter domains were then articulated in the course outlines as objectives and measured against the scales and descriptors.

Case study 4 – Company request (Quality assurance):
The scorecard that we used back home to measure quality doesn't seem to be as effective in this new non-English speaking context. Can BUPLAS help us with our quality assurance processes to make sure that we pick up English language problems effectively for further support as well as provide a QA score that is meaningful? (QA Manager PESAsia)

Currently, the O&O industry uses a reductionist approach to scoring for quality. Typically a QA scorecard will contain between 35 and 50 individual items that the QA personnel simply check yes or no. Some of the items are of low importance to communication success e.g. the exact wording of the opening; while other items are fundamental to the service success e.g. 'did the customer feel s/he was being served in a professional manner?' The scorecards investigated made no allowance for ranking or weighting of the communication areas probed. As well, there were numerous overlaps in the kinds of questions being asked. For a full discussion on the scorecard see (Lockwood, Forey and Elias forthcoming). It was felt that a set of scales and descriptors tailored to the communication requirements of the agents would:

(i)   provide a standardized framework for carrying out the QA process;
(ii) foreground the important considerations in communication success
(iii) provide a principled approach to the QA assessment processes for both judgmental and developmental purposes.

The Development of the BUPLAS Speaking Scales and Descriptors

Once the multidimensional need for language assessment was understood, the author of BUPLAS started with the priority need for developing a set of speaking and writing scales and descriptors to assist the different stakeholders at the key points in the business to measure their candidates for the variety of purposes as described above. The domains of these descriptors needed to reflect the requirements of the industry, which were, predictably, focused on very good interactive skills. The scale and descriptors also needed to reflect a theoretical construct for communicative language competence.

In drafting the BUPLAS I was not only mindful of this interactive skills domain, but also the discourse skills domain that early research into the descriptions of the call centre exchanges, had shown to be problematic (Forey and Lockwood 2007). Pronunciation and language accuracy and range were also key domains to measure for basic language proficiency. The literature on communicative language testing (Bachman 1990; Canale and Swain 1980; Savignon 1983; Weir 1990) combined with knowledge of the business requirements, informed the final domain selection which are outlined in the following section.

'Communicative competence' (Canale and Swain 1980; Canale 1983; Savignon 1983) comprises a number of elements which will be discussed below. These components provide a rich interpretation of what is present in good communication and go far beyond the limited view that good grammar and clear pronunciation is all that is required. Canale (1983) writes of the nature of linguistic communication as:

(a) being a form of social interaction and therefore normally acquired and used in social interaction
(b) involving a high degree of unpredictability and creativity in form and message
(c) taking place in discourse and sociocultural contexts which provide constraints on appropriate language use and also cues as to correct interpretations of utterances
(d) being carried out under limiting psychological and other conditions such as memory constraints, fatigue and other distractions;

(e) always having a purpose (for example to establish social relationships, to persuade or to promise);
(f) involving authentic, as opposed to textbook-contrived language, and
(g) as being judged as successful or not on the basis of actual outcomes

(Canale 1983:3–4)

The following features were selected as important for the domain selection for BUPLAS to meet the kinds of business needs described above:

Language competence (ability to use grammar, vocabulary and the phonological features of the language)
Discourse competence (ability to recognize and construct the flow of a spoken or written text)
Sociolinguistic competence (ability to understand the intercultural nuances)
Interactive competence (ability to make appropriate functional interaction, and to move between transaction and interaction)
Strategic competence (ability to repair language breakdown, particularly in spoken language)

Specifically in the call centre context, these competencies mean the CSR has the ability to:

1. interact well and build relationships with customers
2. make appropriate language choices
3. construct text in a way that is understandable to overseas customers
4. talk with phonological features that are easily understood by the customer
5. maintain control of the call
6. understand the nuances in what the caller says in order to gauge how best to service the caller.

Native English speakers generally have these language and communication skills, but for some NNES speakers these communicative competencies needed to be explicitly identified, explained and taught. Because of the insistence of many, particularly USA accounts, to have native speaker-like varieties of English in their CSR workforce, it was decided to add the pronunciation domain as a separate one, although 'global intelligibility' was highlighted as the desirable benchmark rather than the perfection of an American accent.

The BUPLAS Scales and Descriptors-speaking

Scales and descriptors were developed for both writing and speaking; however, this article will take speaking ones as our example.

The BUPLAS criteria for speaking are comprised of **four domains for spoken communication**:

- Pronunciation, stress and intonation
- Language accuracy and range
- Discourse competency
- Interactive fluency and strategic competency

These domains align with a communicative approach to assessment and most notably incorporate the interactive domain so important to the BPO industry. The scales go from 1 (low) to 5 (high). Assessors use a half way marking scale of .5 where there are features of both descriptions.

It was decided for the practical reasons of training, calibrating and reporting to have two versions of the scales and descriptors: One called the 'elaborated' scales for assessors to use in their marking and calibration sessions, and the other, the 'conflated' version for other stakeholders in the call centre (including head office overseas) to use in interpreting the scores.

Once the scales and descriptors were developed for speaking, they were piloted over a range of workplaces and refined. In writing the text for the descriptor, the author was aware of the need to use plain English as far as possible so that all stakeholders, not just the trainers, could read and understand the profile descriptions.

Discussion

The scales and descriptors, once developed, provided a framework for the call centres to benchmark their (prospective) employees for a range of purposes. The author worked with the various stakeholders on how to assess language for the specific purpose of the business. For example, the phone recruiters simply wanted a yes/no exclusion decision and had targets of 'knocking out' 50% of applicants; the interviewers of the client accounts wanted a granulated report which would highlight hireability or trainability; the trainers wanted diagnostic information for training and for strengthening the content of the curriculum; the QA personnel wanted specific diagnostic information from the assessment to feed into coaching support and so on. The advantage of using the same scales and descriptors meant that, for the first time, recruiters, trainers and QA personnel were using the same language and benchmarks to talk about the needs and success of the front line CSRs. It therefore provided a much-needed systematic language assessment reporting tool where all business stakeholders were using the same metalanguage to talk about communication issues.

This model deviates from traditional language assessment products and processes in a number of ways. First, while the scales and descriptors had been written to reflect the language abilities of the candidate along a scale of 1–5, some call centres and client accounts wanted the descriptors to be tailored more to the communication priorities within the accounts. For example, some client accounts have very complex products and services, so clear and organized explanations were critical to the success of the call. Other requests that resulted in domain description tailoring were soft skills requirements for customer service and even intercultural sensitivity (as it is manifested in language) which were written into the domains of discourse and interactive capacity. This tailoring was done by the consultant only and companies were discouraged from tampering with the scales and descriptors without expert consultancy advice.

The second way in which this model pushed the boundaries of traditional language assessment approaches was that non-language specialists (e.g. HRO, account managers and quality assurance personnel) were trained up and calibrated as language assessors. The consultant wanted the call centre to be able to operate as independently as possible using the scales and descriptor, therefore transferring this expertise to key personnel was seen as critical to the success of embedding the assessment approach within the business. The one thing that became non-negotiable in the training up of non-specialist assessors was that the language level of the non-language specialist needed to be very high (BUPLAS 4–4.5). Occasionally, and at the early insistence of the call centres, potential assessors, as low as BUPLAS 2.5, were sent to BUPLAS training and calibration workshops with frustrating results. This benchmark level for BUPLAS training entry is very confronting for the call centre management who often recruit HRO and QA personnel, phone screeners and even on-the-floor communications coaches whose language level is very low. One of the call centre senior managers admitted that it is often the case that their non-performers get moved into quality assurance functions such as coaching.

The third way in which this model varies from traditional language assessment approaches is that key stakeholders often request for the domain weightings in BUPLAS to be varied according to the needs of the client account. For example, in a client account which is particularly sensitive e.g. debt collection, insurance claims where there has been a death etc. the domain of interactive capacity is seen to be of particular importance. Another example may be where a company (e.g. IT support) has a complex product or service that requires clear explanation or instruction; here the discourse domain may be highly valued.

Assistance with language task construction for the purposes of assessment is also a requirement of this model. For example, at recruitment, traditionally a face-to-face interview involves the interviewers asking the candidates a list of questions – this has been the modus operandi for assessing communications. Devising scenarios for short roleplays at an interview where a candidate works as a pair or even threes has provided HRO recruiters with improved evidence of language performance capability for the work in call centres.

Investigating the business requirements for assessment, embedding the scales and descriptors and transferring the knowledge to the key company stakeholders are the three hallmarks of the CA approach.

Over the last 5 years and since the consultancies described in this chapter took place, the BUPLAS scales and descriptors have been embedded and transferred into a large number of call centre in the Philippines. The main challenges for CA and BUPLAS relate to both the quality issues of embedding and transferring the tools and processes, and also the business model for this new kind of assessment. It is important for an external party such as Future-Perfect Business English Specialists to maintain a 'presence' within the company to ensure internal calibrations are carried out regularly, that new business needs are met by assessment and that moderation studies are also carried out. Also companies need to accept the fact that the costing model, while much cheaper than a per-head flat cost, needs to account for the above on-going services supplied by external experts. This can be done through a license arrangement and regular consultancy visits. As well, further research and development needs to take place to ensure validity and reliability of the tasks and the scales and descriptors. Copyright has also become an issue where companies have simply photocopied the tasks, the scales and descriptors with no training and no license.

While there is plenty of anecdotal evidence from the companies who use BUPLAS concerning improvements in their recruitment, training and quality assurance processes, a full impact study has just begun.

Conclusions

While the CA approach and the use of the BUPLAS scales and descriptors have not undergone formal evaluation to date, anecdotally, companies based in Manila report great success in that it provides a systematic approach to measuring language across and within each part of the call centre business. For the first time recruitment, training and quality assurance personnel are using a common metalanguage to talk about the communication levels of the CSRs. In an industry that measures everything it does, from the average call handling time to first time resolution, a measure for customer satisfaction and communications success is seen as a crucial metric to report on. Clearly there are many areas of further research and development around this model. A formal evaluation of how BUPLAS is soon to be undertaken. It would also be of great interest to see how BUPLAS has affected the communications training programmes i.e. the 'washback' into the curriculum and training approaches which have previously put strong emphasis on accent neutralization and the 'drilling' out of discrete first language interference mistakes. In addition, the impact on the business requires further investigation. Has the very low recruitment rate in HR improved as a result of a communications assessment process that looks for what potential candidates can do with language and how trainable (as well as hirable) they may be? Have the quality assurance processes locally improved and is the diagnostic information finding its way back into more effective training and coaching programmes? The impact of BUPLAS and CA is a rich area that currently requires more detailed and in-depth research investigation.

References

Bachman, L. F. (1990), *Fundamental Considerations in Language Testing*. Oxford: Oxford University Press.

Bachman, L. F. and Palmer, A. S. (1982), The construct validation of some components of communicative proficiency. *TESOL Quarterly* 16(4), 449–465.

Bachman, L. F. and Savignon, S. J. (1986), The evaluation of communicative language proficiency: A critique of the ACTFL oral interview. *Modern Language Journal* 70(4), 380–390.

[BPAP] Business Processing Association of the Philippines. www.bpap.com.ph (Accessed February 2008).

Bramley, P. and Pahl, J. (1996), *The Evaluation of Training in the Social Services*. UK: National Institute for Social Work.

Brindley, G. (1984), *Needs Analysis and objective Setting in the Adult Migrant Education Program*. Sydney: NSW Adult Migrant Education Service.

Brown, J. D. (1995), *The Elements of Language Curriculum: A Systematic approach to Program Development*. New York: Heinle and Heinle Publishers.

Canale, M. (1983) 'On some dimensions of language proficiency' in Oller, J. W. (ed.) 1983: 333–342.

Canale, M. and Swain, M. (1980), Theoretical bases of communicative approaches to second language teaching and testing. *Applied Linguistics* 1(1), 1–47.

Davies, A. (1988), Communicative language testing. In Hughes, A. (ed.) (1988) *Testing English for University Study*. ELT Document No. 127. Modern English Publications.

Dominguez, C. (2006), Bridging the gap. http://www.bpap.org/bpapreserach.asp (Retrieved on 10 October 2006).

Douglas, D. (2000), *Assessing Languages for Specific Purposes*. Cambridge: Cambridge University Press.

Dudley, E., A. and St. John, M. (1998), *Developments in English for Special Purposes: A Multidisciplinary approach*. UK. Cambridge: Cambridge University Press.

Elder, C. (2001), Assessing the language proficiency of teachers: Are there any border controls? *Language Testing* 18(1), 149–170.

Forey, G. and Lockwood, J. (2007), I'd love to put someone in jail for this. An initial investigation of English needs in the Business Processing Outsourcing (BPO) Industry. *English for Specific Purposes* 26(3), 308–326.

Friginal, E. (2007), Outsourced call centers and English in the Philippines. *World Englishes* 26(3), 331–345.

Goldstein, I. (1993), *Training in Organisations: Needs Assessment, Development and Evaluation*. Pacific Grove, California: Brooks/Cole Publishers.

Gonzalez, A. (2008), A favourable climate and soil: A transplanted language and literature. In Bautista, L., Bolton, K. (eds.) *Asian Englishes Today: Philippine English-Linguistic and Literary Perspectives*, 13–25.

Greenleaf, B. and Ferrer, J. (2006), English language acquisition and assessment in call centre environments. Paper presented at *Talking across the World: English Communication Skills for the ITES Industry Inaugural Conference.* AIM, Manila, Philippines, 25–26 February 2006.

Hamp-Lyons, L. and Lockwood, J. (2009), *The Workplace, the Society and the Wider World: The Offshoring and Outsourcing Industry* in Language policy and language assessment, Bernard Spolsky (ed.) 2009 volume of the Annual Review of Applied Linguistics, Cambridge University Press.

Hughes, A. (1989), *Testing for Language Teachers.* Cambridge, UK: Cambridge University Press.

Kirkpatrick, D. (1994), *Evaluating Training Programs – The Four Levels.* USA: Berrett-Koehler Publishers.

Lockwood, J. (2002), Unpublished PhD thesis *Language Training Design and Evaluation Processes in Hong Kong Workplaces.* Hong Kong University.

Lockwood, J. (2004), *Language Audit Report for Call Centre X, Philippines.* Submitted by Lexicon Consulting Group Ltd July 2004, 1–29.

Lockwood, J. (2008), What does the Business Processing Outsourcing (BPO) industry want from English language assessment? *Prospect* 23(2), 60–75.

Lockwood, J., Forey, G. and Elias, N. (2009), Call centre communication: Measurement processes in non-English speaking contexts. In Belcher, D. (ed.) *English for Specific Purposes in Theory and Practice.* USA: University of Michigan Press.

Lockwood, J., Forey, G. and Price, H. (2008), Englishes in the Philippine Business Processing Outsourcing Industry: Issues, opportunities and research. In Bautistia, M. L. and Bolton, K. (eds.) *Philippines English: Linguistic and Literary Perspectives.* Hong Kong: Hong Kong University Press, 157–172.

Lumley, T. and Brown, A. (1996) Specific purpose language performance tests: Task and interaction. *Australian Review of Applied Linguistics* 13,105–136.

Margellan Alliance (2005) *The Philippines as an Offshore Delivery Location.* Manila: John Clements Consultants.

McDowell, C. (1995), Assessing the language proficiency of overseas-qualified Teachers – The English Language assessment (ELSA) In Brindley, G. (1995) *Language Assessment in Action* Australia: NCELTR.

McNamara, T. (1990), Assessing the second language proficiency of health professionals. Unpublished doctoral thesis. Department of linguistics and language studies, University of Melbourne.

McNamara, T. (1996), *Measuring Second Language Performance.* London: Longman.

McNamara, T. (1997), Interaction in second language performance assessment: Whose performance? *Applied Linguistics* 18(4), 446–466.

NASSCOM – McKinsey Report (2005), (retrieved from www.nasscom on 17 June 2007).

Nunan, D. (1988), *Syllabus Design.* Oxford: Oxford University Press.

Reeves, N. and Wright, C. (1996), *Linguistic Auditing: A Guide to Identifying Foreign Language Communication Needs in Corporations.* Clevedon, UK: Multilingual Matters.

Revell, R. (1994), From control to management: Practices and trends in English for occupational purposes. In Boyle, J. and Falvey, P. (eds.) *English Language Testing in Hong Kong.* Hong Kong: The Chinese University Press.

Savignon, S. (1983), *Communicative Competence: Theory and Classroom Practice* Massachusetts: Addison-Wesley Publishers.

Tuchman, M. (2004), *Updates and Downdates: Call Centre 2010 in the Asia-Pacific Region.* Manila ITES 44-40 Special Publication.

Weir, C. (1990), *Communicative Language Testing.* Hemel Hampstead, UK: Prentice Hall.

Willing, K. (1988), *Learning Styles and Strategies in Adult Migrant Education.* Australia NCRC.

Chapter 15

Language Assessment in Call Centres: The Case of the Customer Service Representative

Alan Davies

University of Edinburgh, UK

Customer Service Representatives (CSRs) working in English-based Call Centres need a high level of proficiency in the language in which they speak to customers, a level equivalent to B2/C1 on the Common European Frame of Reference (CEFR) scale. However, such proficiency is not sufficient for interacting with customers: they also need satisfactory clarity, intelligibility and rapport. The ability to speak a variety of English that is indistinguishable from that of an educated native speaker of the language, especially with respect to pronunciation, is not a prerequisite. The present chapter considers how the crucial demands of clarity, intelligibility and rapport can be assessed and recommends how to proceed with such assessments. One important suggestions is that the Call Centre industry promote and flag the World Englishes skills of their highly qualified CSRs, whose command of English is every bit as good as that of an educated native speaker.

Language has many functions, both cognitive and social. Joseph (2004) proposes two essential features: 'communication and representation' (p. 19). Representation is about the self, involving identity, and has to do with our understanding of the world. Communication reaches out to others and concerns the interchange of information. Representation is typically conducted in the spoken language and serves to mark the speaker's primary identity. For most people this is expressed in the speaker's first language (L1). Communication, on the other hand, is carried out in both the spoken and the written language.

In L1 English situations, many speakers for whom English is their L1, will use a local variety of English to express and demonstrate identity. But for written communication purposes, they are more likely to use Standard English (Davies 1999); and for spoken communication an approximation thereto. Similarly, speakers of English as a Second Language (ESL) are likely to use their local World Englishes variety for in-country spoken communication and a Standard

variety for in-country formal written communication. Across national boundaries, unless the speaker has adequate proficiency in the interlocutor's L1 (say,
French speakers to German speakers), given the current prevalence of English,
the likelihood is that written communication will be in Standard English and
that for spoken communication across boundaries speakers will use a hybrid in
order to engage in a mutually intelligible spoken language. Although it is more
likely that everyone will use their own version of World Englishes, a slightly
more formal version than the variety they use to mark identity.

So far so good, one might say. Just as we all accommodate to others, adapt our
speech on one or other dimension (fast-slow, +/– local references, etc), so ESL
speakers need to accommodate to interlocutors across boundaries in English,
which may mean adopting some such variety as English as a Lingua Franca
(ELF) (Jenkins 2007). But this is less easy than it sounds. Whereas a formal
English for communication, whether spoken or written, is not difficult to access,
a less formal variety, intended for communication, is more fugitive. This is the
problem with ELF which rightly makes a claim for international communication by way of a lingua franca version of English as attested by corpus data
(Seidlhofer 2001) but which fails to make clear exactly what is and what is
not ELF.

Since ELF is no-one's responsibility, in the sense that it has no native
speakers, it presents in an acute form a dilemma of all local World Englishes
(WEs) varieties of English. Users of these varieties, Singapore English, Indian
English, Nigerian English (and so on) may be unsure whether to use their local
WEs, however effective they may be as markers of identity, when communicating internationally. (Much the same could be said for varieties of mother-tongue
English such as Glasgow English.) What such WEs lack is a recognized standard-
like version of their own WEs, which is credible and has currency outside their
own identity group.

ELF may be the answer for those who are happy to wear their identity on their
sleeve.

But when the speaker feels the need to disguise their identity and avoid
being placed in their own locality, ELF is not an option since users of ELF
do not wish to disguise their provenance and are happy to be recognized
by their local identity. What is the case of the call centre customer service
representative?

Given that the primary task of call centre customer service representatives
(CSRs) is conversation, it is to be expected that commentary on their activity
focuses on their language use and needs. One such issue is the choice of
a variety of English. Thus Morgan and Ramanathan (2009) comment on
the debate about which spoken English should be taught in schools in India.
Should it be 'that spoken by those educated in the English-medium. Or that
spoken by vernacular-medium teachers who have themselves had their education in this medium' (p. 78). These authors are concerned with the politics of
language policies in India as they influence the work of the call centre. As they

remark, there is a need to recognize the dilemma teachers in India find them-selves in, caught, as they are, between the claims of native speaker (NS) and non-native speaker (NNS) Indian English.

Writing about the call centre situation in the Philippines, Friginal (2009) notes that the industry in that country faces challenges, one of which is 'the actual skill level (that is communication skills in English) of the pool of Filipino customer service agents' (p. 55). The rapid growth of the industry has meant that there are now fewer candidates available with high-level English profi-ciency. This makes the assumed requirement 'to project and act sufficiently like an American' (p. 58) even more difficult. There was always a cross-cultural problem; now there is in addition a language problem. An English-rich society such as the Philippines where English is the educational medium, is an obvious location for a call centre industry. And yet it has major problems:

> . . . the English-in-education policies in the Phillipines still leave gaps in train-ing its professionals in the acquisition of fluent speech. Specific pragmatic features . . . contextual domains of usage, and cultural sensitivity are, as expected, not thoroughly learned in schools. (op cit: 65)

But, as Friginal also recognizes, the problem is not just a matter of inadequate language competence. There are other factors, 'including establishing rapport, personalisation of support, comprehension and correctness of information in transactions are equally important' (ib: 66).

For that reason, Lockwood, Forey and Price (2008) argue that 'training needs to be provided for new recruits that factors in the development of specific com-petencies for the CSR . . . , while at the same time (it) acknowledges the linguis-tic diversity of English in the global work place' (p. 20). And Hood and Forey (2008), discussing the dynamics of call centre interactions, maintain that their analysis of speaker interaction observing the co-articulation and interdepend-ence of linguistic choices could throw light on 'other locations of conflict-reso-lution and consensus in talk, contributing to the body of research on, for example, counselling sessions . . . courtrooms . . . or talkback radio . . .' (p. 17).

The chapter by Lockwood, Forey and Elias (2008) is one of the few attempts to grapple with call centre assessment for selection and monitoring. They address the issue of the Quality Assurance (QA) technique used in training, arguing that: 'the outsourced call-centre industry has become a victim of inap-propriate ELT methodologies that have been prevalent in the school system in Asia for many decades . . . (and which is) inappropriately focused on discrete grammar rules and accent neutralization which has little to do with the cus-tomer service interaction.' (p. 7). They propose that measurement should be based on the model of communicative competence described by Canale and Swain (1980), citing the Business Processing Language Assessment Scale (BUPLAS) as an example of best practice. A scale such as this, they claim, provides an appropriate assessment tool which permits transparency. It is, they say, intended to allow the understanding of 'the complete text and (its assessment) in a clear and objective manner which is explicit to the assessor and the CSR' (p. 27).

Unlike ELF, call centre discourse between CSR and customer is not mutually supportive. In ELF encounters the power differential between the participants is likely to be quite low. Both participants are interested above all in conducting an academic/business conversation. The aim is to engage felicitously and with mutual support in order to reach some kind of resolution which may or may not lead to the signing of a contract or the offer of a position. In the work of the CSRs there is a major power imbalance. For both the CSR and for the overseas customer, the latter is in charge and what that means is that the CSR must present not just as a near native speaker with high English language proficiency, but as deferential and enduringly polite.

This, then, is the dilemma for call centres, for their customer service representatives and even more for their employers. Since they must appear internationally credible and not be located within any one jurisdiction, they need to present themselves as neutralized near native speakers of some version of Standard English and not as Singaporean or Filipino or Indian so as not to give the impression to the customer in, say, Asia that they are speaking from a town next door. Of course, if the customer is him/herself local then they might expect a local speaker. But since that may not be so, and since the local like the international caller may prefer to interact with someone who appears both neutral and at the same time authoritative, the logic must be that in selecting and training front office staff, the emphasis must be on selecting those whose English, including pronunciation, is near educated native speaker.

But hold on! Are we really saying that to be authoritative you have to be neutral? Are we really saying that someone clearly identified by his/her speech as a local WEs speaker, cannot sound authoritative? That judgment (or prejudice?) would exclude many post-colonial professionals, politicians, etc. Call centres themselves must surely stop pretending that their operations are all based in the UK, USA, Canada and Australia rather than where they really take place, in India, the Philippines and so on, thereby enabling themselves to focus on their CSR recruitment and selection, in their training, on issues such as clarity, intelligibility and rapport with their interlocutors. Of course, it is likely that those selected will already have a near-native command of English. There should be no stigma attached to having a local accent, always assuming that there is no problem of intelligibility in telephonic communication.

If this is agreed, then selection and training of CSRs should be concerned above all with their clarity of diction, intelligibility of speech and their rapport/empathy with potential interlocutors. Note that I am not saying that the CSR's general proficiency in English is unimportant. On the contrary, I am taking for granted, as I noted earlier, that they are likely to possess a high level of English on traditional proficiency tests such as IELTS, TOEFL. They are likely to be placed at least as a high B2 or a low C1 on the Council of Europe Foreign

Language Scale (CEFR 2001). But I am saying that level of proficiency is not adequate in itself for the demands placed on CSRs and that they also need to be judged in terms of clarity, intelligibility and rapport. For that a panel of at least three judges will be required:

1. a judge who is representative of standard British or American English
2. an educated speaker of a WEs which is not their own, for example a Nigerian for an Indian call centre
3. a potential non-academic customer from a large client country, for example Mexico, preferably belonging to an older age profile since most CSRs are likely to be in their 20s and 30s and it is important that they should make themselves easily understood by older customers and be able to put them at their ease.

An international pool of such judges should be established. They would interview by audio or, preferably video, always making use of the same protocols. These would not need to be specific to different call centre work since that expertise would be a matter for the training programmes. What the protocols would focus on is whether the CSR can respond clearly and intelligibly to straightforward questions from the judges and at the same time put the judges at their ease, empathizing with them in their roles as potential interlocutors.

Beyond near-native proficiency I have suggested three aspects that should be assessed: clarity, intelligibility and rapport. The first two could be accounted for by (a) reading aloud and (b) comprehensibility under interview conditions. It is the third aspect, rapport, which is less easily assessed, since rapport is very much an individual matter and not easy to generalize about.

I want now to look in more detail at each of the aspects and how they can be measured:

1. Clarity: this refers to the form of what is said not the content. While it is not very easy to distinguish form and content in discourse, it is none the less important to try. This could mean using a test of very discrete phonological contrasts to determine if the candidate is capable of making the necessary distinctions that underlie the clarity of spoken English. Note that I am not recommending a test based on RP or any other prestige accent. What I am suggesting is that the candidate be required to make the phonological distinctions that make for clarity to an international audience. It may be that a test involving larger units than phonemes would be more appropriate, a test perhaps of sentences where stress, intonation and phoneme resolution matter.
2. Intelligibility: if clarity refers to the form, intelligibility refers to the content of what is said. An effective way of testing this is to provide the candidate with

one half of a simple dialogue, the part of the customer. The candidate is then given a few minutes to decide what s/he will say in response to each of the questions and/or comments that his interlocutor says. One member of the rating panel plays the role of the customer. It is of course important that the task is very simple and does not require knowledge of any customer specialism. What matters is whether the candidate can speak sensibly in response to the interlocutor's remarks.

3. Rapport: it is one of the most important features or characteristics of unconscious human interaction. It is commonality of perspective and means being on the same wavelength as the person with whom you are talking. But most of the evidence for rapport building appears to be visual, in particular the use of body language. This is unhelpful for a telephone encounter. But it would work for a video encounter. Rapport has close links with empathy. The basic idea of empathy is that by looking at the facial expressions or bodily movements of another, or by hearing their tone of voice, one may get an immediate sense of how they feel (as opposed to more intellectually noting the behavioural symptoms of their emotion). This is all very well but it remains unclear how we can measure rapport and empathy. It seems that one of the chief measures used by psychologists is self-report (Davis 1983). But there are also the more sociolinguistic features of accommodation and politeness, both of which are indications of rapport and which lend themselves to measurement.

What emerges from this brief account of ways of addressing clarity, intelligibility and rapport in cost-centre assessment is the need for further investigation, especially with regard to rapport. What could be done is to investigate how the more discrete methods for clarity and intelligibility could be used as criteria against which to assess methods which can be shown to be linguistically identified with the discourse and the culture of the call centre CSR. For the investigation of rapport it would be desirable for all interviews to be video recorded which would permit the existing psychological measures to be used as criteria.

Conclusion

I have argued that while traditional language testing in the selection and training of CSRs is essential, it is not sufficient. What is also needed is the assessment of their clarity, intelligibility and rapport. I have made some suggestions of how this might be done. I have also pointed to the dilemma of the current call centre industry which creates problems for itself by its pretence that its operations are based in the West. This pretence creates assumptions on the part of the majority of its customers which cannot be fulfilled.

References

Canale, M. and Swain, M. (1980), 'Theoretical bases of communicative approaches to second-language teaching and testing'. *Applied Linguistics* 1, 1–47.

CEFR. (2001), *The Common European Framework of Reference for Languages.* Cambridge: Cambridge University Press.

Davies, A. (1999), 'Standard English: discordant voices'. *World Englishes* 18/2, 171–186.

Davies, A. (2009), 'Assessing World Englishes'. *Annual Review of Applied Linguistics* 29, 80–89.

Davis, M. H. (1983), 'Measuring individual differences in empathy: Evidence for a multidimensional approach'. *Journal of Personality and Social Psychology* 44, 113–126.

Elder, C. and Davies, A. (2006), Assessing English as a Lingua Franca. *Annual Review of Applied Linguistics* 26, 282–301.

Friginal, E. (2009), 'Threats to the sustainability of the outsourced call center industry in the Philippines: Implications for language policy'. *Language Policy* 8, 51–68.

Hood, S. and Forey, G. (2008), 'The interpersonal dynamics of call-centre interactions: Do-deconstructing the rise and fall of emotion'. *Discourse and Communication* 2/4, 389–409.

Jenkins, J. (2007), *English as a Lingua Franca: Attitude and Identity.* Oxford: Oxford University Press.

Joseph J. (2004), *Language and Identity: National, Ethnic, Religious.* Basingstoke: Palgrave Macmillan.

Lockwood, J., Forey, G. and Elias, N. (forthcoming), In Belcher, D. (ed.) *English for Specific Purposes in Theory and Practice.* Cambridge: Cambridge University Press.

Lockwood, J. Forey, G. and Price, H. (2008), Englishes in the Philippine Business Processing Outsourcing Industry: Issues, opportunities and initial findings. In Bautiasta, Ma Lourdes S. and Bolton, K. (eds.) (2008), *Philippine English: Linguistic and Literary Perspectives.* Hong Kong: Hong Kong University Press, 219–242.

Morgan, B. and Ramanathan, V. (2009), Outsourcing, globalizing economics, and shifting language policies: Issues in managing Indian call centres. *Language Policy* 8, 69–80.

Seidlhofer, B. (2001), Closing a conceptual gap: The case for a description of English as a lingua franca. *International Journal of Applied Linguistics* 24, 209–239.

Part V

Beyond the Workplace: Social Implications

Chapter 16

Language Globalization and the Workplace: Education and Social Implications

Gail Forey

The Hong Kong Polytechnic University, Hong Kong

The chapters in this book make reference to many issues with respect to globalization, language and the workplace. The focus so far has been on call centre interaction, related specific language and assessment issues. However, it is important to consider the impact of the Business Processing Outsourcing (BPO) industry more broadly, on education, politics, the economy, social issues and language beyond the boundaries of call centre interactions or the organizations themselves. The impact the BPO industry has had in the broader social context is clearly evident in countries such as India and the Philippines, and generally speaking Asia has benefitted economically from this surge in global business. To understand the 'megatrends' of the economy and its effect on life in Asian societies that have seen explosive growth in BPO we need to travel beyond the doors of the industry. We need to gain insights into the wider social, educational and political implications of the industry.

Reporting Economic Growth

An extensive report carried out by the McKinsey group for NASSCOM (NASSCOM is the trade body and chamber of commerce for the IT-BPO industry in India – see www.nasscom.in NASSCOM 2009a) states that the addressable market for global sourcing will triple in size from a current USD 500 billion to USD 1.5–1.6 trillion in 2020, an incremental growth of 80%. The NASSCOM report states that 'the industry can have an unparalleled impact on India's economy and society by 2020' (NASSCOM 2009a:17). Such findings and predictions are reflected in numerous other studies and reports on both India and the Philippines (Arackaparambil 2004; Danlog 2006; Durfee 2004; Taylor and Bain 2005).

In 'the past 10 years India accounted for more than 50% of the global low cost workforce' (NASSCOM 2009a). India is internationally the leading BPO and Offshore and Outsource (O&O) destination; their prediction for 2010 is an

employment totalling '30 million urban employment (. . .) Significant job
creation in rural and non-metro areas' and increase in the gender of the workforce where 50% of the workforce will be women (NASSCOM 2009a). A 50%
increase of women in the workforce is a staggering number and the implications of such a huge shift in the workforce will have a tremendous effect on
family life, along with many other social issues. The drive and determination of
this industry is explicit. They promote slogans of change which assess the present
and predict 'megatrends' for the future. For example NASSCOM (2009a) identify a range of problems such as healthcare, education and public services, and
at the same time offer the ITES industry as a solution to such problems, e.g.:

- 50% of Indians do not have access to primary healthcare – Technology can
  provide it at half the cost of traditional solutions
- 80% of Indian households do not have bank accounts – Technology can
  enable access to 200 million families
- India faces a 3x shortage in teachers – Technology can address this through
  remote solutions
- 40–50% of public food distribution in India does not reach the targeted
  groups – Technology can ensure efficiency and transparency

NASSCOM (2009a)

As can be seen from NASSCOM's comments and solutions they believe that the
BPO industry will have a tremendous impact on technology, families, food,
healthcare and other areas of life in India.

The situation in the Philippines is comparable, in their Roadmap for 2010
the Business Processing Association of the Philippines (BPAP – NASSCOM's
equivalent in the Philippines), estimated 40% growth per year from 2008
to 2010. Reports on the Philippines indicate that the BPO economy grew from
USD 1.5 billion in 2004 to USD 3.3 billion in 2006, and employed 235,000
full-time employees at the end of 2006 (BPAP 2007). The Philippines plans to
continue to develop aiming to capture 10% of the BPO industry by 2010 with
anticipated revenues of about USD 13 billion and direct employment of close
to one million people (BPAP 2007). The estimated number of employees for
the industry is 900,000, plus 1.2–1.5 million indirect jobs (BPAP 2007). These
indirect jobs include the cleaners, maintenance, food and beverage, extra
transport workers and many other required jobs to support and maintain the
status quo of the industry.

The Philippines and India share the same vision. In India, NASSCOM's
(2009a) vision for employment by 2010 is 30 million urban employment (direct
and indirect). The estimated revenue for the industry within the Philippines is
US$13 billion, or the equivalent of 8.5% of the national GDP, which for a very
small country is a 10% global market share of the BPO industry (BPAP 2007).
This is an astounding amount of growth when you consider that at the end of
2006 the BPO industry in the Philippines employed 235,000 people, earned

USD 3.3 billion in revenue, which equalled roughly 2% of the national GDP (BPAP 2007). It is indeed important to remember at this point that the majority of this work both in the Philippines and India is English-related work, of which call centres functioning in English language are only part of the bigger picture of the BPO industry. Other services include medical transcription, animation, accounting finance and other back office work, to name but few of the very many jobs which have been O&O to what is now moving from the Business Process Outsourcing Industry to the Knowledge Processing Outsourcing Industry (KPO). The incentive, the rhetoric and figures for the Philippines are similar to India, both profess to be supporting and assisting many different areas of social fabric of their country.

Much of the research in the ITES industry neglects issues related to the social engineering which has taken place in order to provide the industry with a capable workforce. Issues related to the social, educational and political impact of the industry have been neglected. Focusing on a discussion of gender and call centres in India, Van den Broek (2004), Ganguly-Scrase and Van den Broek (2005), Baxi (2009:6) argue that 'in academic discourse in India call center literature has been said to be largely gender blind'. I would add that this neglect is not only true in India and the Philippines but also in many other developing O&O destinations. Research on the BPO, KPO and O&O tends to be centred around management, human resource or IT journals, with a focus on the workforce management systems, recruitment, attrition, technical support, the interpretation of matrix, etc. (Dietze et al. 2002; Hampson, Junor and Barnes 2009; Thomas, Bloor and Frankland 2007; Warhurst and Nickson 2007).

Many of the studies within the industry report statistical findings. In addition, whenever you step in to a BPO organization terms such as 'matrix' and the 'calibration of matrix' seem to dominate the discussion. Matrix in this sense refers to the statistical backbone of the industry, an industry which, due to the highly evolved tech support, is able to count everything in statistical terms regarding the average handling time (AHT), the number of people waiting, the length of time each person waited, the number of average calls per day, the peak periods, surges and estimation of approaching peaks in the number of users and how this relates to the number of customer service representatives (CSR) needed to answer calls, etc. Anything that can be counted is counted and placed in a matrix and then compared and calibrated to other matrix. This is true of the quality assessment measures used to review the handling process of individual calls. Lockwood, Forey and Elias (2009) outline the problems with the traditional quality assurance 'scorecard' used to assess the effectiveness of the call. Lockwood and Davies (see Chapters 14 and 15 this volume) outline a number of concerns about the assessment tools, and specifically the inappropriacy and complexity of language assessment tools found in the industry. Within the field of assessment in language the majority of the research has been undertaken in academic contexts (see Bachman 2000; Hamp-Lyons and Condon 2000; McNamara and Roever 2006, etc.), or assessment and policy, for example in the work of

Shohamy (2006) and MacNamara and Roever (2006), who discuss government policy of immigration in relation to language assessment. A limited amount of research has focused on language assessment in the workplace (Douglas 2000; Taylor and Bain 2003; Lockwood 2008; Lockwood, Forey and Elias 2009; Hamp-Lyons and Lockwood 2009). The relevance of language assessment in the O&O industry is extremely high stakes and can impact the service level agreement between the BPO and its vendor – meaning that contracts between a host company and a third party provider may be won or lost depending on the score of an assessment tool which will include some items directly related to language. The recruitment of staff for employment in the call centre industry is directly linked to a language assessment tool. When working as a CSR the monthly incentives offered to staff and even the continued employment of individuals are linked to some form of language assessment. However, little if any research is available which takes in to consideration the credibility, appropriacy and validity of language assessments (see Hamp-Lyons and Lockwood 2009 and Lockwood this volume).

However, if we consider briefly the research which has been emerging from the industry in recent years there seems to be little related to applied linguistics, English language, training, sociolinguistic studies. Only a few studies, if any, have discussed the relationship between language, globalization and the workplace which is directly relevant to the BPO, KPO, O&O industry. The earlier work within applied linguistics came from the UK where the research focused on language and call centres domiciled onshore in the UK call centres, servicing UK customers (Cameron 2000a, 2000b; Adolphs et al. 2004). More recently, studies have included the O&O call centres, and focused on issues related to training and language. Cowie (2007) and Cowie and Murty (this volume) discuss issues related to phonology, accent neutralization and training. Friginal (2007, 2009, Chapter 12 this volume) using data collected in the Philippines presents an interesting account of call centre interaction from a corpus-based perspective. Data collected in the Philippines is also used to analyse linguistic features in call centre interactions such as the generic structure (Forey and Lockwood 2007), errors and issues of Filipino English (Lockwood, Forey and Price 2008); the ebb and flow in a two-party interaction of interpersonal meaning (Hood and Forey 2008). English language assessment as part of the quality assurance measures is debated by Lockwood, Forey and Elias (2009), Lockwood (2008). However, few studies in these O&O destinations discuss the sociolinguistic impact of English, globalization and the growth of the ITES industry on life in these countries.

Within the field of sociolinguistics or globalization a tremendous amount of work has been undertaken with respect to English as a lingua franca (ELF) (Cummins and Davsion 2007; Pennycook 2007; Philipson 2007). A number of these studies are situated within the field of ELF in educational contexts (see Mauranen 2006a, b, c, 2007; Mauranen and Rantar 2008; Kirkpatick 2007a, 2007b, etc.). As Seidlhofer (2007:137) states English in Europe is seen as having 'de facto status as an auxiliary language for global communicative purposes rather than as a traditional foreign language'. Seidlhofer (2007) and others focus on the influence and the variety of World Englishes (WE), and argue that WE necessitates greater adaptability for those who speak English as a first and second language around the world. Fewer studies are available which focus on ELF in the workplace (Nickerson, Chapter 3 this volume, 2005; Cheng and Mok 2005; Lung 2008; Rogerson-Revell 2008; Jensen 2009 and others), and a limited number of these focus on the impact of O&O and the English language (Graddol 2006). The growth and the 'megatrends' of this industry have a direct bearing on education, politics, economics and social life (see NASSCOM 2009a).

In order to maintain the required standards for business, and to achieve this growth, the biggest challenge faced by the industry is 'talent' (BPAP 2007; NASSCOM 2005, 2009a). Moreover, as noted above the development from a business to knowledge processing work creates a demand for more complex tasks, and thus more professional, highly skilled employees, who also have a high level of English communication skills. Both India and the Philippines are being proactive in aiming to address this problem. NASSCOM and BPAP have both explicitly stated the need for the government's involvement in developing a high calibre fluent English workforce, both O&O destinations industry leaders state that the 'slow pace of reforms in education' (NASSCOM 2009a:12) are the major drawbacks for development. Both strongly urge the Government to undertake educational reforms which facilitate increased private participation in higher education (BPAP 2007; Gonzales 1997, 2004; Hidalgo 2004; NASSCOM 2009a). NASSCOM (2009a) in their report recommends that the Indian Government allocates 2% of their national budget for 'research, and to create quality institutions, to increase PhD holders to 200,000 by 2020. In order to achieve this, the industry must increase R and D spending and co-invest with universities to drive research' (NASSCOM 2009a:17).

NASSCOM outlines specific plans to facilitate growth:

1. Develop the potential of 'near hires'
2. Create an awareness of career opportunities
3. Tap alternative labour pools – housewives, retirees, non-graduates, career switchers
4. Helping students to fund education
5. Make college and high school curricula more related to industry

(NASSCOM 2009)

Industry members (such as NASSCOM, BPAP and many other organizations) along with the Governments of both countries have been actively involved in promoting joint collaboration between educational institutions and the industry in order to develop the talent pool. Later in the chapter a collaborative effort between a bank and a university will be discussed, and the benefits of this partnership will be highlighted. In this particular collaboration undergraduate students are enrolled in a programme 'earn as you learn'. These students spend 50% of their university life in the workplace, in this case the BPO of a large multinational bank, learning practical skills and undertaking tasks, and 50% of their time is based on traditional Business Administration studies at the university towards a Bachelor of Arts degree. However such incentives and collaborative endeavours are not the norm. To some extent, this model provides a leading example to others in the field.

In the chapter, I draw on data collected in a focus group interview with these students along with data from other interviews with a range of stakeholders from the BPO industry. The development of this industry has resulted in increased financial opportunities for those employed in, or supporting the industry and a change in other areas of work and life. In the discussion section, I portray some of the social implications caused by the changing face of the O&O industry and examine issues related to education, financial opportunities, family life and health. Finally, concluding remarks are offered and a call, which is supported by NASSCOM, BPAP (in their reports at least) and others, for funded and more systematic research of the sociolinguistic impact of the industry is recommended.

Background to the Study

The data for the present study have been collected over more than five years' involvement with members of the industry as part of a larger series of research projects (Call Centre Communication Research, CCCR, at the Hong Kong Polytechnic University, http://www.engl.polyu.edu.hk/call_centre). Initial research engaged with the BPO industry in the Philippines, and has extended to include studies in India, Hong Kong and China. In the larger project the research team has visited more than 10 call centres in a range of organizations, observing and discussing industry processes, interviewing a range of stakeholders and collecting data on call centre interactions. To date, over 300 calls have been transcribed in English, 100 English calls from the Philippines, over 100 calls in Cantonese, 100 English calls from Hong Kong. In addition the CCCR has organized three international conferences in the Philippines, India and Hong Kong providing additional opportunities to interact with representatives from a wide range of BPO organizations.

Against this background of accumulated knowledge of diverse aspects of the BPO industry in a number of countries, I draw in this chapter on sets of interview data to explore questions of the broader social impact of the industry from the perspective of those working in the industry. To truly understand what is happening, it is essential to include a discussion of the impact of the 'megatrends' of the BPO industry on those directly involved.

The interviews were undertaken in two types of organizations. Organization A is a third party operator in the Philippines. A third party operator is a BPO organization contracted to do work for a vendor. The third party runs the call centre or other back office work for that vendor, undertaking service level agreements set by the vendor. These interviews were conducted with six trainers (T) and two customer service representatives (CSRs).

A second set of interviews were undertaken in a captive call centre, BankA. A 'captive' call centre is one in which employees are hired directly and the business is run in-house. BankA is situated in India, and is part of a larger global bank which directly runs the operations of their call centres and back office support around the world. At BankA, the data includes interviews with six CSRs, three senior managers who work in the area of Communication Development, Learning and Development, Leadership and Development, Human Resources, as well as three trainers (T) and seven students (S) working and studying at BankA.

All interviewees gave their informed consent to participate and most agreed to the interviews being audio recorded. All data is de-indentified other than for country and position (e.g. CSR-customer service representative, S-student, SM-Senior Manager) plus number. All interviews were conducted in English as all the participants were expert users of English. The interviews varied in length from a minimum of 30 minutes. One whole night was spent with trainers in the Philippines and 3 days with the SMs in India. The interviews were wide ranging and included questions about the influence of the call centre industry on the individual's life. While only a proportion of the content is discussed in this chapter it does, nonetheless, illustrate the complexity of the social impact of the industry, and provides important insights into what the globalization of English language work through employment in a call centre in Asia means for those involved.

The BPO Industry and Education

As noted previously, both BPAP and NASSCOM and many other studies in the area echo that the main threat to growth in Asia is the necessary 'talent pool'. The main requirement and now it seems the main drawback is that the CSR is a proficient English language speaker. Presently in the Philippines nearly all of the employees hired as a CSR and other positions in the BPO industry are university graduates from nearly all fields of education. However, the situation in India, a more mature market, is slightly different. In India, the industry has exhausted the large numbers of university graduates it employed in the early days at the start of BPOs, and as a response to increase the talent pool NASS-COM has established a new mandate to encourage women back to work and to entice employees directly from school and from other professions (NASSCOM 2009a:18, 2009b). In India, the plan is to hire a wider range of employees from different backgrounds. One response to increase the numbers is to cast the net and search for new talent further a field. Initially, in both the Philippines and

India the industry mushroomed in cities which had a large university population and now that resources in these cities have been drained, the industry has
spread to what they term as 'second and third tier cities', i.e. cities which may
not be as advanced and which may not have as large a number of university
graduates.

There is not only a widening of the net to geographical locations, but also an
effort to entice workers from other professions. When interviewing the trainers
in the Philippines five of the six trainers were teachers or university lecturers.
In India the majority of the trainers were from the teaching profession and
others had been raised through the ranks on the floor. In all cases those that
had previously taught, whether in secondary or tertiary institutions, were lured
to the Call Centre industry (and happy there) due to financial gain and an
improved, positive work environment. The Vice President for Learning and
Development at BankA stated that

> The background to the trainers is quite mixed. The only requirement for
> trainers is they're good communicators; many come from the floor, to call
> coaches, to junior trainers, to senior trainers. [sic] (India SM L&D)

Thus, as outlined above, the aim of NASSCOM and BPAP, as well as many other
institutions is to increase education by developing training and assessment tools
which will support the language proficiency of 'near hires', 'help students to
fund education', and 'make college and high school curricula more related to
industry' (BPAP 2007:19). The focus on improving and supporting education
seems to be limited to a few initiatives. One major limitation is that many of the
English teachers are leaving education to work in the industry. There is a one
way movement of educational expertise from the schools and universities to the
training rooms of the industry. It is highly unlikely that the educational terrain
will change dramatically unless the benefits and career prospects within the
teaching profession are drastically improved. Furthermore, at present little
research, is emerging from tertiary institutions in India or the Philippines which
reports and supports applied linguistic or pedagogic knowledge in the field.

However much the industry calls for investment in education and research,
there seems to be limited action within education. One innovative and
pioneering initiative in India which has recently been introduced by an international bank and other large global organizations is a partnership between industry and universities where students study part-time in both the university and
business as part of their undergraduate degree. These innovative moves are
inspiring educational change. As introduced above, BankA has partnered a
local tertiary institution and introduced a 'earn as you learn scheme'. One
student pointed out that 'what happened previously was BankA found a huge
gap between universities and business' (BankA S3). BankA recruited 60 students,
from 6,000 applications, for a BA in Business Administration where 50% of the

studies are undertaken at the university and 50% as an internship within the Bank. BankA sponsored the students and paid the students a stipend:

- Yr, 1 Indian Rupees 2,500 per month
- Yr 2 Indian Rupees 3,200 per month
- Yr 3 Indian Rupees 3,700 per month

Due to the stipend received, the students have gained their independence and were able to pay their tuition fees themselves, as well as have a small amount of disposable income. They felt that the opportunity afforded to them made their parents 'proud' and the friends 'jealous'. In a focus group interview for over an hour with 7, of the soon to graduate students, the impression and feedback from the students very near the end of their degree was extremely encouraging. Six out of the seven students wanted to continue to be employed by BankA. The other student wanted to do an MBA and become an entrepreneur. Unanimously the students repeatedly echoed that the studies undertaken in university were 'bookish'. The students found that

> Whatever we learn in the school is entirely different . . . how you present yourself is so different in work. We have learnt so many different things here [in the call centre], reports, memos, letters . . . (BankA, S5)

The university students repeatedly stated the positive benefits of this collaborative venture, the ability to extend their knowledge and skills to practical and applicable areas. The students appreciated the academic challenge of tertiary education and in fact one student highlighted the double-edged benefits of the venture when she said

> It's like two ends of a rainbow, at one end of the rainbow you learn bookish knowledge in high schools and universities, and at the other end of the rainbow you learn practical valuable information which is so applicable to the workplace. (BankA, S2)

During the focus group interview the term bookish was constantly repeated and when probed for clarification of what exactly the students meant by the term bookish the students were very clear that what they learned in university was completely unrelated to the everyday work of the BPO industry. As stated previously India is a more mature market than the Philippines and NASSCOM and other BPO, O&O institutions have been fighting the battle for a greater synthesis between industry and education for quite some time. However, according to these seven students and many of the others interviewed there still seems to be a huge rift between what is required within the industry and what is included in pedagogy.

Thus in a brief review of one particular aspect of education and the BPO industry it seems that there is still a long way to go to improve the working relationship and positive support of the industry and education. First, there is a clear indication that the professional environment and benefits offered to teachers needs to reflect the salary and benefit package offered to trainers and managers in the industry. When the industry is a private enterprise and many of the organizations are offshore organisations then the remuneration and economical relationship between industry and government needs to improve, in a way there should be a more direct funding relationship between multinational businesses and education. Professional and highly qualified teachers are essential to ensure that a high standard of English is taught at all levels of education. From the data collected and previous work in the field it appears that the language, curriculum and objectives in education are quite distinct when compared with the needs of the industry. Greater attention should be given to review and perhaps if necessary revise what is being taught with respect to communication and language in all educational institutions. An additional question which also surfaced when reviewing the present situation was that although many of the trainers come from educational fields, many originate from non-language degrees, also quite a high number of trainers have progressed through the ranks on the floor, i.e. from CSR, to coach, to trainer. Many of the trainers have limited knowledge of language and intercultural training, as well as adult training, curriculum planning and material development. Much of the training is developed around 'gut' feelings rather than systematic, informed planning. There are limited professional training certificates offered to workplace trainers (see Hamp-Lyons and Lockwood 2009 for a more detailed discussion). There should be international standards and training certificates for workplace trainers, which are run and accredited by official and recognized bodies.

The BPO Industry and Financial Opportunities

In this section, based on the data collected, I provide a brief snapshot of how the BPO has to some extent impacted the life of those working in call centres in India and the Philippines. The discussion and influence of the impact of the BPO industry should be reviewed critically as the numbers interviewed are very small and the organizations we visited are some of the 'better' employers who were happy to showcase the work they had undertaken. However, the picture painted from the interviews carried out are revealing and worth investigating further.

It is undeniable that employment problems have been reduced due to the growth and development of the BPO Industry in India and the Philippines. Employment in the BPO industry has provided an opportunity which was probably only to be found as an overseas worker prior to the evolution of the industry. As one of BankA students stated before the BPO 'only 20% reached their dreams, I'd guess 55% can reach their dreams now' (India S3). The optimism and fortuity proffered to those that join the industry are quite staggering.

At one of the top third party providers in the Philippines we were told that they had 400 applicants a week of which only 1–3% were hired, another 5–10% were near-hires, and with some intense training focusing on English they might be suitable for recruitment.

The financial reward is the biggest attraction for those working in the industry. As pointed out by one CSR 'the salary of a new CSR is even higher than an experienced business manager' (Ph CSR1). On a number of occasions we were told by those working within the industry that a CSR can afford the latest models of mobile phones, play stations and other gadgets. As many of the employees are young fresh graduates with limited responsibility they enjoy a high disposable income. It was also stated by a number of interviewees that a CSR is recognisable by the up-to-date gadgets and clothes they wear. After spending a night shift with some CSR and trainers, returning to our hotel at 6am the call centre manager giving us a lift home pointed at some people and said that you can tell a CSR at a glance, just by the gadgets they carry and the clothes they wear, 'in the Philippines, if you see a person wearing jacket, jeans and sport shoes in the early morning, he/she must work in call centre' (PhT4).

Many appreciate the stress found by the nature of the job, dealing with demanding customers, surveillance, time constraints and the night shift are evident, but also many of those we interviewed also added that the stress is counterbalanced by the financial reward 'working in call centre is stressful, but it can allow you to purchase the house, the car and support the family' (Ph CSR2). Many of the trainers we spoke to in the Philippines and India stated that the BPO industry was a better working environment than the schools. The Philippine trainers compared the lack of resources and support in the school with the better environment, enthusiasm of the students and positive work ethic of the industry.

As a counterargument to the positive implications of greater financial reward, the attrition rate does not reflect a stable and happy workforce. The attrition rate is frequently referred to 'as 20%-40% in some firms, while the top ones averages at least 15%' (BPOIndia 2009), 26% Philippines (BPAP 2007). As one CSR in a Human Resources Manager in the Philippines pointed out 'compensation attracts many young adults, but also the turnover rate is huge. In some companies the annual attrition is 100%, the average about 26%', (Ph, Human Resources Manager). There are many stories of 'burnouts' from constant night shifts and the stress of the work. One ex-CSR who we met at one of the conferences was proud of the fact that she had 'a normal job now', she no longer had to work nights. If night shift and 'normality' are antagonistic then the long term prospects for newly hired fresh graduates is a point which needs to be reviewed. Another explanation for the high attrition rates was offered by a few informants who stated that 'the true fact is a BPO is a bridge to get the global exposure, part time source to grab funds and reach his dream career' (India S5). A number of the CSRs we interviewed said that the reason they were working in the call centre was to improve their English before travelling overseas for postgraduate (mainly MBA) studies. Thus the job is sometimes viewed as a 'stop gap' to gain exposure, work experience, improve their English and save some money 'they stay for a while, then apply to study overseas' (India, SM LandD).

In addition, another economic and positive benefit of the industry is the independence that it has offered women in both India and the Philippines. Cameron (2000a), Van den Breok (2004), Baxis (2009) refer to the feminine nature of the call centre industry and that 'women have been seen to be hired into call centres based on feminine and socially constructed values of empathy, courtesy and softness attributed to women' (Baxi 2009:6). However, within the industry in the Philippines and India, there does not seem to be a focus on hiring women simply due to a linguistic underpinning that they are more empathetic on the phone. Rather the drive to hire women is pursued in order to hire the best talent pool possible. The industry sees the drive to hire women as more of an economic of an economic necessity which may conflict the gender cultural norms of a country such as India. As promised in the new NASSCOM Report (2009b), one aim of the industry in India is to increase the number of female employees by 50%. As one of BankA students pointed out 'girls and boys have got the opportunity now to choose their future as the generation views of the industry have changed people love the jobs now' (India S. 5). This change in gender stereotyping and the freedom given to women was clearly enunciated by one of the students from BankA who said

> parents have changed their views, my mother wanted to join the BPO's but my grandfather told her 'no way', then I got this place and my family have changed their views about the industry. Even my mum has now got a job in the BPO. (India S1)

In the last decade the industry has faced huge challenges in social acceptance. Previously, many parents and academics did not encourage graduates to join the industry. However, the financial reward, good press and focus on educating the public about employment opportunities have lead to a general change in the acceptance of this industry.

Thus it is clear from reviewing reports, articles, facts and figures about the industry along with the stories of those working in the industry that the greatest benefit is financial reward, but at what cost? In the following section I discuss the implications of this financial reward on a range of different issues such as family and health.

BPO Industry, Family and Health

Whether we are studying the overall impact of the industry or issues related to family life, a common denominator is the economic gain for the country and the individual. In what follows we discuss some of the drawbacks and benefits on family life and health. First we consider how economic gains impact the family. It is interesting to pose a question which reflects the present situation of young graduates working in this industry. What happens if a fresh graduate, in their first job is earning more than their parents have earned, how would this impact family life?

For example, one of the Indian trainers, and a number of the trainers in the Philippines were very proud of the fact that now they earned more money than their lecturer who had been teaching at university all their life. One Indian Trainer stated

> I was appointed as a lecturer. I earned 5,000 Rupees, when I came here I got 15,000 Rupees. If you're a lecturer with a permanent job you'd definitely never get 15,000 Rupees . . . Here there's lots of learning, lots of good things that I wouldn't have done in college. In college I would do my PhD and that's it . . . At the University I used to have to wear a sari, even when I was so young, I felt so old . . . I'm happy. (India T3 – Shanti)
>
> (Shanti referred to a monthly salary 5,000 Indian Rupees which is roughly equivalent to US$105)

It is clear to see when talking to the trainers and those employed in the call centre industry that the financial reward is high. If we consider T3's comments above, then it raises a number of questions, to do with tradition and academia. The Trainer is able to have greater freedom and independence from the traditional 'old fashioned' dress, and academia has lost someone who was hired young and would have stayed at University to complete a PhD, probably with a stable future in academia. At BankA, in India trainers receive 300–800K Indian Rupees a year (roughly US$6,280–16,750), with an average of around 500K Indian Rupees (roughly US$10,500). A college lecturer would receive on average 100–200K Indian Rupees per year (roughly US$2,093–4,190). The attraction of the industry goes beyond the salary, it is linked to the working environment, future career paths and working with highly motivated students. Thus it is easy to see why a number of academics and teachers have been inclined to change their career. In addition, if we consider the average starting wage for a CSR in either the Philippines or India the salary is much higher than the average national wage. For example in the Philippines the average entry-level wage for a CSR is around PhP13,000 (Philippine Pesos) (US$275) per month, which is nearly double the minimum wage (BPAP 2007). This wage can quickly rise to around PhP20,500, excluding bonuses and benefits.

The same trainer, T3, also went on to say how her work has affected her family life. In India, following a tradition where the wife usually prepares her husband's meals, Shanti, stated that her husband 'prepares his breakfast, his lunch, we have dinner together and he drops me here'. Shanti is generally going to bed to recover from a night shift when her husband is starting his day, which as stated involves preparing his meals and leaving for work. Let's consider a Philippine Trainer – Gloria, she has a 2 ½-year-old son, who is just waking up when she arrives home from work. They have some quality time together; Gloria can take him to school then returns to bed. Her choices are to sleep for a full 6–8 hours or to sleep 4–5 hours or less, and then spend time with her son, before returning to work in the evening. Many of the interviewees stated that the industry becomes more difficult when the children are older and attending school, as it is then difficult for parents to attend meetings or school events as they are working in the evening when such activities frequently happen. Naturally the benefits of economic reward bring with them many positive implications for a family.

One of the battles the industry faces is trying to persuade the population of the validity of working in the ITES industry. During our interviews we were constantly told that for many of the older generation and tertiary professors actually advise young adults to choose an alternative career that is not within the ITES industry. BPAP points out the need to educate the public about the benefits of this profession, 'the industry will help overcome some misconceptions about the industry among young people (and their parents and counselors), increasing the number of candidates vying for open positions' (author's own parenthesis, BPAP 2007:xix). It appears in the Philippines that the ITES industry does not have a very positive reputation. In India where the industry is more mature it seems as though opinions have started to change. As one of the trainers pointed out:

> 5 yrs ago, it was a challenge for families to send their children to a call centre. There have been some changes, and families are more open to call centre work, exposure is developing. In Bangalore and other more mature venues this obstacle has been overcome. (India Trainer 1)

In the first Talking Across the World conference we organized, one of the questions from the floor during the final panel discussion was 'how will the call centre industry overcome the reputation that the only type of women who works at night, is the type of women you wouldn't want your daughter to be?'. The delegate here was insinuating that call centre female workers could be seen to be associated with other ladies of the night such as sex workers. This and a number of other negative battles are issues the industry has to struggle against. NASSCOM feels very strongly that the issue of a greater gender balance in the workplace are something that need to be addressed. In their recent report Gender Inclusivity in India: Building an Empowered Organisation (NASSCOM 2009b), NASSCOM provide statistics, current trends and practices, a model for gender inclusion aimed at increasing the number of women in the ITES industry, along with recommendations for governments, companies and various stakeholders within the industry. In much of the material within the industry as stated above, the biggest problem facing growth and development is 'talent', by encouraging women into the ITES industry numbers of potential employees simply doubles.

Even in the UK in an industry magazine one article starts off by stating:

Call centres have been given a bad reputation – if you ask someone if they would like to work in one, you can bet their response would be negative. They can be seen as dull, boring places to work, where each day is like groundhog day, monotonous, and drags on. (Call Centre Helper.Com 2009)

One issue which is prevalent in the ITES industry as pointed out by Taylor and Bain, (2003, 2007) is the Taylorist principles, with an emphasis on a strict division of labour, limited and mundane, repetitive job demands, where there is narrow control over work, compounded by a high workload, pressure to meet average handling times, where surveillance is part of every minute of the day, among a range of other pressures. Other pressures found within the industry include limited promotional opportunities, social stressors, customer abuse, a constant contradiction between 'quality' and 'quantity'. These factors are echoed in the poor reputation faced by the industry in their onshore and off-shore destinations. However, it is precisely the choice of offshore destinations which has instigated the growth of this industry in Asia and around the world. Many from these offshore destinations are prepared to face and surmount these 'Taylorist' work environment. The informants we spoke to were prepared to face the social stressors in order to remain in their home country rather than become an expatriate overseas worker.

By remaining in their own country and taking work within the ITES industry a vast majority of fresh graduates can remain in their local environment and earn a decent salary. Above we have considered the impact on family life, from the stories of a few informants who are married and may have children. As many of the employees are fresh graduates, we should briefly consider how the night shift effects a young single adult's personal and social life. Consider the BPAP Road Map for 2010 (BPAP 2007) where they state that the industry needs to grow by 40% and in doing so recruit 600,000 many of whom will be fresh graduates. How will these fresh graduates spend their social time, when they are working evenings and sleeping during the day? One Account Manager during an interview reported that he often had difficulty in meeting his friends as he worked night shifts. Another Philippine Trainer was pretty explicit stating that rather than meet friends, often at the weekend he would catch up on sleep. A number of our informants also spent quite a bit of time sharing with us their health concerns related to working nights, the inability to sleep, the change of physical and psychological expectations. A number of informants discussed how they trained their body to cope with 4 to 5 hours' sleep rather than the 6–9 they used to have, as pointed out by one Filipino Team Leader

Before working in call centre I used to sleep 9 hours a night. Now I've trained my body to manage with only 4-5 hours. I consider the health issues, by eating more healthily, taking vitamins and working out in the gym more often. (Ph Team Leader)

Many of our informants freely shared with us their concerns and methods to overcome the change in sleep patterns and also eating habits. 'Coffee resigns as king' where caffeine in the Philippines was frequently seen as a source to help get through the nights. One Filipino Trainer stated 'if there is a call centre, there is a Starbuck (coffee) nearby'. Walking around Manila during the night shift you are often faced with small groups of CSRs on their breaks from 11pm to 6am, having a cigarette break, snack or meal at one of what seems to be American fast food restaurants. Snacks are available constantly on the floor, food is often provided by the company as buffet style, because few restaurants are open between 11pm to 6 am. Often the CSR goes out for 'LUNCH' at 1am to have a 'morning buffet'. In the dining hall at BankA there was a Weight Watchers booth encouraging employees to join. It is not only the food, but more the social life which is being affected by the globalization of English. In the Philippines a new social life has emerged where bars and restaurants offer happy hour at 6am. New language such as a 'morning beer' is also evolving.

> We go to pub at 6am in the morning, we chat with our colleagues and relax. We laugh at our bu's (buddies) mistakes which means we don't take the stress home. (Ph Team Leader)

The situation is slightly different in India, and the social scene does not seem to be as pronounced, or as easy to spot for an outsider. In both countries, many of the CSRs and ITES industry members are aware of the health issues related to the work and try to address these issues. Organizations also aim to support and offer solutions to the unsociable hours within the industry. Frequently people with family, if possible are offered day shifts, gyms and sporting facilities are sometimes available onsite.

Conclusion

The tremendous benefits brought about by the ITES industry in the Philippines and India have created social, political and economical shifts in the lives of individuals and in the country as a whole. Language, globalization and the pervasive impact of English is highly evident within the ITES O&O world. In this chapter I have provided a brief insight to the impact of English as a lingua franca within the industry and demonstrated, to a limited extent, how the face of English language and the explosion of the ITES industry has changed life in India and the Philippines. A number of studies within business, economics, IT and HR have discussed the 'megatrends' of this industry from a workplace perspective. However, in this new emerging market little is known about the broader impact on society. Limited funding is available to academics or research bodies to study the real impact on education, family, politics. The industry members ardently aim to impress possible investors of the benefits, the growth, the financial gain of O&O work to such destinations, but at what costs? Many organizations appear to take the social and health concerns of their employees in to consideration and introduce initiatives to combat these issues, but where is the independent enquiry which is not associated with the financial gain of developing the ITES industry?

Throughout the book we have documented subject matter related to language, recruitment and culture within training and the workplace. As researchers in the field we also need to consider the relationship between all of these issues with the sociolinguistic impact. There are issues related to language, culture and management style which need to be investigated. Within organizations in the Philippines and India, who are collaborating or representing Western multinationals, there are often comments about the management style and communication which need to be studied. How has the economic crises of 2008/2009 impacted the growth and development of such organizations in Asia? How is change management implemented in these organizations? What resources are used to address the levels of stress experienced by the CSR and other employees within the organizations? How do customers in the domicile country perceive the O&O industry? What can be done to educate and encourage customers in the domicile destinations to be more open and adaptable when using English as a global language? How is the training, curriculum and development implemented? Many of these questions have only been briefly introduced and some preliminary investigations have been initiated in the ITES industry. However, as a new emerging industry which has only been developed in the last 30 years there is still a great deal left uncovered.

> The negative socio cultural implications of call centre growth have been framed around the psychological impacts of the imposition of American identities, health hazards of night shifts, the rise of a new Americanized middle class cut loose from Indian realities. (Baxi 2009:5)

If we are to consider globalization and the workplace and the influence of English as a lingua franca within the ITES industry there is still a lot to learn.

References

Adolphs, S., Brown, B., Carter, R., Crawford, P. and Sahota, O. (2004), Applying corpus linguistics in a health care context. *Journal of Applied Linguistics* 1(1), 9–28.

Arackaparambil, R. (2004, 3 September), Jobs outsourced to Indian firms may not go to India. *USA Today*. Retrieved 18 January 2005, from http://www.usatoday.com/teach/techinvestor/industry/2004-09-03-further-outsourcing_x.htm

Bachman, L. F. (2000), Modern language testing at the turn of the century: Assuring that what we count counts. *Language Testing* 17 (1), 1–42.

Baxi, P. (2009), Intersecting Realities: Women in Call Centers in Gurgaon India. *Paper Presented at the Annual Meeting of the American Sociological Association*, Montreal Convention Center, Montreal, Quebec, Canada, 11 August 2006 retrieved 26 May 2009 from: http://www.allacademic.com/meta/p105220_index.html

BPAP. (2007), *Offshoring and Outsourcing Philippines: Roadmap 2010*. http://www.bpap.org retrieved 12 July 2009.

Call Centre Helper.Com. (2009), Creative ideas to improve the call centre, source: http://www.callcentrehelper.com/creative-ideas-to-improve-the-call-centre-2594.htm retrieved 24 June 2009.

bpoInida.org. (2009), Attrition in Indian BPO Industry. http://www.bpoindia.org / research/attrition.shtml   retrieved 20 August 2009.

Cameron, D. (2000a), Styling the worker: Gender and the commodification of language in the globalized service economy. *Journal of Sociolinguistics* 4(3), 323–347.

Cameron, D. (2000b), *Good to Talk? Living and Working in a Communication Culture*. London: Sage.

Cheng, W. and Mok, E. (2008), Discourse processes and products: Land surveyors in Hong Kong. *English for Specific Purposes* 27(1), 57–73.

Cowie, C. (2007), The accent of outsourcing: The meanings of 'neutral' in the Indian call centers. *World Englishes* 26(3), 316–330.

Cowie and Murty. See this volume.

Cummins, J. and Davsion, C. (eds.). *2007 International Handbook of English Language Teaching*. New York: Springer.

Danlog, A. (2006), Call Centers: Boon or Bane for New Graduates? Retrieved 19/10/2006, from http://www.livinginthephilippines.com/call_centers.html

Dietze, P., Fry, C., Sunjic, S., Bammer, G., Zador, D., Jolley, D. and Rumbold, G. (2002), Using Ambulance Attendances to Recruit People who have Experienced Non-Fatal Heroin Overdose'. *Drug and Alcohol Dependence* 67(1), 99–103.

Douglas, D. (2000), *Assessing Languages for Specific Purposes*. Cambridge: Cambridge University Press.

Durfee, D. (2004), Newswatch: Research India Ink. CFO, February.

Forey, G. and Lockwood, J. (2007), 'I'd love to put someone in jail for this'. English in the Business Processing Outsourcing (BPO) Industry. *English for Specific Purposes*. In press.

Friginal, E. (2007), Outsourced call centers and English in the Philippines. *World Englishes* 26(3), 331–345.

Friginal, E. (2009), *The Language of Outsourced Call Centers: A Corpus-based Study of Cross-cultural Interaction*. Amsterdam: John Benjamins Publishing Company.

Ganguly-Scrase, R. and Vandenbroek, D. (2005), Globalisation, Liberalisation and the Transformation of Women's Work in India. *TASA Conference Proceedings*, University of Tasmania, 6–8 December 2005.

Gonzales, A. (1997), The history of English in the Philippines. In Bautista, M. L. (ed.), *English is an Asian Language: The Philippine Context*. Manila, the Philippines: De La Salle University Press, 25–40.

Gonzales, A. (2004), The social dimensions of Philippine English. *World Englishes* 23(1), 7–16.

Graddol, D. (2006), *English Next: Why Global English May Mean the End of 'English as a Foreign Language'*. London: British Council.

Hamp-Lyons, L. and Condon, W. (2000), *Assessing the Portfolio: Principles for Practice, Theory, and Research* Cresskill, N.J. : Hampton Press.

Hamp-Lyons, L. and Lockwood, J. (2009), *The Workplace, the Society and the Wider World: The Offshoring and Outsourcing Industry in Language Policy and Language Assessment*, Bernard Spolsky (ed.) 2009 volume of the Annual Review of Applied Linguistics. Cambridge University Press.

Hampson, I., Junor, A., Barnes, A. (2009), Articulation work skills and the recognition of call centre competences in Australia. *Journal of Industrial Relations* 51(1), 45–58.

Hidalgo, C. P. (2004), The Philippine short story in English: An overview. *World Englishes* 23(1), 155–168.

Hood, S. and Forey, G. (2008), Co-constructing emotion: The interpersonal dynamics of call-centre interactions. *Discourse and Communication* 2(4), 389–409.

Jensen, A. (2009), Discourse strategies in professional e-mail negotiation: A case study. *English for Specific Purposes* 28/1, 4–18.

Kirkpatrick, A. (2007a), *English in Southeast Asia: Literacies, Literatures and Varieties*. Cambridge: Cambridge Scholars Press (co-editor with David Prescott, Azirah Hashim and Isabel Martin).

Kirkpatrick, A. (2007b), *World Englishes: Implications for International Communication and English Language Teaching*. Cambridge: Cambridge University Press.

Lockwood, J. (2008), What does the Business Processing Outsourcing (BPO) Industry want from English language assessment? *Prospect* 23:2.

Lockwood, J. Forey, G. and Elias, N. (2009), Call centre communication: Measurement processes in non-English speaking contexts. In Belcher, D. (ed.). *English for Specific Purposes in Theory and Practice*. Michigan: Michigan University Press, 143–164.

Lockwood, J., Forey, G. and Price, P. (2008), Englishes in the Philippine Business Processing Outsourcing Industry: Issues, opportunities and initial findings in Bautista, M. L. S. and Bolton, K. (eds.) *Philippine English: Linguistic and Literary Perspectives*. Hong Kong: Hong Kong University Press, 157–172.

Lung, J. (2008), Discursive hierarchical patterning in Law and Management cases. *English for Specific Purposes* 27/4, 424–441.

Mauranen, A. (2006a), Signalling and preventing misunderstanding in English as lingua franca communication. *International Journal of the Sociology of Language* 177, 123–150. Special Issue, ed. by Christiane Meierkord.

Mauranen, A. (2006b), Spoken discourse, academics and global English: A corpus perspective. In Hughes, Rebecca (ed.) *Spoken English, TESOL and Applied Linguistics*. London: Palgrave Macmillan.

Mauranen, A. (2006c), Speaking the discipline. In Hyland, Ken and Bondi, Marina (eds.) *Academic Discourse Across Disciplines*. Bern: Peter Lang.

Mauranen, A. (2007), Investigating English as a Lingua Franca with a Spoken Corpus. In Campoy, Mari Carmen and Luzón, María José (eds.) *Spoken Corpora in Applied Linguistics*. Berlin: Peter Lang, 33–56.

Mauranen, A. and Ranta, E. (2008), English as an Academic Lingua Franca – the ELFA Project. *Nordic Journal of English Studies* 7(3), 199–202. NJES.

McNamara, T. and Roever, C. (2006), *Language Testing: The Social Dimension*. Malden, MA and Oxford: Blackwell.

NASSCOM McKinsey (2005), *The NASSCOM McKinsey Study 2005*. Retrieved from www.nasscom.com.in 17 June 2007.

NASSCOM (2009a), Perspective 2020: Transform Business Transform India. (Executive Summary) http://www.nasscom.in retrieved 27 May 2009.

NASSCOM (2009b), Gender Inclusivity in India: Building an Empowered Organisation. http://www.nasscom.in retrieved 27 May 2009.

Nickerson, C. (2005), English as a lingua franca in international business contexts. *English for Specific Purposes* 24, 367–380.

Nickerson, C. See this volume.

Pennycook. (2007), ELT and Colonialism. In Cummins, J. and Davsion, C. (eds.) (2007), *International Handbook of English Language Teaching*. New York: Springer, 13–24.

Philipson. (2007), English, no longer a foreign language in Europe? In Cummins, J. and Davsion, C. (eds.). (2007), *International Handbook of English Language Teaching*. New York: Springer, 123–136.

Rogerson-Revell, P. (2008), Participation and performance in international business meetings. *English for Specific Purposes* 27(3), 338–360.

Seidelhofer, B. (2007), Common property: English as a lingua franca in Europe. In Cummins, J. and Davsion, C. (eds.). (2007), *International Handbook of English Language Teaching*. New York: Springer, 136–153.

Shohamy, E. G. (2006), *Language Policy: Hidden Agendas and New Approaches*. London: Routledge.

Taylor, P. and Bain, P. (2003), 'Subterranean Worksick blues': Humour as subversion in two call centres. *Organization Studies* 24(9), 1487–1509.

Taylor, P. and Bain, P. (2005), 'India calling to the far away towns': The call centre labour process and globalization. *Work, Employment and Society* 19(2), 261–282.

Taylor, P. and Bain, P. (2007), Reflections on the call centre – a reply to Glucksmann. *Work, Employment and Society* 21(2), 349–362.

Thomas, M., Bloor, M. and Frankland, J. (2007), The process of sample recruitment: An ethnostatistical perspective. *Qualitative Research* 2007; 7; 429–446.

Van den Broek, D. (2004), Globalising Call Centre Capital: Culture and Work Identity. *Labour and Industry* 14(3), 59–76.

Warhurst, C. and Nickson, D. (2007), Employee experience of aesthetic labour in retail and hospitality. *Work, Employment and Society* 21(1), 103–120.

Index

Note: Page numbers in *italics* denote figures and tables.

CPSIA information can be obtained
at www.ICGtesting.com
Printed in the USA
LVHW022307010523
745836LV00002B/6